A Blueprint for
Worker Solidarity

THE WORKING CLASS IN
AMERICAN HISTORY

Editorial Advisors
James R. Barrett, Thavolia Glymph, Julie Greene,
William P. Jones, and Nelson Lichtenstein

*For a list of books in the series, please see our
website at www.press.uillinois.edu.*

A Blueprint for Worker Solidarity

Class Politics and Community in Wisconsin

NAOMI R WILLIAMS

UNIVERSITY OF ILLINOIS PRESS
Urbana, Chicago, and Springfield

© 2025 by the Board of Trustees
of the University of Illinois
All rights reserved
1 2 3 4 5 C P 5 4 3 2 1
∞ This book is printed on acid-free paper.

Publication was supported by a grant from the
Howard D. and Marjorie I. Brooks Fund for
Progressive Thought.

Library of Congress Cataloging-in-Publication Data
Names: Williams, Naomi R., author.
Title: A blueprint for worker solidarity : class politics and
  community in Wisconsin / Naomi R Williams.
Description: Urbana, Chicago : University of Illinois Press,
  [2025] | Series: The working class in American history |
  Includes bibliographical references and index.
Identifiers: LCCN 2024018757 (print) | LCCN 2024018758
  (ebook) | ISBN 9780252046247 (cloth) | ISBN
  9780252088322 (paperback) | ISBN 9780252047510
  (ebook)
Subjects: LCSH: Working class—Wisconsin. | Working
  class—Political activity—Wisconsin. | Labor movement—
  Wisconsin.
Classification: LCC HD4855 .W49 2025 (print) | LCC HD4855
  (ebook) | DDC 322/.20977596—dc23/eng/20240514
LC record available at https://lccn.loc.gov/2024018757
LC ebook record available at https://lccn.loc.gov/2024018758

Contents

Acknowledgments ix

Introduction: Working-Class Identity
and Postwar U.S. Society. 1

1 Building Racine's Labor Community 19

2 Labor Politics and Solidarity in the 1950s 43

3 UAW Local 180 and the Attack on
New Deal Liberalism. 63

4 Race and Shifting Class Boundaries in Racine 87

5 Cross-Sector Solidarity Amid a Shifting Landscape. 103

6 Racine's Labor Community and Deindustrialization 129

Conclusion: How We Get Free 159

Notes 163

Bibliography. 197

Index 205

For Danita

Acknowledgments

I must begin by thanking the working people of Racine, those I met and spoke to during the Wisconsin uprising, those whose interviews I read, and those who agreed to interview with me. I acknowledge and honor the fighting spirit, enduring solidarity, and adaptable approach to labor politics that truly provide a blueprint for the economic justice fight that continues today. I hope my respect and honor are conveyed in these pages.

This started at the University of Wisconsin–Madison, and my committee continues to be a source of both inspiration and direction. I am grateful to William P. Jones, Christina Greene, Jane L. Collins, Colleen Dunlavy, and Tony Michels. Will Jones continues to challenge and encourage my work and his probing questions and thoughtful reflections have made this a much better project. It was an honor to work with the late Camille Guérin-Gonzales, who showed so much enthusiasm for this project.

I also thank and acknowledge the enduring community of intellectuals and activists I met while in Madison, who remain friends, allies, critics, and supporters. Leslie Abadie saved my life multiple times and kept me on track to completion. Many thanks and much love to Geneviève Dorals, Simon Balto, William and Marci Scott, Matt Reiter, Charles Hughes, Jillian Jacklin, Jess Kierstein, Vikram Tamboli, Holly Y. McGee, Carrie Tobin, Rachel Gross, Vaneesa Cook, and so many others. Geneviève: Thank you for being a dear friend; all the coworking and talks over whiskey helped make this a better book. Doria Dee Johnson has joined the ancestors, and her memory and example continue to shape my research and writing. Thank you, Jana Valeo, it was so cool writing about your grandfather, Tony, and interviewing your dad. That we both were working at UW, is still incredible to me. Much love to all my comrades in the TAA: Adrienne

x   Acknowledgments

Pagac, Eleni Schirmer, Sigrid Peterson, Kevin Gibbons, Nancy Rydberg, Lenora Hanson, Gina Spitz, Heather Rosenfeld, Michael Billeaux, Alex Hana, Dan Liu, and all the TAA members.

As a first-generation student, I had no thought of graduate school and I owe a debt of gratitude to the nurturing and supportive environment at the University of South Florida History Department. Many thanks to Drs. Robert Ingalls, David K. Johnson, Lou Ann Jones, Frances Ramos, and Joanna Dyl. Dr. Fraser Ottanelli continues to be a dear friend and collaborator. Jeff Perry, who continues to inspire me, has turned into a lifelong friend as well as a valued colleague. His work ethic and determination help show me how to be a better historian.

I acknowledge the scholars who have helped me shape my approach to the craft, understanding Midwestern labor history, and centering workers' voices. Many thanks to Heather Ann Thompson, Joe William Trotter, Jr., Crystal Marie Moten, Keona Ervin, Ashley Howard, and William P. Jones.

This project would not have been completed without the financial support of the University of Wisconsin Graduate School and History Department. The History Department funded a trip to Racine, Wisconsin, and Detroit to conduct archival research and collect interviews. I also received two Vilas grants from the graduate school to present early versions at conferences. I especially benefited from a Mellon/ACLS Dissertation Completion Fellowship, which provided a year of support to finalize chapters, conduct follow-up interviews, and attend two conferences. I spent over a month at the Walter P. Reuther Library and Archives at Wayne State University. I would like to acknowledge the helpfulness and professionalism of the staff there, especially William LeFevre and Louis Jones. The archives at the Wisconsin Historical Society are extensive and the help and support of the staff made researching, as I also worked as a teaching assistant, easy and mostly stress-free. The staff at the Monticello Public Library allowed me to monopolize their only microfilm machine for many months as I read years of newspaper articles from *Racine Labor*.

I am honored to have received the inaugural John A. Peters Fellowship from the Friends of the U.W. Madison Libraries in 2016. I owe special thanks to Laurie Wermter, whose work as a research librarian for the UW Library system and member of the Wisconsin Labor History Society introduced me to scholars and activists essential to the completion of this work. Her bibliography of Wisconsin Labor History is a wonderful gift. The support I have received from the Wisconsin Labor History Society also helped this project, and I am proud to be the 2010 recipient of the graduate student Zeidler Academic Award for Research Papers in Wisconsin Labor and Working-Class History. I finally met Roger Bybee, labor journalist and

Acknowledgments

lifelong activist, at the 2021 Wisconsin Labor History Society conference. His comments, suggestions, and support are much appreciated.

I am also grateful for the community of scholars and activists involved in the Labor and Working-Class Studies Association. Many thanks to Lane Windham, Jon Shelton, and Jessie Wilkerson, who presented at multiple conferences with me. Thanks as well to LAWCHA members Tom Alter, Liesl Orenic, Julie Greene, Joe McCartin, Adan Mertz, Dennis Deslippe, Marisa Chappell, and many others. I would also like to thank the participants of the Newberry Library Urban History Dissertation Group. The opportunity to share and workshop so many interesting chapters-in-progress over three terms was both intellectually stimulating and productive. I would also like to thank the Newberry Labor History Seminar organizers Peter Cole and Liesl Orenic and commenters, including Jon Shelton, Toni Gilpin, and others.

I must also thank the community of scholars and activists who welcomed me at Georgia Tech and SUNY Brockport: Doug Flamming, Dan Amsterdam, Mary McDonald, Willie Pearson, Amy D'Unger, Bill Winders, Jennifer Singh, Laura Bier, Anne Pollock, John K. Marah (may he rest in peace), Michael Boston, Milo Oburn, Karen Podsiadly, Kristen Proehl, Heather Packer, Amy Guptill, and Brittany Profit-Rheinwald. Thank you, too, to the faculty community at Rutgers who have helped see me through this process. Thank you to the senior scholars who read and commented on early chapter edits: Donna Murch, Dorothy Sue Cobble, and Janice Fine. Thank you to Fran Ryan, Becky Givan, Danielle Phillips-Cunningham, and all the faculty and staff in the Labor Studies department. Special thanks to SaunJuhi Verma, Sheri Davis, and Tami Lee, for welcoming me into your crew. Your community has been a great space to test out ideas and to think deeply about Critical Race Theory, Intersectionality, and doing the work of activist scholars. Respect!

The COVID pandemic outbreak, economic shutdown, and murder of George Floyd could have derailed this project. I will be forever grateful to the Black feminist scholars who started a daily writing and sustainability group. Thank you to Donna Murch and Crystal Hayes for creating such a welcoming space. This manuscript made it to my editor because of that community. Dominque Courts: Thank you, you were seen and loved! I appreciate every moment we got to work together to make this world a better place and share intellectual ideas, write together, and build community. Rest in peace, Dom.

Thank you to the editorial team at the University of Illinois Press. It was a dream to publish my first book in the Working Class in American History series and I appreciate the reality come true. Thank you, Alison

Syring, Leigh Ann Cowan, and the whole editorial team, for seeing this project to completion. Many thanks to editor extraordinaire Vaneesa Cook for being a generous and thoughtful contributor along the way. Vaneesa read so many versions of all these chapters with her usual humor and keen eye. A special thank you to Gary Huck for the perfect cover design. I am grateful to the anonymous reviewers at *Labor: Studies in Working-Class History* and UIP. And to the series editors. Your thoughtful and encouraging comments made this a much better historical narrative. All remaining errors and omissions are my own.

Finally, I offer thanks to my family, who aren't always sure of the work I do, but who support me and my passions. Thank you Eary, Niecy, and Dorothy. Thank you, A'sia Howard for being a cool little sister, who I am still getting to know. Phillip Williams, Jr., I miss you every day and I am so sorry that you didn't live to see this in print, but it does exist. Thank you, Daddy, for always accepting me for who I am and loving me all the more for it. Much love to the aunts, uncles, and cousins who taught me so much and who have sustained me over the years. And thank you to my best friend, biggest supporter, and sharpest critic, Danita. She encouraged me to go to graduate school, to pursue my passion, and to tell the stories of working people (even if she wanted the stories to be much shorter). Danita, your love and devotion give me strength and courage. Ohana.

A Blueprint for
Worker Solidarity

INTRODUCTION

Working-Class Identity and Postwar U.S. Society

Leading up to the 2012 presidential elections, Patrick Caldwell, a reporter from *The American Prospect*, visited Racine, Wisconsin, to better understand a state that political analysts have described as the "most schizophrenic battleground" in the nation.[1] The majority of voters in Racine opted for George W. Bush, Paul Ryan, Scott Walker, as well as Barack Obama throughout the decade. In June 2012, they voted against recalling their Republican Governor Scott Walker but recalled their Republican state senator. Racine, a small industrial city that sits along Lake Michigan between Chicago and Milwaukee, has a long history of unionization and was widely known as a progressive union town with militant labor activists who created a local political environment that supported working-class issues. But the Racine that Caldwell visited in 2012 seemed like the barren wasteland of abandoned manufacturing plants and retail shops that depictions of deindustrialized North American cities typically invoke. Plant closings, increased management resistance to organized labor, mass layoffs, shrinking local and state budget expenditures, and conservative political agendas, which have undermined the gains of the labor movement, took a heavy toll on Racine's labor community over the last few decades.

The Racine that Caldwell saw in 2012 offers lakeshore beaches, a zoo, abundant parks, and an art museum. It has plenty of fast-food restaurants, cafés, and bars, lining its main street, housed in the traditional cream brick buildings typical of the Milwaukee area. The general aesthetic, however, is a mixture of quaint, refurbished structures that one would expect of a touristy beach town with the old, outdated storefronts and houses of a city struggling to renovate since its industrial heyday. The Racine Labor Center still stands in the middle of a sprawling parking lot on Layard Avenue, as a one-story, nondescript building of plain brick and stone without much natural lighting. The city, in short, reflects a diversity of natural beauty, tourism, and artistic elements, but also functionality and low tax rates.

Racine also has a complex political environment. On his visit, Caldwell encountered Democrats seeking to appeal to white middle-class voters who were undecided about their upcoming presidential vote. Democrats felt good about their chances due to the resurgence of political activism over the previous two years since Governor Walker's attack on public sector workers in the state. In "The County that Swings Wisconsin," Caldwell implied that activists and the voters they swayed were responding to nostalgia for a bygone era when unions had the political power and clout to influence local, state, and national elections. But Racine County Democratic Chairwoman Jane Witt explained, "I think there are a lot of people who are loyal to the unions, even if their own company doesn't have one anymore . . . There are a lot of union sympathizers."[2] The 12,000 people who signed up with the American Federation of Labor (AFL)-Congress of Industrial Organizations (CIO) affiliated group Working America leading up to the election confirmed Witt's sense of pro-union attitudes in Racine. Democratic Party members joined forces with Working America to rally these union supporters to reelect Obama and send Democrat Tammy Baldwin to the U.S. Senate.[3]

Caldwell's situating of postindustrial Racine in nostalgic terms is emblematic of a declension narrative that seeks to explain the collapse of union power in the 1970s. Scholars have pointed to the decline of class politics during the 1970s and argued that class lost its meaning as a tool to mobilize working people to collective action or to the voting polls. Related and overlapping theories point to the successes of the civil rights and women's movements of the 1960s, which shifted social and political debate toward individual rights in lieu of group identity. Others suggest that the political ties between labor and the Democratic Party deteriorated and rank-and-file union members lost their militancy and courage in the face of deindustrialization, corporate resistance, and conservative backlash. Similarly, the failure of liberal Democrats and policymakers to adapt to the changing economic conditions of the world economy and adjust domestic policy to minimize the resulting turmoil caused working people to lose confidence in the labor-liberal coalition.[4] Yet, the mobilization around Working America in 2012 is evidence of a continuing legacy of working-class identity and class politics in Racine.

I first learned about Racine's labor community at a campus-community labor reception during my first semester at the University of Wisconsin-Madison. I met sociology professor Jane Collins, who was finishing *Both*

Hands Tied, and when she learned that I was interested in examining local history around labor, politics, and worker mobilization, she told me the story of the Black and Brown women who went on strike at St. Luke's Hospital in Racine in 1976.[5] After many of them were laid off in the 1990s, they became active in the welfare rights movement, the topic of her book. Jane shared a draft chapter and the news clippings covering the strike. We were both intrigued by frontpage *Racine Labor* pictures with white, male United Auto Workers (UAW) workers walking the picket line with the women SEIU workers. The story I knew of white industrial workers in the 1970s was one of neglect or hostility to service workers, especially those of color. Yet, in Racine, there was a concerted effort to bring SEIU workers into the community. The UAW locals not only walked the picket lines, they also donated funds, opened office space in the Racine Labor Center, stepped in with a lawyer to help with bargaining until they could "Racinize" the SEIU state leadership, and supported new organizing, even as they fought against plant closures and downsizing at local manufacturing plants. What made this community different? Why did white industrial workers see value in supporting organizing and strike activity in the service sector? How did workers in Racine overcome internal racial divisions to build an inclusive working-class community? I wanted to meet these activists, hear their stories, and put their experiences into the context of the political, social, and economic landscape of the late twentieth-century United States.

I first met Racine worker activists in 2012 while protesting the unjust Act 10 in Madison, Wisconsin, at the state capitol. Act 10, which became law in June 2011 after several legal challenges, changed the public employee collective bargaining laws first enacted in Wisconsin in 1959 by listing a set of prohibited bargaining subjects and limiting contract negotiations to wage issues. It also required public worker unions to undergo certification with the Wisconsin Employment Relations Commission on a yearly basis and prohibited state and local governments from collecting members' dues payments.[6] Policymakers designed these legal changes to destroy public worker unions by depleting their financial and time resources. This attack by a Republican governor on public worker unions mirrored the actions of private corporate employers in the postwar period. Like the tactics of Racine's industrial leaders in the 1950s, Governor Walker eliminated tools that workers' unions used to gain some sort of economic security and power in the workplace. The political and economic attacks on private worker unions in the postwar period weakened the labor movement and opened the door for the twenty-first-century attack on public sector unions. These continued attacks on an embattled and weakened labor

4 Introduction

movement illustrate the ways in which conservative policymakers and politicians understand and fight against the power of organized workers to effect change in U.S. society.

A Blueprint for Worker Solidarity details the ways workers in Racine built, maintained, and adapted a robust working-class community and shaped the local political economy from World War II to the 1980s. They helped build the Wisconsin Democratic Party, fought for fair housing and education, ran for local political offices, and held politicians accountable to the working people in the city. They forged coalitions with racial and gender justice organizations, and they organized deep and wide across employment sectors in the city. Their legacy is part of what makes Wisconsin such a key state in national politics today. And worker activists' experiences offer clear lessons on the value of broad-based adaptable class politics and the struggle for economic justice at a time when coalition building seems more difficult than ever. They sustained a vibrant working-class community deep into what many still point to as labor's decline. The lessons they provided highlight how we can support workplace democracy and economic freedom in the twenty-first century.

Those activists included people like William Jenkins and Tony Valeo whose life experiences are spread throughout the book. William "Blue" Jenkins grew up in Racine after his parents migrated north. His was the only Black family in an Italian neighborhood. Jenkins was a popular and precocious child and local sports star. His family provided information and welcome to other Black families during the Great Migration. He learned early, as most Black children do, that his race limited his opportunities in the city. Yet, he encountered people who stood against discrimination. He learned from his father, a former unionized coal worker, that solidarity meant not crossing picket lines. These early lessons shaped Jenkins into the kind of person who stood up for those less fortunate and encouraged others to act in solidarity. Jenkins was active in the Racine NAACP and helped shape the local chapter into a working-class haven during its early years. While popular in the foundry where he worked and often called to lead work stoppages in his department, it took many years before Jenkins was elected to a union leadership position. When he was elected, he helped transform his local and the larger Racine labor community to address racial equity, expand bargaining to community concerns, and build coalitions with other likeminded union leaders in the garment workers and teamsters unions. Jenkins spent his whole life fighting for workers' rights. After retiring, he served in community-based activist groups and won a seat on the school board during a debate over taxes and public education.[7]

Introduction
5

Anthony "Tony" Valeo's family came from Southern Italy. He came of age during the Great Depression and, as his son recalled, worked his whole life so other workers would not experience such devastation. Valeo spent most of his career at the J. I. Case Company. He worked his way up to union leadership and oversaw the union through some tough negotiations and a pivotal 1960 strike. After retiring, he worked as a UAW international representative and organized and served on the board of several community-labor coalitions. Like Jenkins, Valeo understood the value of bringing workplace issues to the larger community and addressing community issues from a working-class perspective. Valeo spent many of his evenings going from door-to-door talking with workers and their families about issues impacting Racine. His son Tom explained that he never resented his father's work in the community but only understood the significance of Tony's work at the memorial service in Kenosha when he was overwhelmed by those who showed up to share their remembrances. So many of the workers I encountered during my research remembered Jenkins and Valeo as influential role models for working people.[8]

Activists also included people like Harvey Kitzman who helped start the largest union local in Racine, became director of UAW Region 10, and led the way in building a broad community of labor activists and their supporters. Kitzman spent his career building, reshaping, and sustaining a sense of class solidarity in Racine and throughout Wisconsin. Loretta Christensen organized workers across industries, sat on the board of the AFL labor council and of *Racine Labor* in the 1950s, and remained an active member of the county's Democratic Party for forty years. Corinne Reid-Owens, "Racine's Rosa Parks," was denied a teaching job because she was Black yet opened that door for others and then herself by the 1970s. Reid-Owens helped lead the NAACP, YWCA, and various community and neighborhood programs and spent her whole life dedicated to helping and empowering the young people in Racine. These and other activists shaped a class politics that sought to encompass the whole community through union organizing, civic engagement, worker education and mobilization, and a political use of the labor history in the city. Using a broad-based class politics that successfully adapted to economic, social, and political changes in the city and nation, labor activists kept the notion of collective class solidarity at the forefront of the city's identity from World War II to the 1980s. Even after the plant closings in the 1980s, the Racine labor movement remained an active voice for the working people of Racine and reinforced the continued relevance of class identity and political action.

While Racine seems like a typical Midwestern Rust Belt town found in the literature on deindustrialization and the postindustrial United States, its relatively diversified industrial base made it more resistant to the market fluctuations that devastated one-industry towns like Akron, Gary, or neighboring Kenosha, Wisconsin.[9] More important to understanding the vitality of the labor community, four factors set Racine apart and played key roles in the enduring labor militancy and lingering sense of collective class identity. First, early organizing beyond industrial settings to include public workers, private service, and white-collar workers expanded the definition of who belonged in the labor community. Second, Black workers' efforts during the long civil rights era helped infuse a racial analysis into working-class politics. Third, the labor strife that persisted in the postwar period belied any illusions of a labor-management accord in local class relations and extended the sense of collective struggle. And fourth, the forty-year history of the publication of the local labor paper, *Racine Labor*, which helped encourage public debate on working-class issues, the political use of the city's labor history, and broad support for working-class issues across diverse unions, shaped a lasting narrative of the valuable role of the labor community in securing economic and social justice for all workers. These four factors facilitated an environment favorable to the building and sustaining of a sense of class solidarity and the adaptability of class politics to changing economic, social, and political struggles over time.

Studies such as *A Blueprint for Worker Solidarity*, of a community in transition from an industrial to a service-based economy, can provide new insights into the ways in which worker solidarity persevered within a shifting capitalist society in the late-twentieth century, a valuable lesson for twenty-first-century worker activists. They reveal the ways in which the meaning of class and class politics shifted in the 1970s as opposed to a simple story of decline like that articulated in the 2012 *American Prospect* article. The continuing identification of Racine as a union town and its residents' memberships in class-based groups like Working America and community-based social justice organizations are legacies of the broad-based working-class politics pursued by people like William Jenkins and Tony Valeo from the New Deal era through the 1980s.

Emergence of Racine's Labor Community

In the nineteenth century, Racine County developed as an agricultural area. Situated at the mouth of the Root River on Lake Michigan, the city of Racine originally provided business and governmental services to the surrounding agricultural areas. However, proximity to Chicago and Milwaukee created an attractive setting for manufacturing industries and many

Introduction 7

firms located their operations in Racine in the early- to mid-twentieth century.[10] Racine's labor movement mirrored the city's industrial growth. Early unions included cigar workers, bricklayers, masons, plumbers, and brewery workers, all members of the elite AFL, which focused on organizing skilled craftsmen. Some activists saw the need to organize unskilled workers across whole plants and industries. For example, in the 1880s, the local Knights of Labor membership totaled nearly 1,000. And during the Great Depression, workers in Racine formed the Racine County Workers Committee to represent unemployed Works Progress Administration (WPA) relief workers.[11]

As workers continued to organize, they formed local unions and sought affiliation with major national and international unions, further solidifying Racine's reputation as a union town. Workers at Racine's largest foundry, the J. I. Case Company (Case), organized themselves into the Workers Industrial Union and, after a 91-day strike, the company finally recognized their union. However, it was not until 1936 when the workers at Case affiliated with the UAW as Local 180 that they saw real gains at the workplace. The UAW, an example of the formation of unions in large industries and not just specific trades, successfully organized various factories during the late 1930s without creating significant conflict with local AFL affiliates. The UAW joined the newly organized CIO in 1935. Like other CIO unions, the UAW in Racine organized workers in industrial settings and the culture of CIO unions inspired workers to become engaged citizens and demonstrate worker unity within local unions, across industries, and with other unionized and nonunionized workers in the areas where they operated.[12] Case was the largest manufacturer in town and remained the most intransigent regarding worker rights. Despite or because of this, UAW Local 180 often led by example in regard to labor militancy and the benefits of persistence.[13] City firefighters formed a union in 1931 and affiliated with the AFL.[14] Building Service Employees International Union (BSEIU) started organizing private service workers in Wisconsin during the 1930s, and BSEIU Local 152 had several units of janitors in schools, office buildings, and department stores in Racine. This organizing helped shape the working-class community that flourished in the mid-twentieth century.

World War II created an unprecedented opportunity for political and social action in the United States by expanding the role of the federal government, facilitating the movement of even more people from rural areas and Southern cities to industrial centers, and bringing unprecedented wealth and power to the United States. Scholars have detailed how federal policymakers became more committed to the government's role in social welfare and economic growth. Federal spending increased the capital holdings of large corporations. As a result, increased wages, a sense of affluence, and a hope for greater access to this affluence spread throughout U.S. society.[15] In Racine a broad range of working-class activists took advantage of the opportunities of the World War II period to demand a voice in shaping the new social, political, and economic landscape.

As Nelson Lichtenstein and other scholars have shown, the massive wartime economic and social changes helped mobilize workers to join unions in ever greater numbers and solidify the labor movement's connection to the Democratic Party. Unionization rates in key industries rose above 80 percent after the war, and by 1953, over one-third of workers outside the farm industry belonged to unions.[16] High wages and low unemployment made joining the union less risky for workers seeking economic gains and workplace democracy. Nationwide, about half a million Black workers joined industrial unions, mostly after migrating from the South or from rural areas, and they led the way in addressing racial issues in the workplace. Black workers were galvanized by New Deal legislation and used the rhetoric of economic and political citizenship to gain access to jobs and unions where they were previously denied access.[17] Blue-collar women workers joined the labor movement as well and used their positions to create better conditions for women throughout U.S. society, eventually leading to legislative changes in the 1960s and 1970s that opened the door for greater economic freedom.[18]

As Black men and white women entered Racine's workplaces in the postwar period, they actively asserted their place in labor unions and established themselves as capable members of the labor community. Most Black women remained in domestic and other low-wage service positions as they were most often last to be hired in industrial workplaces. This did not limit Black women's social justice activism. Crystal Moten details Black women's economic activism in Milwaukee during this time in *Continually Working*.[19] In Racine, workers consolidated their postwar economic gains by demanding more from employers at the bargaining table and backing up their demands with work stoppages and strikes. Worker activists also used their new political power in local politics and entered public debates on social and economic conditions affecting the community. Activists elected labor-endorsed candidates to local and statewide offices, demanded seats on the boards of charitable institutions, and lobbied for legislation to protect public sector collective bargaining rights. Workers pushed a class agenda that would benefit all organized and unorganized workers in the city. Labor liberals used the postwar growth and prosperity to push for an expansion of economic citizenship rights for a larger portion of society.

Introduction 9

As Paul Whiteside, an active union organizer in the area from the 1930s through the 1980s, emphasized, "When you got control of a thing, you got the majority in an area, you tend to be more aggressive."[20]

While the labor movement experienced an unprecedented position of power in U.S. political and economic debate in the postwar period, it did not go unchallenged by conservative business leaders and politicians intent on minimizing labor's influence. Weaknesses within the New Deal labor laws and attacks on collective bargaining mitigated labor's ability to consolidate its power more fully. Along with weaknesses within the labor law, the conservative political and corporate backlash of the postwar period limited labor's influence. In Racine, the long-lasting battles with paternalistic managers at companies like Case and the history of civic engagement among workers created an atmosphere of militant resistance to efforts to weaken federal labor laws or undermine the political power of organized labor. In fact, Racine's labor community helped successfully reverse a right-to-work law in the 1950s, similar to the 2012 Act 10 law, which led to the recall election for Governor Scott Walker.

As the 1960s dawned, Racine's labor activists sought to build on the successes of the postwar period and continued their efforts to push liberals to hold to the promises of New Deal liberalism, mainly active support of workers' efforts to gain full economic citizenship rights. A strike at Case, coupled with the ongoing struggles at Kohler and the political battle surrounding it, fueled the notion of continued class warfare. Unions organized new members in the low-wage service sector and public workers prefigured the labor militancy that would take hold across the nation in the 1970s. Black and Latine activists built on the inroads they made in the postwar period and helped reshape the sense of class identity in the city to more fully incorporate race and gender.

The economic, political, and social changes of the postwar period helped facilitate gains in the fight for racial equality in the United States. As the federal government became more actively engaged in intervening in crises, civil rights activists seized the opportunity to intensify their demands for equity. Black activists used the democratic rhetoric of the war period to challenge the federal government to act on behalf of citizens left out of the new social contract. Scholars have noted the ways in which the civil rights movement opened "the American workplace."[21] As historian Jacquelyn Dowd Hall has documented, Black workers understood that civil rights and workers' rights were two connected aspects of the freedom struggle.[22] In Racine, labor activists actively participated in the civil rights and women's movements of the 1960s, which helped the larger labor community more smoothly adapt to shifting social identities while maintaining a commitment to class solidarity. While internal challenges of racial conservatism and political differences existed, the active participation of Black workers, public workers, women, and those in the service sector, helped legitimize a wide diversity of workers as members of the working-class community.[23] This is part of the blueprint for twenty-first-century activists who struggle to dismantle systemic barriers and to organize across lines of identity.

Labor activists reshaped their sense of class solidarity as political debates around discriminatory hiring practices and housing grew in the city. This adaptive solidarity laid the foundation for the political battles of the 1970s. Some labor activists and labor unions have worked hard to adjust their strategies to meet goals of not only changing American workplaces but also creating a more democratic society. The historiography of the period demonstrates the ways in which the labor movement used creative coalitions to bring about workplace and societal improvements. Jefferson Cowie describes how the changed American landscape played out among workers as more diverse workplaces expanded opportunities for building solidarity across race and gender lines. As he points out, "The new worker emerging in the 1970s was not, however, a simple reincarnation of the 1930s proletarian of popular historical imagination." As workers sought to understand their economic situation and the new politics of race and culture, they reacted in multiple ways, often revolting not only against corporations but also intransigent union leadership as exemplified by the strike against General Motors at Lordstown. Although Cowie bemoans the inability of liberals, especially those in the Democratic Party, to capitalize on working-class political expression, he acknowledges the rank-and-file militancy of the period.[24] So, while the environment had changed, working-class activists played an active role in shaping political and economic issues in American society, *especially* on the local level. In Racine, rank-and-file workers' activism continued into the 1970s and facilitated organizing in new sectors and within changing work environments. This is the story that Lane Windham details in *Knocking on Labor's Door*. She shows the ways workers continued to organize and seek out unions to improve workplace democracy and economic power. What changed was not workers' efforts but their ability to win. Victories were few because of increased corporate resistance and the failure of liberal policymakers' political will to support labor's efforts.[25]

By 1972, Racine County ranked second in Wisconsin for the number of manufacturing establishments, yet industrial jobs declined due to workforce reductions and corporate restructuring. Some plants had moved from the city to the county to capitalize on lower tax rates, while

Introduction 11

others had shifted out of state to the South or overseas. With the decline of well-paying industrial jobs, the Chicago and Northwestern Railroad ended commuter service from Chicago to Racine in 1970 and many retail establishments closed during this period as well.[26] While industrial jobs declined, public sector and low-wage service sector jobs increased.

Racine's workforce also shifted as more Mexican and Mexican American workers moved from Midwestern farm employment into factories and new migrants also took entry-level jobs in the region's meatpacking plants and foundries. Women's employment increased as industrial jobs declined and the service sector grew, shifting the makeup of many unions and presenting the opportunity to expand labor organizing in new sectors.[27] At the same time, organized labor maintained a prominent voice in Racine's political and social debates and actively supported the efforts of low-wage service workers and public employees to achieve more dignity at work and economic security in uncertain times.

Labor activists in Racine effectively shaped a narrative of a broad-based class community that legitimized the role of public and private service employees to demand better wages and working conditions as industrial employment declined and low-wage service sector and public worker activism grew. While industrial unionism was seen as crucial to the maintenance of middle-class incomes for workers, many policymakers, intellectuals, and conservative pundits debated the rights of public employees to join unions, especially their right to strike.[28] Although Wisconsin was the first state to enact legislation enabling public employees to bargain collectively, strikes were prohibited. Joseph McCartin has rightly compared the militant nature of public worker unionism in the late 1960s through the early 1970s to industrial unionists in the 1930s. Teachers, firefighters, police officers, sanitation workers, as well as clerical workers flocked to public sector unions during this period. Strike activities were also impressive, with 478 strikes in 1975 alone.[29] In Racine, public workers organized earlier than at the national level, opening the door to a wider understanding of who belonged as members of the labor community.

Racine's activists maintained a vibrant labor community, a militant class politics, and managed to adapt to the changing environment while also continuing to focus on fighting against economic inequality and exploitation into the 1980s. Between 1977 and 1987, manufacturing jobs in Racine County declined by 15 percent, and most of this decline came in the city of Racine itself. By the early 1980s, Racine's downtown had over one million square feet of empty business space. These depressed conditions limited the city's ability to attract new businesses and visitors.[30] Yet, the labor community continued to actively fight against the effects of deindustrialization

12   Introduction

with diverse tactics. Workers went on strike to push back against management resistance, stayed politically involved in local and national elections, organized new workplaces, and formed coalitions with social justice and political groups. While their efforts did not ultimately lead to a reversal of the economic instability wrought by weakened labor contracts and plant closings, it did sustain a sense of class solidarity and commitment to push forward a working-class politics that they hoped would change the political landscape to one where a broad-based economic and social agenda could proceed. This is the spirit that Caldwell encountered in 2012, and it remains an important lesson for scholars and activists today. The stories we tell and the frames in which we construct our narratives can either give workers' voices a clear expression or stifle them into an uncomplicated declension narrative.

Racine's working-class community demonstrated a remarkable ability to adjust to the changing economic and political landscape in the second half of the twentieth century. A long history of class struggle and the political use of the city's labor history helped maintain a sense of shared experiences within the community. The broad-based working-class politics that fueled labor activists' engaged involvement in political debates garnered some level of control in allocating resources for working-class residents. An increasing number of workers with unions behind them, improving—in limited and disjointed fashion—the economic, social, and political conditions for all workers in the city helped create and maintain a productive working-class identity. Labor activists' expansive understanding of who belonged in the working class, including the language, actions of solidarity, and struggles for economic and political power, demonstrate the continued importance of a working-class identity and solidarity that went beyond typical narratives of labor's lost power during the transformations of deindustrialization. Racine's activists also adapted to the economic and political times by showing a continued willingness to build coalitions within the labor community, with liberal politicians, and with other social justice organizations. *A Blueprint for Worker Solidarity* traces the history of these developments and analyzes how class remained a salient force in the changing political, economic, and social landscape.

Postwar Liberalism

The story of Racine's labor community is intricately tied to the complexities of New Deal liberalism and the relationship between labor activists and their liberal allies. The New Deal era reshaped U.S. liberalism, made it the driving force of the political landscape, legitimized government

Introduction 13

intervention in the private sector, and built its strength on a coalition of Democratic politicians, labor leaders, intellectuals, and marginalized racial groups.[31] After World War II, labor activists used their power to continue to push New Deal policies even further to aid more and more of the working class.[32] In his 1941 State of the Union address to Congress, President Franklin D. Roosevelt linked the militaristic efforts of winning World War II with solving the economic and social ills of the nation. In place of fear and inaction, Roosevelt asserted that people everywhere should enjoy freedom of speech, freedom of worship, freedom from want, and freedom from fear. For activists around the world, Roosevelt's speech seemed like a call to action. For labor activists, this speech and Roosevelt's plan for an "Economic Bill of Rights" seemed to confirm that Roosevelt supported their demands for a broad-based economic citizenship and that the federal government would support their efforts to gain those citizenship rights.[33] In states with significant industrial sectors such as Wisconsin, labor activists helped propel the Democratic Party to power and demanded government involvement as part of their economic rights after World War II.[34]

New Deal liberals adopted policies of active government to manage and regulate the economy, provide social welfare programs, and redistribute private power. New Deal liberals supported and promoted the growth of the labor movement. As the postwar economy continued to grow, politicians and policymakers shifted their attention away from economic inequality to focus on other matters, such as Cold War foreign policy and anticommunism. Union activists had broader goals beyond allying labor to the Democratic Party. Activists sought to "transform it into a coherent liberal political party."[35] In the postwar period, activists in Racine continued to push their liberal allies to take a firm stand on the side of workers' struggle to gain greater economic freedom and workplace democracy.[36] In Racine, the idea of economic security for all that emerged within the context of New Deal liberalism remained salient, and labor activists often used the rhetoric of economic citizenship to embrace labor liberalism. Black workers in particular helped bring racial analyses into the labor community's agenda, keeping unions relevant throughout the end of the twentieth century.

Deindustrialization

The literature on deindustrialization points to the devastating effects of plant closings, global capital expansion, and mass layoffs on industrial workers and their communities. *A Blueprint* relies on Barry Bluestone and Bennett Harrison's analysis of deindustrialization as a process within capitalist society in their work *The Deindustrialization of America*. The authors show how corporate decisions and the battle for industrial control over the economy led to a steady movement of capital and the massive "dismantling" of basic industry across the U.S. by the late 1970s. Their extensive research shows the devastating effects of plant closings on communities through widespread loss: jobs, municipal tax revenue, and population. The authors also highlight the ways in which corporate decisions have detrimental outcomes for seemingly booming areas that should have been reaping the benefits of reindustrialization. Using Houston, Texas, as an example, Bluestone and Harrison show how the competition between cities, and throughout the nation for industrial growth, led to poor city planning, housing shortages, and increased income disparities.[37]

Workers responded to deindustrialization and global capitalism's shifts with a range of responses, including building cooperatives to keep manufacturing plants, fighting for policy changes, collectively bargaining for economic protections, and fighting to repair damages to their communities.[38] Scholarship also shows how grassroots mobilizations and collective action worked across the Rust Belt in the United States.[39] Scholars who incorporate workers' memory and community identity into their analyses help argue against a strict declension narrative in the story of deindustrialization. For example, this literature highlights the connections between memory and worker identity. From oral histories, Steve May and Laura Morrison conclude that workers explain deindustrialization as corporate abandonment of the social contract, yet workers retain their sense of pride in themselves as they adjust. Centering workers' experiences illustrates the ways people considered themselves to be agents instead of victims in their narratives. "Workers' investment in the political system" can be maintained even as factors of deindustrialization break their trust.[40]

Building on this literature, *A Blueprint* explores the determination of workers to continue to fight for economic justice and maintain a voice in the local political economy as more and more industrial jobs left the city. In Racine, this process started in the late 1950s and then climaxed in the early 1980s. When they could, workers in Racine leveraged their collective power to shape the economic and social landscape as employers increasingly had to search for new ways to limit workers' resources.[41] Throughout the most severe dismantling of Racine's industrial sector, even while workers lost power on the shop floor, they held on to the working-class militancy that had aided them through the earlier period. At the end of the 1980s, workers felt encouraged by the political victories they had managed at the local and state level. Over the second half of the twentieth century, Racine's labor community learned to adapt to the major political, economic, and social transformations of the era without losing sight of the need to combat economic inequality and exploitation.

Workers did lose power at work and in local, state, and national political battles, but defeat came not because they failed to adapt or limited their militant activism but due to larger economic and political changes out of their control. This story matters in today's continuing battle for greater economic, social, and political empowerment in the United States. It offers an example of the ways in which a broad-based definition of who belongs in the labor movement, coalition building, and militant resistance to economic and political conservatives can help cultivate and sustain collective actions for holding on to some gains and the political motivation to continue to fight when new opportunities emerge: A blueprint for today.

Terminology

Throughout the book, I use the term *labor community* (or working-class community) as Racine labor activists used it over the decades of my study. The most dynamic, engaged activists expressed their vision of the city's labor community to include all workers and those who wanted to work. This meant craft workers, industrial laborers, public workers, office staff and technicians, private service workers, and those unemployed or under-employed who relied on social service programs for survival, all stood within the labor community. While a sense of collective identity and class solidarity requires the engagement of rank-and-file workers, Racine's labor leaders and engaged activists provided the motivation, commitment, and direction that kept bringing in new members and inspired others to action. Of course, this vision was complicated as Black and Latine workers struggled to break into the better-paid, safer positions. This vision was also made more difficult by the refusal of the building trade locals in the city to welcome nonwhite workers into apprenticeship positions until the late 1970s. However, the consensus among the core group of labor activists was to incorporate as many workers as possible into the community, aided by early organizing in the public sector and private service industries, and their participation in other social justice movements.

Activists strictly enforced the boundaries of the labor community during strikes or other labor actions when met with resistance. Union leaders and rank-and-file members would shun strikebreakers or other workers who spoke and/or acted against class interests. While all workers did not always walk in lockstep with the circle of engaged activists, the labor community's ability to garner the support of its members to participate in rallies, Labor Day celebrations, sports and other social events, write

16 Introduction

letters to the editor, engage their political leaders, vote for labor-endorsed candidates, grant interviews with journalists and researchers, and to sign membership cards and actively seek jobs in unionized workplaces shows the value of using the broader term of labor community. The broad-based working-class vision pursued by the Racine labor community influenced local politics, charitable and social justice organizations, as well as social issues such as housing and education. It also increased the number of workers with the power of unions behind them, and improved Racine's economic and social conditions. The Racine labor community transformed the local political economy and centered working-class issues in economic and social debates.

Latine is the gender-neutral term I use when referring to Mexican, Mexican American, and/or Puerto Rican Racinians as a group. I use Latine because it originated among queer people within the LGBTQIA+ community in Spanish-speaking countries. It is truer to Spanish grammar and easier for native speakers to pronounce than Latinx (another commonly used gender-neutral term).[42]

Sources

This story of Racine's labor community is based on archival research of local union records, political organizations, and social justice groups, particularly the Racine branch of the National Association for the Advancement of Colored People (NAACP). My sources also include records of the UAW and Service Employees International leadership and countywide labor councils. *Racine Labor*, the *Racine Journal-Times*, and other newspapers provided the backdrop for the census data, local business and industry records, and local electoral politics. *Racine Labor*, the weekly newspaper published by a group representing most of the city's unions, provided another avenue for activists to communicate with the public, to maintain an active voice in political, economic, and social debates both local and national, and to sustain the historical narrative of Racine as a union town with an active working class.

A Blueprint for Worker Solidarity centers the perspective of worker activists who lived and worked in the city. I have used oral history records collected from Racine-area worker activists, starting in the 1950s and through the 1990s, which are held at the Wisconsin Historical Society and the Walter P. Reuther Library at Wayne State University. I have also interviewed members of Racine's working-class community to gain insight into memory, space, and identity. Together with the stories, interviews,

Introduction 17

and letters in *Racine Labor*, these perspectives informed and deeply influenced the direction of the book. Workers' lived experiences illustrate the ways collective action shaped Racine's political economy and support the argument for dynamic working-class politics fighting for all forms of social justice. Readers will notice a lack of first-person accounts from women workers. No women who I approached would agree to participate in formal interviews for this book. While women were recognized as legitimate workers, the culture of Racine's labor community kept men in most of the leadership positions. Women advocated for their rights, and sat on executive boards and committees in labor organizations, but rank-and-file women had few opportunities to advance to leadership positions. I did speak informally with women workers and their perspectives shaped my analysis.

I begin the story of Racine's labor community with workers' growing power in the period leading up to and after World War II. Workers used the rhetoric of economic security to organize more people into the community, militantly forced manufacturing companies to accept collective bargaining, and helped create Wisconsin's Democratic Party. Black workers moved into the city and brought racial justice demands to their unions. This led to decades of working-class solidarity to fight against business leaders' and their conservative allies' attempts to push back against New Deal liberal labor laws. Black workers and women across racial lines continued to add depth to the labor community's political analysis by demanding race- and gender-conscious theories of change. Their efforts created the space for more organizing and cross-sector support. Solidarity and expansion shaped Racine's labor community agenda into the 1970s. As the process of capital flight and restructuring took its toll in the 1970s and 1980s, workers sought to reshape the local political economy by keeping class politics at the center of debates, electing more labor activists to local office, and supporting the growing immigrant worker population. The loss of good union jobs due to deindustrialization and the failure of state and federal politicians to provide protections for working people left Racine's labor community to fight a losing battle with heavy conservative pushback. Yet, their determined efforts helped Racine's workers retain more economic and political power through the last decades of the twentieth century. Their story illustrates the continuing importance of collective working-class identity and the value of broad-based coalitions for economic justice. *A Blueprint for Worker Solidarity* also suggests the value of new interpretations of the labor movement during this period of low-density and "decline."

CHAPTER 1

Building Racine's Labor Community

William Jenkins remembered that most Black people arriving in Racine between the 1930s and the 1950s came straight from the South or just after a stop in Chicago because, "This was a good workplace, awful good place for work."[1] Jenkins had moved with his family to Racine in 1917. The family settled in the mostly Italian neighborhood on the north side of town near the railroad station. Jenkins decided not to pursue a college athletic scholarship because his father's death meant he was needed at home for economic support. Instead, he went to work in Racine's industrial sector. After accepting a job at the Belle City Malleable foundry in 1939, Jenkins became an active member of UAW Local 553 during World War II.[2] The lessons he learned from his father, his outspokenness and willingness to speak out for others, and his UAW membership, sparked over forty years of William Jenkins's role as a leader in the Racine labor community. The work he and other labor activists did in the postwar period helped build a broad-based and robust labor community that maintained its relevance for working people in the city for the next half century.

This chapter examines the ways worker activists like Jenkins built Racine's labor community and shaped working-class political agendas leading up to World War II and the immediate postwar period. It begins by looking at early organizing and how President Franklin D. Roosevelt's rhetoric around the New Deal and particularly his 1944 presidential address galvanized Racine's activists to become engaged citizens in the local political economy. Labor unions banded together and supported a vibrant press, workers helped revitalize Racine's Democratic Party, and they fought against conservative business leaders and Republicans seeking to roll back New Deal labor gains. A close look at UAW Local 180 and the workers' relationship with J.I. Case's management team illustrates how Local 180 helped shape the terms of debate around class politics in the city. This battle led to a 440-day strike in 1945. World War II spurred population growth and expanded Racine's industrial workforce as many Black workers moved into town and took jobs at local foundries. Women across racial lines found new job opportunities in Racine as well, and along with Black men, helped bring racial and gender analysis to the local labor community. Labor struggles leading up to and after WWII, workers' political engagement, and the efforts of Black and women workers to democratize unions and the city, helped labor activists build a broad-based labor community in Racine.

Economic Citizenship and WWII

In Racine, the idea of economic security for all that emerged within the context of New Deal liberalism remained salient, and labor activists often used the rhetoric of economic citizenship throughout the decades. Labor liberals took a "total person unionism" approach to building and shaping the labor community during this period. They understood that working-class politics needed to influence and shape the city's broader political economy and that unions needed to do more than focus on shopfloor politics. In his biography of Harold Gibbons and Ernest Calloway, Robert Bussel details how their vision of engaged citizens meant treating workers as "total persons" with "both economic and social needs." Gibbons and Calloway "sought to create a community bargaining table where empowered worker-citizens negotiated with St. Louis's economic and political elites." Workers needed to be civically engaged, which meant addressing the community's economic, social, and political environment.[3] Similarly, Racine's worker activists took on these challenges in their unions and community and created a culture of active civic engagement.

Workers started organizing and building community in conjunction with industrial development. A Knights of Labor local assembly was one of the first organized worker organizations in Racine, with about 1,000 members. In 1886, the county assembly held a successful rally with 10,000 people and endorsed a slate of candidates for fall elections. They combined forces with local Democrats and had a mostly successful slate of candidates elected, including the first Black elected official in Racine County, P. B. Thomas, who won as coroner.[4] Early trade unions affiliated with the American Federation of Labor (AFL) and included local cigar workers, bricklayers, masons, plumbers, and brewery workers. The building laborers had originally been part of the Knights of Labor but organized as Local

108 in 1888. One of the largest early unions was the Molders, Local 310, recognized in 1897, which had more than 400 members by 1912. Cigar makers, Local 304, organized the first Labor Day celebration in Racine in 1892 and helped found the Racine Trade and Labor Council (RTLC) in September 1894.[5]

Started by seven local unions, the RTLC by 1901 had delegates from twenty-two separate unions, representing 2,200 members. The Council focused on building support for working people in the city, supporting union shops, and adding to the built environment. After raising funds and finding land, RTLC member unions dedicated the new building on 27 October 1912.[6] Located downtown, Union Hall contained a bar, night club, bowling alley, and a variety of meeting rooms.[7] These unions took a heavy blow during the crisis of the Great Depression as members lost their jobs and production slowed across the city. Yet, early organizing meant that Racine's labor community was able to carry forward with some momentum. During the Great Depression, workers formed the Racine County Workers Committee to represent unemployed Works Progress Administration (WPA) relief workers.[8] This early activity paved the way for the fledgling community to be prepared for the fast-paced expansion surrounding World War II.

Racine's worker activists participated in a wide variety of activities related to economic citizenship, workplace democracy, and building working-class solidarity. Leaders were proud of the fact that unions cooperated across racial, ethnic, and labor affiliations to publish the weekly newspaper, hold special events, and plan yearly Labor Day celebrations.[9] Leaders prioritized community improvement. The RTLC voted in 1946 to meet with "other civic organizations" to utilize the recreational centers to provide an outlet for young people.[10] Also in 1946, Racine UAW-CIO education director Hugh Reichard felt confident to write in a column for CIO's political education magazine *Ammunition* that Racine, a "cradle of industrial unionism," was "where UAW members man the city council and elect the mayor of their choice."[11] Union members in Racine ran for public office, they lobbied the city and county to improve housing availability, and they sponsored Boy Scout troops and youth baseball teams. In 1949, the Teamsters local initiated a drive among area unions to sponsor a room at St. Luke's Hospital and donated $400 of the necessary $2000 to see it through.[12] As labor activist Paul Whiteside remembered, the high rates of unionization and activism in Racine and Kenosha empowered the working class communities to use their collective power. Nearly all the major industrial plants were organized: skilled trades workers had been organized since the turn of the century and often collaborated with industrial unions, the Teamsters had organized most of the truck drivers in both cities, public worker unionization was widespread in the area, and service workers in the janitorial industry had high levels of union representation. As Whiteside stated, "when you got control of a thing, you got the majority in an area, you tend to be more aggressive."[13] Because Racine's union members were in a relatively strong position, they felt confident in pursuing broad-based social justice issues that would benefit the whole community.

Working-class activists provided Racinians with an alternative view of local news to counter the negative press labor received in the *Racine Journal Times*, the daily paper, and to keep the community abreast of news related to working-class issues. Starting in the 1930s, the labor community sponsored the *New Day* and then *Racine Day* but producing daily news journals proved too expensive. When the *Racine Day* had to shut down in the late 1930s because of high operating expenses, representatives from the RTLC, a body of the area's AFL unions and the United Automobile Workers Council #8, got together and decided on a weekly format, which started the sixty-year run of *Racine Labor* in 1941. Loren Norman, a former Illinois mine worker, labor organizer, and journalist, was the first editor of the weekly. The newspaper operated as a cooperative, with each local that held subscriptions receiving voting rights at annual meetings. It had no formal ties to any labor organization or particular union, despite the large contingent of UAW locals in the area. Instead, the aim of the paper was to appeal to the whole city and still be recognized as a paper for working people and labor activists.[14] Even during conflicts on the national level between the AFL and CIO, and later the UAW and CIO, the publishers maintained their commitment to inclusiveness of all labor news, regardless of affiliation. Local union members also held a weekly radio show on WRJN reporting about plant conditions, layoffs, bargaining committee updates, and other issues of interest to the working class.[15] Local 180 sponsored an annual Christmas dance and used the funds collected in entrance fees to buy gifts for needy children in the Racine community. In the 1940s, members contributed to the needs of the children at the Taylor Orphanage through the welfare committee.[16] These public activities helped foster the labor community's role in Racine's public life.

Labor activists' community and civic involvement went beyond local matters as union members sought to influence state politics and continued to push a working-class agenda to benefit not just the labor community but the city, state, and nation as well. While Democrats at the national level received most of labor's support during the New Deal period, in Wisconsin, the Progressive Party and progressives within the Republican Party garnered more support than the conservative-led Democratic Party. It was not until debates surrounding World War II led to a split in the Progressive Party that many young liberals and war veterans who joined together in the University of Wisconsin's Young Progressive Club worked with those seeking to reform and revitalize the Wisconsin Democratic Party.[17]

Gaylord Nelson, John Reynolds, Horace Wilkie, James Doyle, and Carl Thompson worked together with other liberals and former Progressives to gain control of the Democratic Party in 1948. Union activists and progressive leaders in each county organized campaign drives to reshape the Democratic membership in the state. Labor organizations began to actively support the Democrats at the local and state levels and contributed significant amounts of financial and manpower support throughout the decade. In Racine, labor activists including Sam Rizzo and Harold Thompson, served on the county's Democratic Organizing Committee. During the 1950 campaign, the Democrats focused their support on Harry Truman and his Fair Deal platform, supported civil rights, social security expansions, and the repeal of the Taft-Hartley Act.[18]

Racine's working-class activists fought to elect local politicians that would speak for the people of the city and called them to task if advances were not made. In the postwar period, class remained the most significant factor in city elections. Corporate executives often held positions in city and state government and sat on the boards of multiple charitable organizations in the city. Their influence impacted management and labor relations well into the second half of the twentieth century. Like worker activists, these industrialists recognized that class conflict operated not just within the plants but in the political arena as well. Both sides saw the need to influence public debate, knowing that victory in one area led to their class politics achieving precedence in the other. Worker activists wanted to counter the political weight of management by fighting and winning seats on the Common Council, the executive board of the United Way, and various other civic organizations.[19] With the election of Francis Wendt as mayor in 1943, labor activists started to gain control of a few Common Council seats.[20] By 1950, active union members served as chair of the finance committee at the city and county level, president of the city council, and as chair for the county courthouse, salaries, health, highways, parks, and zoning committees.[21]

World War II created an unprecedented opportunity for political and social action, as the federal government's wartime investment drove the growth of manufacturing and brought dramatic economic, political, and social changes to Racine and across the nation. The resulting prosperity legitimized government involvement in private manufacturing for members of the labor community and their political allies. Like many mass-production urban areas, Racine's industrial output exploded due to government defense contracts. Increased production called for new and refurbished factory sites. For example, the federal government built new facilities so that the J. I. Case Company could produce bomber wings and gun carriages. Allis Chalmers Manufacturing Company received federal funding to build new facilities to complete its forgings contract, and the Massey Harris Company expanded its tractor facilities to build gun motor carriages, light tanks, M4s, and various tank parts. Other companies that received federal contracts include Sperry Gyroscope Company, Belle City Manufacturing, Neleon Brothers and Strom Company, and Twin Disc Clutch Company.[22] With these new economic opportunities, the population of Racine County increased from 90,217 to 109,585 between 1930 and 1950.[23] This influx of jobs, people, and income complicated existing political lines as labor activists sought to solidify their position with their political allies. In Racine, labor activists used the momentum to negotiate favorable labor contracts for union members, expand government protection for workers and the social safety net, and resist pushback from conservative business leaders and politicians. They met heavy resistance, which fueled labor strife, while also opening the way for workers to gather public support among political, social, and religious allies.

In Racine and across the nation, conservatives sought to retain the status quo or even shift power away from these goals. While some industrialists and business leaders supported the administration's efforts to restore economic stability with federal regulations that reduced competitive price wars, other conservative business leaders challenged Roosevelt's New Deal policies, especially the National Labor Relations Act (Wagner Act), and any attempts to interfere in their business prerogatives. Once the economy did start to recover, some business leaders started to resent what they saw as the loss of "management prerogative."[24] As Nelson Lichtenstein points out, if anything is exceptional about the U.S. labor system, it is the "hostility managers have shown toward both the regulatory state and virtually all systems of worker representation."[25] The National Association of Manufacturers (NAM), a key organization opposed to government regulation and unionization, understood itself to be involved in a "knockdown, no-holds-barred fight against labor unions by every possible means" and stood at the forefront of the attack on the Wagner Act.[26] The Business Advisory Council also objected to the Wagner Act, "which contained what they thought were dangerously radical provisions that could require corporations to bargain with unions and require workers to join them."[27] Such corporate resistance suggests how fraught the relationship between labor and management remained in an era that some scholars often associate with cooperation between the two sides.[28]

In an important victory for NAM and others, the 1947 Taft-Hartley Act placed legal restrictions on unions and helped re-shift the balance of power away from unions and the state and toward corporate America. The new amendment undermined the importance the Wagner Act placed on collective bargaining as an effective tool in equalizing the playing field in the labor-management struggles for control at the site of production and in the larger economic, political environment. Instead, Taft-Hartley made individual rights just as important as collective bargaining. It imposed new legal restrictions on labor unions and granted employers more rights, increasing the power imbalance in labor-management relationships.

The Act also codified efforts to curtail the Congress of Industrial Organizations (CIO)—the leader in industrial unionization—through its anti-Communist measures. Communists had played important parts in helping to organize workers within CIO union locals, but after Taft-Hartley, unions could no longer tolerate such political diversity. The law required union members to sign affidavits showing they were not affiliated with the Communist Party. This allowed those opposed to Communism to push out many active union leaders and organizers.[29] Finally, Taft-Hartley limited the spread of unionization by outlawing union shops, which would have required all workers to join the union that won representation at a particular workplace, thus creating space for state-level right-to-work laws.[30] In his study of the U.S. labor movement, Lichtenstein concludes, "Taft-Hartley thus did much to depoliticize the unions by curbing interunion solidarity and ghettoizing the power of the labor movement" and devalued the idea of worker organization "independent of managerial influence."[31] Taft-Hartley and the NLRB's rulings in the postwar period changed the scope and meaning of collective bargaining and weakened the power of trade unionism.[32] The new legal restrictions limited the effectiveness of labor's efforts to promote the ideology of working-class solidarity in the postwar period for many unions. Yet, these restraints galvanized other unions, as we will see. While this political landscape limited labor's leverage in the fight for economic democracy, workers never expected the legal apparatus supporting collective bargaining to solve all their issues. They considered collective bargaining rights as just one tool in their arsenal.

Conservative political backlash also limited the labor movement's range of effective strategies and sought to change the public debate by delegitimizing union leaders. For example, Lichtenstein argues that the postwar liberal and labor alliance failed to achieve any of its goals and was too unorganized to overcome entrenched conservative resistance to expanding economic citizenship rights. Conservatives used the rhetoric of menacing union bosses as vindication for their resistance to collective bargaining, which weakened labor's position in the public arena. As a result, the coalition of the labor movement and the Democratic Party forced unions to separate collective bargaining from political debate to protect the fragile relationship. Some unions, especially at the national level, refused to take strong political stances in support of such issues as civil rights or Cold War foreign interventions in order to avoid conflict. Union leaders focused on getting the best labor contracts concerning wages and fringe benefits coupled with attempting to adhere to a "labor-management accord" by suppressing rank-and-file militancy, which led to a business-model approach to bargaining. Union bureaucracies grew to service their members as organizing, political education, and community outreach took a backseat.[33] It also created divisions between unionized workers and those without union support. These external and internal changes weakened the labor community's position and strengthened that of their political and class opponents.

Local 180 and Racine's Labor Struggles

In Racine, even the myth of a labor-management accord did not exist. The largest employer, The J.I. Case Company (Case), was led by Leon R. Clausen, who actively fought against workers' right to collectively bargain and resented any government involvement in private industrial matters. As the largest employer, organized by the largest and most powerful UAW local, this relationship had a considerable influence on class politics in the city. The continuing battle for workplace democracy at Case galvanized the broader labor community to remain vigilant, recruit more allies, and nurture the working-class community. After starting the firm in Rochester, Wisconsin, in 1842, Jerome I. Case moved his agricultural manufacturing firm to Racine two years later.[34] Leon R. Clausen became president of the company in 1924 and remained as president and then chairman of the board for the next thirty years. Known as a "rugged individualist," Clausen remained opposed to collective bargaining and any type of government or worker involvement in business affairs. He personally resisted all the workers' efforts to form a union or to bargain collectively.

Workers at Case initially tried to organize into a union in 1906 but management successfully defeated their efforts and started blacklisting any workers who tried to organize. During the Great Depression, workers again attempted to organize with the help of members of the local Socialist Party, but the company retaliated by firing over a thousand of the four thousand workers. Finally, in 1933, workers managed to organize into an independent union after a ninety-one-day strike, but negotiations with the company did not meet many of their demands. The workers affiliated with the American Federation of Labor in 1934 after another strike but joined the newly-formed United Automobile Workers in 1937 as UAW Local 180 under the leadership of Harvey Kitzman. They became the first unit of what would become the Agricultural Implements Division of the UAW.[35]

During World War II, the federal government demanded a one-year contract between UAW Local 180 and the company in an effort to keep war production on schedule, but Clausen's refusal to recognize workers' basic bargaining rights persisted over the next two decades.[36] As the local labor paper editorialized, Clausen "fought the UAW tooth and nail throughout his career."[37] After finally relenting and granting bargaining rights in 1936, Case management, led by President Clausen, rejected Local 180's request to collect automatic dues deductions from paychecks or to require all members of the bargaining unit to join the union as requested. However, inspired members kept voting to keep these key issues on the bargaining table as well as to capitalize on the gains made by other UAW unions across the automobile industry.[38]

So, in the industrial heartland, which has been associated with the labor-management accord in the postwar period, local conditions in Racine resembled the continued employer resistance typically associated with plants in the South and West. The difference between the hope generated by the rhetoric of postwar liberalism and the reality of class struggle sparked continued worker activism and fueled workplace and political battles to extend economic citizenship. This was true across the nation.

Worker activism had pushed forward the passage of the Wagner Act and gave it political relevance. From the very beginning, however, activists recognized the limitations of the Act, and continued to pursue avenues outside of collective bargaining to gain economic and political power. Despite resistance from business leaders, conservative politicians, and Southern Democrats seeking to protect their economic, social, and political power structure, the labor movement expanded and gained a powerful voice in national politics. Industrialists, like Clausen, resisted government regulation and workers' collective bargaining efforts, further galvanizing the labor movement in Racine and across the nation. For example, the tremendous growth of the labor movement, as well as the institutionalization of labor relations within the New Deal state, transformed Oakland, California's labor community into a political and social force. To consolidate their power, activists extended unionization in Oakland to the mass of unorganized workers and created a conflict with a local business association that facilitated the 1946 general strike.[39] In Chicago, the Packinghouse Workers' Organizing Committee's battle for union recognition, despite heavy resistance, led to more and more workers becoming committed to the union and willing to engage in long-term fights with management.[40]

Members of Local 180 set the tone of labor militancy and activism that coalesced in postwar Racine. Harvey Kitzman led UAW Local 180's bargaining committee in weekly negotiation meetings. Kitzman was born on a farm in rural Wisconsin in 1906 and completed the eighth grade before leaving school to help with farm work. At seventeen, he left home to pursue a baseball career. When a car accident ended his baseball career just two years later, Kitzman started work at the Ajax Auto Works in Racine. He became interested in labor activities during Hoover's presidential campaign because management tried to pressure all the employees to vote Republican. Outraged, Kitzman started educating his coworkers on the need for political activity based on class interests. Kitzman moved to Case in 1929 and worked there as a bar operator for the next nineteen years. He helped organize the first successful union and served as president for ten years. Kitzman and his coworkers fought to establish the union, get recognition as the official bargaining unit by management, and to set the best possible working conditions, wages, and benefits for all employees. Kitzman recalled that, during the 1930s, many working-class activists did not have clear ideas about what sort of mechanism would be successful in their attempts to negotiate with management. But, workers organized because "people saw the opportunity to become human beings and not machines . . . the opportunity to redress when you had a grievance because you were not satisfied with what the foreman was doing or what was going on . . . and this is what motivated people to flock to the union in the early days by the hundreds."[41] Kitzman served as president of Local 180 until 1947, when he helped establish the UAW farm implement division. In 1949, he was elected to his first term as director of UAW Region 10, which represented over 50,000 union members in Wisconsin, Minnesota, Montana, North Dakota, South Dakota, and Wyoming, by providing administrative and organizational support to UAW locals.[42]

UAW Local 180 union members worked for years to gain a contract more in line with national standards. Even during the war, Local 180 members staged work stoppages and sit-ins in an effort to gain better working conditions. Their representatives had voted against the no-strike agreement that International leaders accepted during the war, and only orders from Walter Reuther, president of the International, could get the workers back on the job when grievance negotiations failed.[43] Even before the war ended, Case president Clausen demanded that city officials provide "law and order" to maintain discipline in the plants after peace was declared. The contract between Case and Local 180 expired in April of 1944.[44] After the war, Case managers still denied workers the benefits that union organizers had bargained successfully for with automotive executives at Ford, General Motors, and Chrysler in Detroit. Weekly negotiation meetings came to a standstill because the company would not accept the all-union shop, a grievance procedure, department-level steward system, and vacation pay that members demanded. The bargaining committee would not agree to a settlement on wages first as the company demanded. Finally, the day after Christmas in 1945, workers at Case went on a strike that would drag on for 440 days. Kitzman remembered that although the company tried to keep the plant running, "it was really marvelous the way people hung together. Not a single soul tried to go in and go to work. They all took the position that this time they were going to do it up right, so we do not have to do it again."[45]

Workers were motivated to get what they recognized as standard contract provisions and Clausen's intransigence fueled their determination to hold out for a better agreement. They picketed through two Wisconsin winters and aggressively defended the plant against strikebreakers. Clausen immediately canceled workers' health insurance, refused to negotiate with the mayor or any other arbitrator, and publicly denounced even the notion of collective bargaining. Workers at Case sought to gain and maintain community support during the strike. Local 180 sent informational letters to other UAW locals within the state, brought complaints to the Wisconsin Employment Relations Board because of management's refusal to accept a union shop, and sent Racine striking Case workers to help maintain momentum at a Case plant in nearby Rock Island, Illinois, which was also on strike.[46] UAW Local 82, representing the workers at Modine Manufacturing Company in Racine, sent a resolution, which resolved "that Local 82 sends its greetings to the striking workers of . . . Local 180 in Racine, and others throughout the country, and declares itself ready to join them in the fight so that Freedom from Want and Freedom from Fear shall be made a reality."[47] The union's inclusion of "freedom from want" and "freedom from fear" illustrated the way in which Racine's labor community embraced the New Deal liberalism of the period.

The public pressure paid off for Case workers when Mayor Francis Wendt sent an open letter to management "condemning their unchristian principles in allowing the group hospitalization insurance to be cancelled" during the strike.[48] Wendt, a longtime supporter of worker rights, had been legal counsel for the UAW before being elected mayor in 1943.[49] The union praised the mayor, contending, "We know that every fair minded citizen in the city of Racine agreed with your statements to the company and the press."[50] Case workers also won support from Fiorello La Guardia, the former mayor of New York and a prominent voice for New Deal liberalism at the national level. As director of the United Nations' Relief and Rehabilitation Administration, LaGuardia urged Clausen to meet with workers and demanded, "You better accept that invitation of the mayor of Racine to meet Monday. I would if I were you. It's just about time to end this," on his national radio show in June 1946.[51] Yet the company, especially President Clausen, refused to even negotiate.

Workers managed to stay away from the plant for so long because the overwhelming majority found other sources of employment. Support from the city and federal governments allowed the 3000 Local 180 members to continue to hold out for their demands. The City, led by Mayor Wendt's initiatives, agreed to hire workers for local public works projects and the International provided financial support. Finally, a federal arbitrator moved negotiations thirty miles north to Milwaukee to take some of the pressure off Case management, which soon led to compromise between the company and the union. The arbitrator convinced both sides to accept concessions, and they finally reached an agreement in March 1947. The company agreed to increase the number of paid stewards, but the union gave up two key demands, the union shop and dues checkoff. They also compromised on grievance procedures and vacation pay. Less than half the membership voted on the weak agreement, but those who did approved it by a margin of nearly two-to-one.[52] The voter turnout was probably low because so many Case strikers felt unsure of the future of their own employment and the union at Case after pushing so hard for changes with such few gains actually achieved.

Despite failure to achieve several key wins, Local 180 members remained committed to the union as the best means to improve working conditions and increase workplace democracy. They continued to participate in sit-down strikes, work stoppages, and officially sanctioned strikes throughout the postwar period. Kitzman remembered, "If we were unable to settle a grievance in which we felt we were entitled to have an adjustment, there was only one other way we could move on it. It was to simply shut the operation down. That happened not once but hundreds of times. This is the way we did our collective bargaining inside the plant."[53] Workers understood the power of their collective action to stop production. They achieved collective bargaining not through formal structures but through work stoppages. And workers steadily came back into the union as employment levels rose.[54] The continued efforts of these Racine unionized workers in the face of extreme resistance by management solidified the efforts

of the 1930s and war period. It situated Local 180 as a model of persever-
ance for other unions in the city and set the stage for Local 180's role as a
leading union in Racine's labor community.

Black Migration to Racine

In addition to legal and political changes, labor activists confronted a burst
of migration to Racine during and after the war. The Black population
in the city increased from 477 to nearly 7000 by the end of the 1950s, an
increase of 72 percent. As with most of Wisconsin's industrial centers,
many Black migrants to Racine during the WWII years came from southern states.[55] Some Black male workers like Jenkins were active members
of the city's industrial unions. Black union membership rose during the
war as they filled the need for production workers. In turn, these workers used their experiences in the Racine labor community to continue to
fight for access to better jobs, more economic security, and more respect
in the workplace.[56] William Jenkins' family's early arrival, and his popu-
larity in the city, placed him in a unique position to help shape Racine's
labor community.

William "Blue" Jenkins' early experiences gave him the confidence
to stand up for himself and others, and he honed a keen understanding
of social politics in the city. Jenkins moved to Racine in 1917 with his
family from Hattiesburg, Mississippi. His father, Frank Jenkins, worked
as a coal miner in Virginia, moved to Hattiesburg for job opportunities,
and came to Racine when Case recruited Black workers from the South
during a strike. When Frank Jenkins discovered that Case hired him as a
strikebreaker, he decided not to accept the job because of his experience
as a unionized coal miner. He eventually found work at the Nelson Brothers' construction company, and the Jenkins family settled in the mostly
Italian neighborhood on the north side of town near the railroad station.
As one of the few Black families in the neighborhood, they opened their
house as the first stop for many Black migrants to Racine, offering them
information on housing, jobs, and what to expect as newcomers. As an
outgoing person and local sports star, "Blue" Jenkins knew lots of people
in the city and had access to diverse subcultures. As a precocious young-
ster, he roamed the city on his own, went to work and taverns with his
father, and mingled with sports stars across the city. He played baseball,
softball, and basketball on local teams in the Black community and was
the only Black player on his high school football team. When his Horlick
High School teammates voted Jenkins captain, the coach stood up for him
when a group of parents protested having a Black player in a leadership

position.[57] As Jenkins recalled this incident in his 1974 interview, he noted it as a reason he wanted a leadership position in the labor community, so he could speak up for others.

After graduation in 1936, Jenkins turned down two college football scholarships in part because he was worried about racial discrimination at state universities and went to work to help support his family because his father had died a few years earlier. He moved around from job to job until he was hired at the Belle City Malleable foundry in 1939 and became an active member of UAW Local 553. The lessons he learned from his father, his outspokenness and willingness to stand up for others, and interactions with other foundry workers and UAW members, led to Jenkins' commitment to union activity and social justice issues throughout his life.[58]

Black men moving into Racine sought jobs in the foundries for secure income during the 1940s. Craft unions and many employers excluded Black workers from skilled jobs, and only the lowest paying industrial jobs offered Black workers employment. Even in the foundries like Belle City Malleable, which served as the city's main employer of Black foundry workers during the postwar period, Black workers had the most dangerous and hardest jobs. Jenkins' father, although skilled in several areas of carpentry and plumbing, was never able to join a building trade union or get a skilled job in this field in Racine.[59] Nonwhite workers found employment in foundries because these were often the hardest, dirtiest jobs available in manufacturing centers, and workers who could find better employment usually did. Although a few Black workers moved up to skilled positions in the foundries during the war, they were often passed up for promotions. Black workers in Racine slowly began to appeal to their UAW locals to address employment and promotion discrimination.

Black workers were more open to using unions to combat structural racism in Racine than in cities with larger Black populations and established Black middle-class institutions. In Detroit, for example, the Black community had vibrant chapters of the National Association for the Advancement of Colored People (NAACP) and the Urban League. Black workers in Detroit usually went through the Urban League or their local ministers to find industrial jobs and to combat discrimination in hiring or union practices. And Ford Motor Company, the largest employer of Black workers in Detroit, made efforts to appeal to Black workers, provide good pay and benefits, and be seen as a benefactor in the Black community. With the history of exclusion from good jobs and the benefits of union membership, Black workers in Detroit had little reason to listen to UAW organizers. As August Meier and Elliott Rudwick show, the UAW had to work hard to recruit support from Black middle-class leaders and to gain the trust and commitment of Black workers. It was not until the UAW took an active role in the 1941 strike to integrate Ford plants outside of River Rouge that Black workers started to shift their allegiance to their local unions.[60]

In Milwaukee, racial tensions in industrial plants stemmed not only from prejudice on the part of rank-and-file white workers, but also because most Black workers only gained entry into industrial employment as strikebreakers or through "exceptional personal contacts with influential whites."[61] With increased employment during World War I, Black Milwaukeeans created their own labor organizations and formed all-Black chapters of existing white union locals. This history of organized struggle within the Black working-class and within the whole Black community to hamper increasing discrimination in social and governmental services in the city, helped propel the efforts of Black industrial workers during and after World War II. Black workers responded favorably to the advances of CIO organizers in the city during this period and kept pressure on the UAW and other CIO unions to seriously address the needs of Black workers in the defense industries.[62] In fact, Black workers' increasing activism across the nation forced employers, unions, and the federal government, to deal with issues of discrimination during and after World War II.

At the national level, when Black workers' efforts for entry into defense work during war mobilization continued to fall on deaf ears, leaders acted. A. Philip Randolph, a longtime labor and civil rights activist, called on Black workers to mobilize for a march in Washington, D.C., to protest discriminatory hiring practices in defense jobs and in the U.S. armed forces. Randolph, Black worker activists, civil rights leaders, and union leaders, planned to bring one hundred thousand protesters to D.C. and demonstrate their determination to demand access to jobs and the economic security the jobs would bring. The success of the mobilization, the strategic lobbying by Randolph, and the need to keep up with war production, led President Franklin D. Roosevelt to sign Executive Order 8802, banning discrimination based on race, creed, color, or national origin in defense industries and in the federal government for the duration of the war and establishing the Fair Employment Practices Committee (FEPC) to oversee enforcement in 1942. The FEPC was very active in the Midwest, holding hearings in Chicago, Milwaukee, and Detroit, negotiating with some employers, and using its limited power to force compliance.[63]

The measured success of the FEPC fueled Black worker activists to continue to push for economic democracy in the workplace and in their unions. Black workers in Detroit's auto industry and in other UAW locals pushed for stronger efforts to strengthen antidiscrimination clauses in employment contracts. Through their efforts and the determination of some international union officials to effect change, the UAW initiated an internal Fair Practices Committee in 1944, put in place to deal with discrimination both in manufacturing plants and in local unions. In the postwar demobilization, fears of a tightened labor market and lingering racial prejudice led to resistance on the part of companies and some white rank-and-file members and union leaders to the inclusion of full antidiscrimination clauses. The Fair Practices Committee apparatus provided an avenue for Black workers and union locals to seek aid in these discrimination cases.[64] The UAW's FEPC efforts placed it at the forefront of industrial unions in this regard and made the UAW a valued organization among Detroit's Black workers.[65] In Milwaukee, the March on Washington Movement that started after the war brought even more Black industrial workers into the UAW ranks.[66]

The labor activism surrounding World War II demonstrated to Black workers in Racine that unions could be forces for economic justice and racial equality. For instance, Jenkins went to Milwaukee in the early 1940s for a UAW Fair Employment Practices Committee meeting. While there, he met people from Detroit who shared how Black workers fought for a greater voice in their union locals and the varied successes they were achieving. The talks he had with them motivated Jenkins to become active in the union.[67] Robert Korstad and Nelson Lichtenstein point out that those Black workers who joined CIO unions during this period were "in the vanguard of efforts to transform race relations."[68] While the UAW's record was a complicated mix of accommodation and resistance, the broad-based social justice rhetoric of the UAW facilitated a growing support for the union among Black workers and community leaders.[69]

Jenkins remembered that he became more vocal in his labor union when he saw the treatment of Black contract workers from the Caribbean during the war. Management "misused those guys. What did they know about union contracts? They were really discriminated against. It was bad," he recalled.[70] During World War II, the federal government instituted an Emergency Labor Importation Program that brought five million Mexican and Caribbean guestworkers to the United States. These migrants fell into a "no-man's land" when it came to receiving the legal protection of U.S. labor laws. Workers were promised better wages and working conditions, yet employers consistently failed to follow through on all their promises. Foreign workers served to rein in domestic workers' militancy, depress wages, and increase workplace strife as workers attempted to maximize the gains of the war economy.[71] While some white workers pushed Belle City to expel the immigrant workers, Jenkins's response was to recruit them into the union. Other Black workers at Belle City started to participate in union activities during the debate over Caribbean workers and access to jobs in the reconversion process when white union members demanded the workers recruited from Caribbean nations be sent home. While Black workers also wanted to protect their jobs and the small amount of seniority they had established, they resented the inherent racism they perceived in white unionists' words. At the union meeting when a member suggested they, "send the s.o.bs back in cattle cars if we have to," Jenkins "got up and I really blew my top. I was cussin' . . . I got pretty excited at that meeting. And after that, the guys started coming to me then."[72] The contract workers did leave after their time at Belle City Malleable but the racial tension shifted power relations within Local 553 as competing leaders sought to gain Jenkins's support. Workers in the plant, both Black and white, increasingly started to look to Jenkins as one of their union leaders because of his vocal stand for all workers during the early postwar period.

Jenkins' position as a leader in Local 553 was solidified when he led a sit-down strike after the war. Belle City Malleable's management had agreed to vacation pay during the war, but they reversed their position when the contract expired in 1945. When bargaining committee members approached Jenkins about leading a work stoppage, he readily agreed. He talked to the workers in his unit, and after several agreed to follow his lead, he sat down in front of his machine in the steel shop. He told the foreman, "So until they make up their mind what they're gonna do, I'm gonna [sit] down here."[73] Several foremen attempted to use white racial solidarity to get the other workers in Jenkins's department back to work because Jenkins was the only Black worker in the unit. When the foremen failed to get the white employees back to their stations, other workers in the plant sat down, including those in the core room, the place where workers manufacture the center cores that were then used to make hollow steel castings.

Without cores, the production line would stop. As Jenkins explained, if the core room did not run, the plant could not operate. The work stoppage proved successful and management reinstated vacation pay. Workers continued to look to Jenkins for advice and guidance, but it was a long time before he was elected to official office. He was determined to "keep running for office in the union until I could be of some use to my people."[74] Jenkins would finally be elected president of the local in 1955 and again from 1957 through 1960. Union delegates voted to elect Jenkins as president of the Racine County AFL-CIO in 1962, and he also served as chairman of the UAW foundry sub-council for District 2. In these positions he extended his already large network of labor leaders, built coalitions, and served as an influential negotiator for racial inclusion in the labor community.[75]

36 CHAPTER 1

Racine's labor activists continued to battle racism and fight for racial inclusion in workplaces and unions throughout the postwar period. In September 1942, the UAW Local 180 executive board asked the bargaining committee to address the reported discrimination against Black workers because management refused to accept them as members of the union.[76] This was a tactic often used by management to foment dissension and break union solidarity. But as more and more Black workers came to Racine looking for steady employment, discrimination and racial tension grew.[77] Local union leaders like Jenkins and Kitzman worked to counteract the racism of other workers, managers, and the broader community. Yet, a few union activists and CIO and UAW rhetoric did not cure all the racial tensions created with the influx of new Black workers during the war years. Employment data suggests that while the Black male population was increasing, access to well-paying industrial jobs did not keep up with the growth. While Jenkins and a few others successfully broke the racial barrier in a few local plants, Black workers in Racine remained in the lowest paid, most dangerous positions.[78] Throughout the postwar years, Black workers and their allies continued to work for change through UAW education programs, social justice organizations like the NAACP, churches, and via direct action.

Unionized workers participated in civic improvement related to racial justice outside of the workplace as well. Local 180 worked closely with the Urban League and NAACP of Racine as they offered names for employment for vacant plant positions. Unlike cities like Milwaukee and Detroit, both of which had larger Black populations and clearly defined Black middle classes earlier in the twentieth century, Racine's Black population did not start to grow to significant numbers until the 1940s and 1950s. Racine's branch of the NAACP was started in 1947 and longtime UAW activists like Jenkins, were involved from the beginning. As a union leader in Local 553 and the NAACP branch president, Jenkins used his dual positions to effect change in the community.[79] Racine UAW members regularly recruited their fellow union members into the NAACP and joined forces to promote racial equity.

This trend was best exemplified by the work of CIO unions. Many CIO union locals worked to improve race relations among members and force employers to honor labor contracts without discriminating against workers based on race. For example, packinghouse workers in Kansas City and Chicago came together across racial lines to force employers to grant Black women equal opportunity to previously all-white positions. Autoworker, packing worker, and electrical unions supported equal opportunity legislation at the state and national level and would often join forces with the NAACP to boycott retail establishments that would not serve Black patrons.[80] Jenkins was very proud of the fact that the entire membership of UAW Local 234 voted to affiliate with the Racine NAACP chapter. Local 234 represented workers at Lakeside Malleable, one of the foundries in the city where Black workers were able to obtain jobs.[81] Black workers in Racine found the most economic security in the industrial plants in the city and used their union membership to fight for social change. *Racine Labor* regularly carried stories about local NAACP activities, membership drives, and other campaigns for racial justice, highlighting the connection between racial and economic justice.

Black workers and their allies continued to provide a racial justice framework for the rhetoric of class solidarity and economic citizenship that shaped the Racine labor community, but it was an ongoing process. For example, Black workers in Racine lived in the least-maintained housing of the city, were severely overcrowded in segregated areas where "slum lords" charged exorbitant rents. After years of struggling to get a housing code passed that would require landlords to maintain basic health and safety conditions, Black working-class Racinians marched through the city in the mid-1950s to obtain better housing options as the population exploded. Corinne Owens, former Racine NAACP president, led the lobbying efforts at the city level. Probably through the support of the YWCA in Milwaukee, Owens conducted a neighborhood survey outlining Black residents' living conditions.[82] When the Racine Common Council repeatedly tabled the proposal for a proposed public housing ordinance to alleviate the worst conditions, Owens organized a march to City Hall to publicize the needs of Black residents. Many new residents still lived in the trailer camps on the north and south edges of the city built during the massive in-migration of the early 1940s.[83]

Yet, without mentioning race as a factor, the local AFL unions passed a resolution asking the city not to allow any trailer camps to be located within the city limits.[84] The AFL unions supported the Racine realtor's association that claimed that low-rent federally-subsidized housing would hurt the private building industry. This decision left Black families segregated on the outside of town in substandard housing with no official plan to build new housing in the city. Meanwhile, *Racine Labor* ran editorials condemning the poor housing conditions that Black families faced, urging the Common Council to act on building public housing in the city to accommodate the growing Black population, and urging real estate agents to practice fair practices when it came to renting and selling to Black residents.[85] While the support from union leaders and editorials in *Racine Labor* provided moral support for Black residents living in

38   CHAPTER 1

extremely overcrowded and neglected dwellings, the real change needed
to come from working-class residents living in all-white neighborhoods
where Black residents could not rent or buy homes.[86] Examples like this
demonstrate the ways in which an all-inclusive working-class solidarity
did not always operate successfully to overcome racial conservatism and
structural racism.

Working Women and Racine's Labor Community

In addition to racial conflicts, Racine's labor community divided over the
question of women's labor rights. For many white and nonwhite women
who found industrial jobs during World War II, the higher wages and
job security ended with the war and the return of troops. Yet, the taste of
access to better-paid, better-protected jobs led many women to become
active in the labor movement. Increased employment possibilities fueled
working women's efforts to gain equal pay, greater access to jobs beyond
traditional "women's work," and protective features such as childcare
and maternity leave.[87] Because of negotiated seniority rules, women, like
the nonwhite men who were first hired during the war, faced the first in,
first out rule of employment turnover. Women have reported the exhila-
ration of the higher wages and greater independence felt with wartime
employment as well as the disappointment of losing those opportunities
in the immediate postwar period. At the same time, however, women used
the empowerment and education they received through union meetings
and negotiations to become involved in the labor movement, in local and
national politics, and in the women's movement. Women filled the ranks
of national unions like the United Electrical Workers and UAW beginning in the 1930s, and by the 1940s, the UAW showed real progress in
representing its women members. Through the efforts of labor feminists,
UAW leaders created the Women's Bureau in 1944, which became a permanent division in 1946 under the Fair Practices and Anti- Discrimination
Department.[88] Articles related specifically to women members and generally educating all membership to the needs of women workers appeared
regularly in *Ammunition*, the CIO member education journal. The regular
feature "Sister Sue Says" covered issues like women's role in local unions,
women's need to attend union meetings, the importance of childcare and
lunchrooms in workplaces, and sharing housework.[89] CIO unions, taking
account of the issues raised in this column, made some effort to represent
women members more fully.

　　Some union leaders and shop stewards worked hard to create an inclusive atmosphere and gain the support of all workers. While women in the

garment industry in Racine organized in the nineteenth century, many of the factories left the city by the 1950s, and women's membership in local unions thereafter declined. Loretta Christensen, a member of the AFL office workers union at Western Printing Company was one of only a few women who held a prominent place in Racine's labor community in the postwar period. In 1937, she was elected treasurer of the Racine Trades and Labor Council, and she was the only female trustee among the twenty-two-member group over the labor newspaper in 1941. She was active with Racine's chapter of the Women's Trade Union League (WTUL), a national organization "dedicated to advancing the interests of working-class women," and its fight for pay equity during the 1940s.[90] The Racine WTUL was formed in 1935 and received a charter from the national organization the next year. The members worked to help organize workers across industries and participated in worker education, sending people to the University of Wisconsin School for Workers. Racine WTUL members also participated in annual Labor Day celebrations, entering a float in the parade each year. It disbanded in 1951 shortly after the national organization dissolved due to the growth in the labor movement and built-in union structures to organize workers that made the organization obsolete.[91] Other women held leadership positions in several local unions, with Geraldine Kamla becoming the first woman to be elected president of a local in the summer of 1954, representing UAW Local 627 at Oster Manufacturing. Women were also on the executive boards of the garment workers union, retail clerks, laundry workers, and communication workers unions in the city.[92]

In Racine, women's employment varied across industries. Most Black women worked in domestic or low-wage service positions in education and healthcare. White women and a few Black women found employment in some of the smaller industrial plants. Western Printing, Webster Electric, and Rainfair employed the most women but were not the only industrial job sites where women worked. In fact, Webster Electric had enough women employees to organize the best players into the winning team in the Girls Industrial Softball League in 1954.[93] This shows that despite the male-centered language and culture there were enough female industrial workers to form a whole league in the area.

Many of the women who entered the workforce during or after WWII reported they became involved in labor or women's issues through their unions. For example, Dorothy Haener, who would go on to help found the National Organization for Women in the 1960s, reported that the UAW local where she worked as a punch press operator and welder in the 1950s offered the encouragement and education necessary for her

40   CHAPTER 1

political activity. Clara Day appreciated the hard work of her steward in Teamsters Local 743 in Chicago and the way organizers worked hard to include racialized minorities and women.[94] These types of efforts by union leaders helped bring women into organized labor and inspired these underrepresented workers to become politically active in other areas.

While labor feminists had been working hard to implement changes within the labor movement and many positive changes occurred, the process took time and the results were mixed. Labor leaders slowly responded to women activists and began to recognize the need to fully integrate women members. In 1940, the Local 180 Executive Board approved a motion to exempt women members from the compulsory union membership meeting requirement for male members, which would surely have limited the amount of worker education and mobilization required to inspire greater political action by women members.[95] In another instance in 1944, Harvey Kitzman complained to the Wisconsin Industrial Commission after the agency approved a request by Case to extend an order to hire female plant workers.[96] The union felt that Case management wanted to keep the women on staff because they could pay them lower wages for similar work. Yet, the negotiation minutes do not record Local 180 requesting equal pay for equal work.

Early in 1945, Local 180 helped five women receive unemployment benefits after a week's layoff from Case.[97] Then in April of 1950, Local 180 called a special meeting of all the women laid off at the Case plants to discuss the issue of gender discrimination. Women had complained about not being called back to work in the repair shop before some men who had less seniority. Union leaders took the matter to the bargaining table with management.[98] When negotiations failed, Local 180 filed unfair labor practices charges against Case through WERC.[99] Case never employed many female employees inside their Racine plants, and it was not until the 1970s that female employment levels increased there in any significant numbers. However, women were demanding more voice in union and workplace decisions.

The first UAW District Conference for women was held in Milwaukee in February 1950. Racine locals at Case, Horlicks Corporation, several diecast plants, and Howard Industries sent delegates. The Retail Clerks local also sent observers to report back to their union. The women's conference had panels on laws affecting women workers, equal pay, seniority, and fair practices.[100] At the same time, every issue of *Racine Labor* included an image of a "pinup" girl, an illustration of mixed messaging.[101] Inclusion of pinup girls in *Racine Labor* points to the continuing socialization of a male-dominated labor community in the city. This was a complicated balance as worker activists sought to adjust their thinking and adapt to new social norms related to work and gender differences. While unions offered women opportunities for greater political involvement and leadership roles, such gains were hard fought successes by women activists. However, the language and actions within the historical record reveal a movement toward greater inclusiveness and recognition of the value of full incorporation of all workers into the Racine labor community. This tension existed across the decades as the working-class community went through processes of shifting understandings of the gendered nature of the workplace, women's ability and desire to have full economic citizenship, and acceptance of women in leadership roles.

Black men and white women made early inroads into the leadership of the Racine labor community, starting and resolving battles that would only come with the intensification of civil rights and the women's movements. Increased manufacturing and the population growth to sustain it offered more opportunities for the labor community to grow. As Black men and white women entered Racine's workplaces in the postwar period, they actively asserted their place in labor unions and established themselves as capable members of the labor community. Most Black women remained in domestic and service positions as they were most often last to be hired in industrial workplaces. Corinne Reid-Owens felt this distinctly when she arrived in 1946 and could not get a job as an elementary school teacher.[102] In Racine, workers consolidated their postwar gains by demanding more from employers at the bargaining table and backing up their demands with work stoppages and strikes. Worker activists also used their new political power to actively participate in local politics. Their efforts in the postwar period laid the groundwork for a strong and vibrant labor community in the 1950s.

Many workers continued to push for economic and social justice issues throughout the postwar period. Workers reached out to union leaders, their religious advisors, community and ethnic civic association leaders, and to any organization they thought might assist them in their efforts for economic security. They wrote letters to their elected state and national political leaders, to the international headquarters of their unions, and to daily newspapers to address their perceived needs. When workers felt their issues were not suitably addressed, they kept moving along the line of available assistance in Racine and through national networks.[103]

CHAPTER 2

Labor Politics and Solidarity in the 1950s

On 22 September 1959, Governor Gaylord Nelson signed the Municipal Employees Relations Act (MERA) giving public sector employees in Wisconsin the right to organize unions and bargain collectively with local governments. MERA was the nation's first state law to grant public employees these rights. Working people's collective efforts through their unions, the expansion of public sector employment, and the role the labor movement played in rejuvenating the Wisconsin Democratic Party led to the passage of the Act.[1] The passage of the state's public worker collective bargaining law shows the political success of Racine's labor community in the 1950s.

While much of the scholarship points to the 1950s economic boom as a period of expanding wages and security for working people, a close look at Racine's labor community adds nuance to this interpretation by examining the ways political and economic changes complicate stories of employment growth and stability.[2] This period of rising wages and general employment stability was also a period of an ongoing battle between capital and labor. In the 1950s, Racine, like the rest of the nation, dealt with coordinated Republican and conservative business attacks against the New Deal order. Antilabor politicians and capitalists came together to pass the Taft-Hartley Act in 1947, amending the Wagner Act to further weaken workers' economic democracy. Some politicians used Taft-Hartley's amendments to enact "right-to-work" laws at the local level. Business leaders' efforts to regain power lost during the New Deal resulted in strategies of maintaining and reifying "management's prerogative" to be sole decision makers in production.[3]

Workers insisted on dignity at work and participation in decisions regarding work rules and hiring and firing decisions. Racine's labor community also fought the effects of corporate restructuring that led to plant closures and relocation. Private and public sector worker organizing, hard-fought bargaining with local employers, and strike activity illustrated the labor solidarity of the postwar period. Along with ongoing demands for dignity on the job, Racine's workers continued to expand their labor community, demonstrated solidarity across unions and employment sectors, played an active role in local and state politics, and marked their place on the city's landscape with a new building, the Racine Labor Center.

In his 1963 interview Harvey Kitzman looked back at his career at Case, and as a UAW executive, proud of the work he and other activists did to build and sustain Racine's labor community. After leaving Case in 1947, Kitzman had a long career supporting workers in Racine and the surrounding area. He stayed active in the Wisconsin and national Democratic Party. He supported Walter Reuther and they shared similar anti-Communist views, which opened Kitzman's path to leadership within the UAW International. He helped set the example of lifelong service to Racine's labor community by continuing to work within the labor movement and politics after his retirement from Case. This legacy continues to inspire members of Racine's labor community and demonstrates the model of engaged citizen and total person unionism that community members valued.[4]

This chapter examines the ways Racine's labor community matured in the postwar period and established itself as the voice of working people. It starts with a look at private sector manufacturing workers and their efforts to solidify the gains of the post-WWII era. Workers at Modine Manufacturing went on strike to protect workplace democracy in the face of a "management prerogative" clause during contract negotiations. Public workers' mobilization and strike activity in the early years of the decade laid the groundwork for expanding Wagner Act benefits to municipal employees. These cross-sector collaborations set the stage for a coordinated pushback against Republican efforts to overturn worker protections. The labor community in Racine was in tune with the impact of corporate mergers and technological changes that threatened job security, which led to labor-management struggles as well. The chapter ends with the six-year battle to gain what at this point were standard labor practices at the nearby, privately-owned Kohler Company while also battling management at Case. The battles at Kohler and Case highlight the continued importance of sustaining the local labor community and how workplace democracy issues shaped labor strife during the 1950s in Racine.

Workplace Democracy
in the Private Sector

By midcentury, Racine had about 230 manufacturing firms employing roughly 12,000 employees.[5] In the early 1950s, workers at local automobile manufacturing firms, foundries, home electronics manufacturing plants, printing companies, outdoor clothing makers, and engine parts manufacturing firms all went on strike or threatened strikes for workplace democracy, better pay, and improved working conditions in the city. For example, UAW Local 391 capitalized on an organizing drive at Webster Electric Company, a local radio manufacturing firm, and won a NLRB election in February 1950 by a victory of 316 to 12. After several months of negotiations, the local signed a contract with management recognizing Local 391 as the official bargaining agent. Workers won a union shop agreement with dues checkoff, health insurance, grievance procedures, vacation pay, and a new seniority provision governing hiring and layoffs.[6] Workers at Belle City Manufacturing, where William Jenkins worked, bargained for and won better pension and wage agreements during several rounds of contract negotiations. UAW Local 85, representing workers at Walker Manufacturing's lawn mower company, signed what was considered at the time the best contract in the area. Members proudly announced that they received a better pension and wage package than some workers at General Motors in Detroit the same year.[7]

Not all struggles were as easily won, however. A hard-fought seven-month strike at Modine Manufacturing Company, a manufacturer of heating and cooling products, in 1952, demonstrated two key factors that would continue to unfold in postwar Racine. First, as U.S. companies began to change management practices and seek to gain profits through the buying and selling of other corporations, ownership and management of local manufacturing plants shifted from local to foreign control. Many family and privately owned companies were sold or relocated, and new managers and owners did not always adhere to local customs and traditions, which led to increased tensions during negotiations and strike activity to achieve workers' gains. While Modine's owners remained local, the management team did not. They approached the 1952 contract bargaining as an opportunity to severely limit the union's power. But there was a countervailing second trend within Racine's labor community: rank-and-file support for striking workers across the area. Union members often walked picket lines with their striking neighbors, sent financial support to other unions' strike funds, and attended rallies and mobilized for workers across industries and employment sectors. Remembering their history, Racine's labor community members understood that only their collective power would force capitalists to give working people a fair share of industrial profits.

While Modine's workers felt the time was right to negotiate a labor agreement in line with similar industrial plants, the new management team felt that their prerogatives should be made explicit. A. B. Modine started Modine Manufacturing in 1916 as a producer of radiators for farm tractors after moving to the area as part of another company three years earlier. Over the years, the company expanded its product line to produce radiators for cars, trucks, and a wide variety of heat transfer needs for industrial installations.[8] The union that became UAW Local 82 had negotiated amicably with Modine's management team for twenty years and represented 800 employees by 1952. The contract expired 16 July and the union approached the company about making changes that would fall closer in line with other automobile industry agreements. However, by September, only a union recognition clause had been successfully negotiated. The company wanted to include a management prerogative clause in the contract and would not negotiate on any other items such as wages, fee scales for piece work, or other economic issues. The management clause listed a set of terms that the company would not negotiate, such as management rights that they considered off limits for bargaining with the union.[9]

Union members recognized that signing this agreement before opening negotiations on a new labor contract would jeopardize their workplace democracy. Workers felt that their only option to protect themselves from the prerogative clause was to insist on a past practices clause that would allow the bargaining team to submit standard operating procedures as starting points for negotiations. When management refused to include the past practices clause or discuss wages or other economic issues, workers voted to strike. Local 82 President Louis Raschke, UAW International Representative Harold Thompson, and other activists in the community blamed the new hardline approach from the company on outside managers not from the Racine area.[10] At the same time, this was a common tactic by antiunion capitalists to limit workers' power in contract negotiations.

Worker activists also argued that management sought to take advantage of political shifts to wrest power from workers. As discussed in the previous chapter, conservative business organizations and Republicans had passed the 1947 Taft-Hartley Act, and Republican Dwight D. Eisenhower won the presidential election of 1952.[11] Harvey Kitzman's speech after his 1953 reelection as UAW Region 10 Director spoke directly to this issue in the Modine strike. He declared, "If the employers think just because they were successful in putting in a Republican administration last November

Labor Politics and Solidarity in the 1950s 47

that they are going to destroy the labor movement, they had better start thinking again because that is not going to happen." Kitzman highlighted the importance many in the labor community placed on fighting back against what they saw as political backlash aimed at labor's gains since the New Deal.[12]

Workers did not allow the cold winter or severe financial hardship to keep them from striking. They cited the need for dignity at work and fair reciprocation of the loyalty they had shown to the company in letters to *Racine Labor*, at union meetings during the strike, and at public rallies. In a letter signed "Modine Worker," one man explained that he worked at Modine's for over twenty years and expected management to recognize the service of long-term employees like him. He wrote that the company had always been fair and that he and his fellow workers wanted the company to continue dealing with them in a fair manner. The wife of a Local 82 member wrote in to encourage the workers to stand firm in protecting the interests of all working people in the city. She explained that she had to take a job to help supplement the family's income and encouraged others to do the same while also admonishing against any shame or guilt in using community charity services to help provide for their families. At a union meeting in March, after negotiations had been halted for nearly a month, member Arthur Kitzman (no known relation to Harvey) asked for a vote of confidence from the floor so the bargaining committee would know where members like him stood. There was a unanimous voice vote in favor of the bargaining committee's efforts.[13]

The Racine labor community gave full support to the Modine employees in part because they recognized that this was a precedent-setting strike. Other UAW locals, unions within the CIO, and AFL-affiliated unions all contributed to the Local 82 strike fund. Members of UAW Local 180, at J. I. Case, donated $100 and pledged another $100 each month until the strike was settled. Local 180 President Tony Valeo reported that Case workers "want to show their gratitude to the other locals which came to their assistance in past disputes." Contributions came from across the city, including auto workers, garment workers, foundry workers, laborers, leather workers, and bookbinders. The letters and resolutions submitted with the donations reiterated the labor community's commitment to helping working people across the city. Steve Olson, President of UAW Local 244 at Massey-Harris, pledged the support of his union in a written statement issued to Modine strikers that emphasized the likelihood that if one company proved successful in overturning hard-fought union wins, it would not bode well for workers throughout the area. As he explained, the whole labor community's interests were closely tied to the workers'

48 CHAPTER 2

success in the strike against Modine Manufacturing. This level of support enabled the union members to endure the long winter months.[14]

Religious leaders also supported the union. After several failed attempts by the U.S. Department of Mediation and Conciliation to broker an agreement, Reverend S. V. Labaj of the Holy Trinity Church stepped in to help in January. The union willingly agreed to work with Reverend Labaj, but he was unable to convince the company to bargain. In March, Reverend John B. Wolf used a sermon at the Church of the Good Shepherd to counsel Modine's managers to recognize that they had forced the workers into a corner and the workers had to stand their ground. While pointing to errors on both sides, he cautioned managers to accept the fact that "business will cut off its nose to spite its face if it attempts to forget the human values involved and supports a campaign of power politics." Despite the determination of the workers to maintain the strike and the public pressure to bargain, Modine's management held firm to their demand for a management right's clause before any other contract negotiations proceeded.[15]

When the Federal Conciliation service added pressure, Modine's management came back to the table. Because the U.S. Navy and other firms needed parts and supplies from the Racine plant, the Conciliation service sent in three representatives to force the company into bargaining. The union bargaining team leveraged this power to keep the past practices clause, and after a series of eight meetings over the course of an intense week of bargaining, an agreement was finally reached on Sunday, 19 April 1953. Local 82 was forced to compromise with a partial no-strike clause. The contract gains included better job security, a new arbitration agreement, fringe benefits, and wage increases. Union members ratified the contract with only twenty-five dissenting votes. The strike took a heavy toll on the workers, union, and the company. It was a slow process of restarting production and getting all the workers back on the job; many workers were laid off until June.[16] The battle for workplace democracy at Modine shows how hard business leaders in the area fought to tilt the collective bargaining power back to their side. In Racine, workers understood the need for unwavering solidarity to protect workers' rights across industries.

Public Workers Expanding the Labor Community

Just as private sector workers fought for democracy at work, municipal and county workers also sought to gain better pay and working conditions through union organizing and strike campaigns in the 1950s. While most policymakers and political leaders by the 1950s saw industrial unionism in the private sector as necessary for a robust economy, public worker unionism remained a highly contested idea. In Wisconsin, the progressive wing of the Republican Party had supported public employees' efforts to organize and bargain over work conditions and to protect the civil service system earlier than other states and the federal government. Republican Governor Philip La Follette voiced his approval of state employee unionization in 1932, giving legitimacy to a small union of state employees that would become the American Federation of State, County and Municipal Employees (AFSCME) in 1936. Public workers and AFSCME activists pushed allies in the Wisconsin legislature to create the first state retirement system in 1943, and by 1947, they had successfully lobbied for the first wage-escalator clause for public employees linked to the Consumer Price Index. So, public workers received regular cost-of-living wage increases. By the end of World War II, AFSCME had a strong foothold in the "city and county governments of Wisconsin's urban centers."[17]

Racine reflected this statewide trend of early public worker organizing and collective bargaining. Racine's firefighters formed the first public sector union in the city in 1931. In 1935 they successfully bargained with the Common Council for a wage increase. The water department employees followed in 1937 by organizing AFSCME Local 63.[18] Other city employees organized the CIO-United Public Workers Local 249, started a major organizing drive during World War II, and went on strike in 1948 to improve wages. Union organizers tried unsuccessfully to organize teachers through the American Federation of Teachers (AFT) in 1916 and 1920, but the labor community stayed closely involved with the school system, arguing for good schools with well-paid, quality teachers, despite the high public cost. The school janitors organized through the Building Services Union BSEIU 152, and, after they won wage increases in 1943, local labor activists demanded that teachers' wages be kept at least at the same level as the janitors.[19] Early organizing and bargaining paid off for Racine's public workers, and by the 1950s, they were seen as an integral part of the labor community by the industrial and skilled trades union activists in the city.

Despite not having legal protections, Racine's public workers' early strike activity proved successful. On 3 January 1952, 200 workers represented by United Public Workers Local 249 walked off the job and stopped all garbage and ash collection, snow removal, and building maintenance. The workers had won increased wages in negotiations with the City Council the previous November but could not come to an agreement on guaranteed annual salaries and cost-of-living increases. Local 249 members maintained picket lines at the Department of Public Works garage, the sewer disposal plant, city hall, cemeteries, and the zoo. Workers kept the

50   CHAPTER 2

heat at forty degrees to prevent water lines from freezing in municipal buildings, but many city offices closed because of low temperatures. The union also kept a skeleton crew at the sewage disposal site and had workers standing by for burials if vaults filled. While many citizens complained on the radio and the local daily newspaper condemned the city employees for initiating a strike, *Racine Labor* supported their right to take necessary action to improve their wages and protect workers. A snowstorm in the middle of the strike left streets impassible, and basketball games and other sports tournaments were canceled. After a twelve-day strike, Local 249 won a two-year wage agreement. Although the strike was successful, some labor activists felt that it lasted longer than necessary due to poor service by union officials and lack of negotiation strategies by both the union and Common Council members.[20]

In addition to reflecting ongoing battles over the legitimacy of collective bargaining and workers' standards of living, the municipal employees strike also sharpened a debate over the role of Communists in organized labor at the onset of the Cold War. Many of the radical union activists of the 1930s had been influenced by the anti-capitalist politics of the Industrial Workers of the World and the Communist Party. However, as union ranks grew, most workers did not share the same radical politics, and those more orthodox Marxist views became a minority in CIO unions. The Cold War environment that facilitated anti-Communism led to the purge of Communists from CIO unions after the passage of Taft-Hartley. Yet Taft-Hartley only exacerbated an internal CIO ideological battle that had been waging since the 1930s. In Racine, most union activists sought to distance themselves from the taint of Communism, even before the Cold War began. In fact, Harvey Kitzman accepted the nomination for President of the Wisconsin CIO council in 1939 to lead the effort to remove Communist board members. It was not until the state CIO conventions of 1946 and 1947 that anti-Communists successfully purged all the Communist leaders from the organization.[21] The national CIO ousted the United Public Workers (UPW), the United Electrical Workers, and other Communist-led left unions from the organization in 1950.[22]

Members of Local 249 in Racine chose at the time to remain with UPW instead of seeking a new charter with another CIO union. However, during the strike, workers expressed disappointment about the lack of support from national UPW representatives and some local supporters blamed the slow negotiations on the UPW representatives as well as the Common Council. One month after the strike, Local 249 members voted unanimously to disaffiliate with the UPW and seek direct affiliation with the CIO, whose Racine locals had offered crucial support during the January strike.[23] Racine activists supported the city workers but judged UPW as operating outside the boundaries of the local labor community. The Racine labor leaders' refusal to accept Communists or organizations that seemed to be led by Communists into the labor community complicates their otherwise broad understanding of who belonged. This can partly be explained by the close relationship between Harvey Kitzman and Walter Reuther, who was a staunch anti-Communist.[24] At the same time, Racine's labor activists did not allow ideological differences to stop them from supporting the UPW members during the strike and accepting them as part of Racine's labor community.

Despite these internal conflicts, other public workers actively engaged in organizing and bargaining for better wages and working conditions during the early 1950s as well. Racine County highway workers, sheriff's deputies, and courthouse employees represented by Teamsters Local 43, sought to increase wages in their 1952 bargaining sessions. After several weeks of intense negotiations and a three-day strike, union and county negotiators came to an agreement. Highway workers, courthouse workers, and deputies all received considerable increases and the cost-of-living scale was duly adjusted.[25] Local firefighters and police officers also worked together during the postwar decade for better pay and safer working conditions. Firefighters and police officers often sought the aid and support of the local labor movement during negotiations. They presented their proposals to the Racine Trades and Labor Council, the representative of AFL-affiliated unions in the city and used the services of Ben Schwartz, a labor lawyer. Schwartz helped many local unions during negotiations, filed charges with local and national labor boards, and settled many interunion disputes in the region. In negotiations with city officials in 1953, firefighters expressed their frustration with the pay scale. They acknowledged the consistent wage increases they had received over the years but planned to present the Common Council with figures demonstrating how far the city fell behind in pay rates compared to other Wisconsin cities.[26] Public workers in the city and county departments used the favorable political economy in Racine to successfully demand better pay and their active participation in urban politics helped establish Racine's image as a robust labor community.

Racine's labor activists sought to push back against a Republican resurgence in Wisconsin to solidify the gains of public workers. During the 1952 election season, the focus was on the attempt to prevent the reelection of Senator Joseph McCarthy, who actively fueled the Red Scare hysteria against anyone on the left at the national level. Racine political and labor leaders joined forces with a statewide coalition of university

52 CHAPTER 2

administrators, business and financial managers, and other labor leaders to form the Wisconsin Citizens Committee on McCarthy's Record. The group included many former Progressive Republicans who supported Robert "Fighting Bob" M. La Follette, Sr. and had since left the Republican Party. The group published a 136-page booklet, "The McCarthy Record," detailing McCarthy's business and political dealings starting with his 1936 campaign for District Attorney. They concluded that McCarthy's "policies and methods reflect a dangerous drift toward alien, totalitarian methods," and that his allegations of Communist takeover of the government were unfounded. Former Mayor Francis Wendt and Harvey Kitzman were two of the seventy-five business, labor, and university officials who signed their support for the book's findings.[27] While McCarthy did retain his Senate seat, Racine activists took pride that he did not win victories in the county or city. In the city, he lost by 4,000 votes, and the county tallied just over 1,000 votes.[28] Working-class activists continued to stay involved in local and state politics and planned a strategy to continue their efforts to elect political leaders that would promote their class issues. In Racine, labor activists did not feel obligated to forgo political goals for the benefit of collective bargaining; they actively campaigned on both fronts.

Political opponents also gathered their allies for action. In 1955, Republican Mark Catlin pushed a bill (named after him) through the legislature that prohibited any political contribution from union dues. William Proxmire had won 49 percent of the vote in his 1954 run for governor with most of his campaign funds coming from labor organizations, which probably led to the new legislation. Local 180 sent members to the State Capitol in Madison to learn more about the Catlin Bill (419A), and they concluded it was "the most backward step the state of Wisconsin or any legislature of the state could take."[29] The law decimated Democratic campaign coffers and limited the labor movement's ability to pursue its agenda. Labor activists felt this bill was part of a larger strategy of politicians and business leaders to pass so-called "right-to-work" laws and restrictions on labor unions that would severely damage unionization efforts in the state. Several states implemented such laws after the passage of Taft-Hartley, which in Section 14(b) allowed states to ban closed shops, an oft-sought contract measure that enabled unions to require all workers to join.[30] As historian Matthew M. Reiter has detailed, conservative business owners in Wisconsin, fueled in part by resistance to the progressive politics of Bob La Follette in the 1920s and 1930s, formed the "bedrock" of the conservative movement in Wisconsin.[31]

For such a law to pass in Wisconsin, known for its progressive politics and high levels of unionization, shows how powerful conservative business leaders and their political allies fought to shift the balance of power among labor, capital, and the state. In September 1955, Local 180 members resolved "that it must be the job of all the people, within and without the labor movement, to oppose this vicious 'un-America' law" and pledged to use all the union power to resist it through a media campaign and direct legislative lobbying.[32] Workers across the state recognized the need to defeat such legislation and supported the Kohler strike in part to keep "right-to-work" laws out of the state. But they had to wait for a political majority to work in their favor. While AFL and CIO councils sought to question the constitutionality of the law through state courts, the law was not repealed until Democrats gained control of the legislature and governorship in 1959.[33]

At the local level, four of the five candidates who announced they were running for seats on the City Council in January 1954 were also active in their local unions, and one was also on the RTLC.[34] While Wendt, with overwhelming labor backing, did not win the 1955 mayoral election, nine of the thirteen City Council seats went to labor endorsed candidates.[35] The biggest success for Racine's working-class political activists came in the 1958 elections. Gerald Flynn was elected as the first Democrat to represent Racine in Congress in sixty-eight years. On the Wednesday after Election Day, Flynn went around to many of the local factories to thank workers as they started their shifts. The election also saw the return of William Proxmire to the Senate, Gaylord Nelson as governor-elect, and labor-backed Democrats filled all the area's state legislative seats.[36]

Successful public employee organizing led to Governor Gaylord Nelson signing MERA in 1959. The cross-sector solidarity and growth of unionization throughout the 1950s also helped lobbying efforts at the state level. AFSCME leaders and their supporters in private sector unions had made significant gains for public employees by the 1950s. Building on the success of the 1930s and 1940s, these activists continued to lobby the state legislature for a law granting public employees bargaining rights against the opposition of state chambers of commerce, the League of Municipalities, and the County Boards Association. In 1958, after electing the first Democratic governor and state assembly in years through the combined efforts of young political progressives and labor union activists, this coalition pushed through legislation that led to MERA.[37] Signed by Gov. Gaylord Nelson in 1959, this law was the first of its kind in the United States to grant collective bargaining and mandate that employers must negotiate with employee-chosen representatives. MERA expanded the role of the Wisconsin Employment Relations Commission (WERC) to provide enforcement and regulation for public employees as it had for private sector workers. However, it did prohibit public employee strikes.[38] Nevertheless, this long sought legislative victory increased the sense of labor power and fueled organizing activity in the area.

Job Security amid Corporate and Technological Changes

Success on the shop floor, in the community, and at the ballot box did not blind Racine's labor community to corporate restructuring, growing capital mobility, and the technology changes that threatened employment levels, economic security, and political power. Starting in the 1950s, the number of managers who came into their positions by working their way through other areas of the company fell, and more managers came with a background in finance. Business schools began focusing on financial and legal training. Corporate boards began rewarding short-term gains. Changes in corporate management decisions regarding short-term profits and finance as well as the battle for industrial control over the economy led to a steady movement of capital and the massive "dismantling" of basic industry across the U.S.[39] The shift in political power toward corporate management also facilitated capital mobility as businesses forced local and state governments to vie for their attention through tax cuts and other incentives that weakened communities' safety nets and put labor in even weaker positions with management.[40] Even though such issues would not become a focus of widespread concern for the public until the 1970s, working-class activists in Racine looked at plant closings and massive layoffs due to corporate restructuring as serious concerns in the 1950s.

Mergers and restructuring led to consolidation of corporations and worker layoffs in the area. A few examples illustrate the impact this had on jobs and worker power in Racine. In preparation for its merger with the Hudson Company, Nash Motors in Racine began laying off workers in nearby Kenosha and Milwaukee in 1953. In February 1954 the company laid off 1,300 employees at the Kenosha plant and several hundred in Milwaukee. What became the American Motor Company was still the largest employer in Kenosha, but workers there recognized their vulnerability in the face of shifting economic trends in the county.[41] Through another merger, Massey-Harris Company became the Massey-Harris-Ferguson Company. Like the Case Company, workers at Massey-Harris-Ferguson had to deal with cyclical unemployment due to lulls in the agricultural cycle.[42] When members of the Amalgamated Meat Cutters and Butcher Workmen of North America Leather Division Local 77 refused to accept the increased production schedule introduced by Eisendrath Tannery management, the company announced it was closing the plant.[43]

In 1956, workers at Case and Massey-Harris-Ferguson faced one of the worst years of layoffs since the postwar reconversion. A report by the Wisconsin Industrial Commission showed that in October 1956 nearly one thousand fewer workers were employed in Racine than October 1955, mainly due to the layoffs in the agricultural implements industry. While textile and garment workers saw an increase in employment, it was not enough to compensate for all the out-of-work employees at Case, Massey-Harris-Ferguson, and other local foundries. The Case Company's downturn seemed more severe than just typical seasonal decline because the company decided to close its plant in Anniston, Alabama, as well as the Racine Main Works facility due to low orders for their farm equipment. The list of unemployed workers totaled 1,630, most of them unskilled workers, including over 300 women.[44] The diversity of industrial sectors helped the overall unemployment levels, but those most excluded or unable to adapt to new technologies, such as unskilled workers and people of color, felt the brunt of the downturn in heavy industry.

Automation and technological innovation also caused layoffs and created as much concern and strategic planning within the labor community as did corporate restructuring. As scholars have shown, workers have dealt with technological change by learning ways to accommodate the changes and protect their power on the shop floor.[45] At the 1953 UAW International Convention, delegates passed a resolution for the union to institute a program of planned study on automation and its impact on workers. The resolution stressed that rapid progress in industrial efficiency concerned "every worker, every citizen in America" and "gives more urgency than ever before to the necessity for finding a solution to the problem of maintaining full employment and full production in peacetime."[46] In 1955, Machinists Lodge 437 invited Erling Johnson, an area engineer, to speak at their union meeting about automation. Johnson warned the skilled workers to prepare for the shock of automation and the devastating effects it would have on workers due to massive layoffs and lower wages. He urged, "Labor has a duty to closely scrutinize all new methods and how far they are to progress with a view to easing the changeover caused by automation."[47] Johnson agreed to study the problem and contribute a series of articles to *Racine Labor* to report his findings. In his January 1956 article he suggested the biggest problem of automation would be economic distribution because technological advances would not only displace some workers but would eliminate whole areas of employment.[48]

In his 1959 Labor Day address, President George Haberman of the Wisconsin AFL-CIO spoke directly to the labor community's concern with automation, plant closings, and corporate restructuring. While he acknowledged the benefits of increased productivity, he also recognized the dangers it caused to the workforce, as young people entered the labor market and workers lived and worked longer while the need for unskilled workers fell. He emphasized the AFL-CIO's efforts to plan for these coming changes and highlighted work with Governor Gaylord Nelson in planning a conference to discuss these issues in 1960. He pointed to plant closings throughout Wisconsin as evidence of the need to increase vocational education, provide adequate recreation facilities, develop conservation plans, and expand economic development.[49] Working-class activists recognized the need to stay abreast of economic and political changes to maintain economic security for workers and the political power to pursue their best interests.

Bolstering the Labor Community

The increasing challenges facing the Racine labor community did not hinder worker activists' commitment to class politics and their intention to maintain an economic, social, and political force in the city. Workers in Racine continued to place their mark on the city's built environment as they had since the early local unions constructed union halls and occupied public space during rallies, strikes, and organizing campaigns. UAW locals and other CIO unions banded together to build the Racine Labor Center so that people would have permanent space to meet and collaborate. In 1956, they purchased seven acres of land and authorized a building at the cost of $300,000.00.[50] The Racine Labor Center gave workers a place to socialize, conduct union business, build solidarity, and feel at home. True to its commitment to broad-based collaboration and cooperation, the building committee, part of the District Council 8, the collection of UAW and independent unions in the city, offered space not only to member unions, but to other social justice organizations as well. Once the building was completed, the NAACP moved its offices into the Labor Center. It had a bowling alley, a bar, and rooms for other social and union activities. It served as a command post for strikes throughout the second half of the twentieth century. It also demonstrated to the city that Racine's workers held a firm commitment to pursuing their class interests.

This commitment to class interests was sustained in social, community, and family events as well. The working-class community's involvement in civic and political events carried over into social events for working

Labor Politics and Solidarity in the 1950s

Racinians. The annual three-day Labor Day festivities were only one opportunity for working people to come together. The bowling, dartball, and golf leagues provided social connections outside of workplaces. It also brought workers from diverse plants together. Many unions reported on social activities in *Racine Labor* and advertised picnics, socials, and parties on a regular basis. In 1952, all the CIO unions got together to hold a dance for union members and their families. The next year, area UAW locals formed a recreation council. Together with mass rallies to support strike activities, these sports teams and other leisure activities went a long way in shaping the sense of working-class group identity across employment sectors.[51]

The most widely publicized case of worker solidarity involved the four-year strike at the Kohler Company, a producer of plumbing fixtures, in Sheboygan, Wisconsin, eighty miles north of Racine. The Kohler Company, like Case, consistently refused to accept worker demands for a union shop and mandatory arbitration as the last step in the grievance procedure. The strike started in April 1954 when management again refused to implement what amounted to standard contract language by this point in U.S. labor relations. The nearly 3,000 workers belonged to UAW Local 833 and felt they were continuing a fight that workers had been waging with the Kohler brothers since the AFL attempted to form a union in 1934. That earlier strike was met with tear gas and gun fire by the company's security force. These company employees killed two men and injured another forty-seven people.[52] Many participants in the 1954 strike were children and family members of the earlier strikers. They could see their struggle across the generations. Workers, management, and union leaders felt that the 1954 battle to keep Local 833 in Kohler Company was a crucial event in the ongoing U.S. class struggle. Workers explained, "we believe we are entitled to the same working conditions, the same degree of security that has become the standard for factory workers across America."[53] Almost immediately, the UAW counsel filed suit with the NLRB for unfair labor violations against Kohler Company and continued to add to complaints for the next four years. Kohler's representatives readily filed countersuits. These lawsuits, finally settled four years after the strike, would play a crucial role in future labor relations at the plant.

As the strike wore on, it became a national issue and both sides recognized the need for a victory. The long, bitter strike, the propaganda from both sides, the coercion that workers faced to return to the plant, and the violence as strikebreakers tried to enter the plant made the strike a sensational news story. UAW Local 833 received the full support of the International. One year into the strike UAW Local 833 released a brochure titled "All My Life My Daddy's Been on Strike to Make My Future Better:

The Kohler Worker's Story," which started with a history of the 1934 strike and explained the violence, fear, and intimidation faced by workers who held onto their pride and determination to gain justice.[54] In April 1955, the company's *Kohler of Kohler News*, a monthly journal "by and for the Kohler Co," offered management's position that "the dignity and worth of the individual American workman is theoretically stressed by unions" and "the vicious methods of power-hungry labor leaders who seek not only to dominate their membership, but seek, within or without the law, to take this nation down the road to socialism, must be understood."[55] Battle lines were drawn and the national debate ensued. The President and Secretary-Treasurer of the UAW gave tremendous amounts of time and resources to sustain the Kohler workers. They initiated a boycott campaign, solicited extra strike fund donations from the network of UAW locals, and sought the aid of John and Robert Kennedy. At the time, John F. Kennedy was serving in the U.S. Senate and was chairman of the Labor and Public Welfare Committee. His brother, Robert Kennedy, was chief counsel for the Democratic minority in the Senate. While JFK offered minimal support, Robert Kennedy provided considerable support for their efforts, especially after he visited Sheboygan and saw that the UAW claims were true.[56]

In Racine, Local 180 members at Case voted to send the striking employees monthly $100 checks to support the strike, they actively participated in the Kohler boycott, and they sent members to many rallies in support of the Kohler workers over the years.[57] Workers from the Kohler Company came to Racine and spoke at several membership meetings, with updates appearing as part of regular meeting minutes. This show of solidarity is most impressive because Local 180 and other Case locals in Rockford and Burlington, Illinois had negotiations break down, leading to several strike votes during the same period. During the three years of negotiations while working without a contract, Local 180 President Tony Valeo trained stewards, pushed back against company efforts to divide the bargaining unit and take all shopfloor authority away from workers, and led multiple close, contentious strike vote meetings. When a two-year agreement was finally signed in February 1956, it had been thirty-nine months since Case workers had a signed collective bargaining agreement. The new plan offered a few economic advancements but met none of the standards of agreements within the agricultural implements industry.[58] Instead of focusing solely on their own internal problems, however, workers at Case linked their struggle with those of the Kohler workers. Meetings often consisted of a comparison of the struggles at Kohler and with dealing with the disparate Case plants.[59] By December 1955, Wisconsin workers had donated $5000.00 to the Kohler strikers. Workers in Racine convinced the YMCA and other

Labor Politics and Solidarity in the 1950s 59

organizations to participate in the Kohler boycott and even threatened to picket and discontinue all union meetings at Eagle Hall, where many unions met, because Kohler products were installed in a recent renovation. Controversy was only averted when the architect proved he did not receive the boycott notice until after the fixtures were installed.[60]

Herbert V. Kohler, president of the company, sought out his allies in the conservative National Association of Manufacturers (NAM), and company spokesmen went on a nationwide tour to various business organizations and conservative political groups.[61] While workers around the country rallied behind the Kohler strikers, Herbert Kohler became a champion among conservative leaders and a rallying point for "right-to-work" proponents. Effective lobbying by conservative forces led to the McClellan Committee hearings looking into corruption in the Teamsters and other unions in the late 1950s in the U.S. Senate. Barry Goldwater, Republican Senator from Arizona, pressured the McClellan Committee into investigating Walter Reuther despite the lack of evidence of financial or other misconduct. Reuther testified for three days in March 1958 for the McClellan Committee. While his testimony and the evidence cleared Reuther and the UAW, it did not lead to major dividends for labor liberalism in the late 1950s. In fact, some scholars point to the McClellan Committee hearings as a significant turning point for conservative opponents of the New Deal order. Kim Phillips-Fein and Elizabeth Tandy Shermer, for example, mark this as a major event in Barry Goldwater's political career, as he solidified his position in the Republican Party while also facilitating an eventual takeover by the far-right members.[62] As scholars have noted, Goldwater used his first term in the Senate to assert the anti-collectivism ideal of the Republican Party's right wing.[63]

Yet, on the local level in Sheboygan, Racine, and other parts of Wisconsin, the Kohler strike and its political outcomes galvanized local class struggles, both in workplaces and in city and state politics. Workers in Racine especially saw the significance of the Kohler strike and its relationship to management intransigence at Case and other manufacturers where the company refused to accept the basic rights of the "social contract" between labor and management that had become the norm. The Kohler strike ended when the NLRB ruled in late-August 1960 in favor of most of UAW Local 833's claims of unfair labor practices against the company. Pickets ended in early September and, although there was no signed agreement between the company and the union, most workers returned to their jobs on 14 September. The legal battle continued until 1962 when the U.S. Supreme Court upheld the NLRB decision and forced the company back to the bargaining table. Finally, a new contract was ratified on 7 October

1962. The new contract provided for dues checkoff, no wage increases, but stipulated increases in fringe benefits, arbitration, and better seniority.[64] The long, hard-fought battle proved significant not only for Kohler employees but as a victory tale in Wisconsin's record of labor history. Labor activists' narrative of the strike remained a powerful incentive to militant action in support of working-class issues in Wisconsin's industrial centers.

Despite the solidarity among workers spurred by the Kohler strike, tensions within organized labor had not subsided. The merger of the AFL and CIO at the national level uncovered some of these local tensions. In January 1956, just a few months after the national merger was complete, Charles Schultz, Wisconsin State CIO President, told the committee selected to work on a merger at the Racine County level that they should proceed as quickly as possible because he expected no delay at the state level. Charles Heymanns, already chosen to be the merged AFL-CIO Regional Director, told the local AFL delegates something similar, adding that the two-year window was too long for Racine, with its "progressive history and . . . pattern of cooperation."[65] AFL unions had offered unyielding support during the Kohler strike and Racine's AFL and CIO unions often flaunted their ability to successfully work together. But there were internal tensions in Wisconsin. What should have been an amicable merger between state and local AFL and CIO-affiliated councils turned into a multiyear contest within the Wisconsin labor movement. At the state level and in Racine County, issues surrounding representation and voting rights, per capita tax payments from affiliated organizations, division of officer slots, and finances and property held up the merger and led to heated disputes within the communities.

By October 1957, it was plain that serious issues would prolong the merger process. In Racine, AFL locals felt that the CIO unions would have an undue advantage due to their much larger numbers. The AFL locals were in better financial situations than the CIO locals and wanted much lower per capita tax rates and a more equitable distribution of delegate votes to counteract the membership imbalance. At the state level, the battle turned bitter over issues of what the AFL building trades called CIO invasion of their jurisdictional territory and attempts to dominate the merged council. At an AFL building trades conference in Wausau, Wisconsin, one delegate warned that CIO building trades workers should not be doing new construction or major repairs in industrial plants, and another argued that CIO delegates to the merger convention wanted AFL money to pay for failing labor newspapers instead of voting to support an AFL newspaper that was solvent. State CIO merger delegates sent a public letter to AFL-CIO president George Meany demanding that he force a merger at the Wisconsin state level. When AFL-CIO national representatives made plans for a merger convention in February 1958, AFL delegates vowed not to attend. Finally, after several months of negotiations, both groups agreed to a compromise on representation and per capita tax issues and sent the final issue of a representative newspaper to President Meany to decide. The first merged state AFL-CIO convention was held in Milwaukee in July 1958. The merged group did leave the convention with successful resolutions endorsing Democrats in the upcoming election, including William Proxmire for his Senate reelection campaign and Gaylord Nelson for governor. In Racine, the battle over representation and per capita tax lasted until late in 1959, when at a meeting arranged by Heymanns, both sides agreed to send the cases to President Meany for arbitration. By early December, the only items left open were officer elections. However, the Racine Labor Council would not receive its charter until 1960.[66] While the merger delays reflect continuing tensions between the historic AFL and newer industrial unions, ultimately the Racine labor community managed to move toward greater unity.

Conclusion

The public- and private-sector labor struggles in the 1950s created a strong sense of solidarity throughout the Racine working-class community. Workers often referenced the early strikes of the 1930s and the violence and deaths involved in those struggles for greater working-class citizenship rights in Wisconsin. These memories and the history of militancy in the community created a continual atmosphere of militant resistance to intransigent corporate power in the decades after World War II. Workers continued to fight for workplace democracy and to demand fulfillment of the promises of the New Deal and Roosevelt's Four Freedoms. Public worker militancy fueled labor solidarity even when ideological and political views differed across unions and employment sectors. Building on two decades of public worker activism, the passage of MERA expanded the power of Racine's labor movement.

Workers remained determined to act in their best economic and political interests, taking advantage of political leverage to gain public employee bargaining rights, adjusting to corporate restructuring, and searching for effective solutions to the adverse effects of automation and plant closings. While Black and women workers made considerable gains, the road to a most-inclusive working-class group identity was not always smooth, as the next chapter illustrates. However, the language of inclusion and direct action in support of racial and gender equity led working-class Racinians onto that path. The continual labor militancy and collaboration efforts by worker activists in the Racine community created a sense of strong solidarity across industries, among private and public workers, and across racial and religious boundaries. By the 1960s, Racine's organized workers had a long history of labor activity to use in shaping urban politics. They kept open lines of communication across employment sectors, supported others' bargaining and strike efforts, and worked to create a more equitable distribution of Racine's resources.

CHAPTER 3

UAW Local 180 and the Attack on New Deal Liberalism

Racinians listening to WRJN radio in the 1960s could expect to regularly hear the voice of Tony Valeo, UAW Local 180 president, giving union and community updates. Valeo led Local 180 through tough negotiations with the intransigent Case management team in the 1950s and spent his whole adult life fighting for economic justice. His energy and devotion to protecting workers' rights was infectious. Anthony "Tony" Valeo was born in Kenosha, Wisconsin on 28 October 1915 to an immigrant family from southern Italy. Unable to find a job after graduation, he went to work for the Civilian Conservation Corps. The Great Depression had a deep impact on Valeo, as it did for many young labor activists in the area, and he dedicated his life to securing economic security for all workers as a result. Valeo finally got a job at Case in 1937 and worked there and within the union until he was drafted into the U.S. Army in 1943. After the war, he returned to Case and served as an active member of the education committee during the 1945–47 strike. Valeo was elected Local 180 president in 1950 and served until 1966 when he was appointed as International Representative to UAW Region 10.

His commitment to bringing people together to solve economic and social justice issues sent Valeo to workplaces around Racine and to workers' homes to help explain the value of unionization, discuss various organizing campaigns, and expound on local union contracts, despite his intense shyness. He saw unionization as the best way to protect people from the ravages of poverty and injustice, and this belief fueled his tireless energy to get working people to stick together and make the world a better place. Outside of his union activities, Valeo served on the Labor Advisory Board to the United Way and as an activist in senior citizen and consumer rights groups.[1] He is remembered as a staunch supporter of workers' rights with a deep commitment to the health and safety of people across Racine and Kenosha. He spent sixteen years as Local 180 president and like Harvey Kitzman, moved into UAW International leadership after he retired from Case. Like William Jenkins, Valeo sat on the board of multiple volunteer organizations. Valeo's lifelong commitment to economic justice and lived experience as an engaged citizen continue to inspire and vitalize activists in the area.[2]

The 1960s began with a high stakes strike between UAW Local 180 and Case, which built on the issues of workers' legal right to bargain collectively and the balance of power among workers, management, and the state that played out during the Kohler strike. While this battle waged, Racine's labor community continued to organize new workers and worked to influence the local political economy. Job losses through economic fluctuations in manufacturing and plant closings led activists to maintain an ongoing conversation about economic and technological shifts that impacted workers and to actively search for ways to successfully protect the economic democracy most had come to expect in the postwar economy. The labor community remained active in local, state, and national political debates and successfully elected liberal Democrats to key offices. Union members stayed involved in their civic endeavors through financial contributions, volunteering, running for office, and advancing class politics.

This chapter details how Racine activists crafted a narrative of the valuable role of the labor community in leading the struggle for economic and social justice in the city, state, and nation. It begins with the strike at J. I. Case Company and the ways this pivotal event shaped local politics and activism, then looks at organizing and strike activity among other industrial unions. Next, the chapter covers labor activists' political use of history, community building, and political education to reinforce labor-liberal ideals of "total person unionism." In Racine, leaders used strikes and labor actions for political and economic education for rank- and-file members and the larger public. The goodwill established in the postwar period coupled with activists' continued involvement in public debate earned widespread support in the city and forced management to come to the bargaining table on multiple occasions. The chapter ends with a look at the ways corporate restructuring, debates about automation, and plant closings impacted the labor community. Despite corporate attacks and plant closings, Racine's labor community remained active and engaged, added new members, and fortified economic democracy in the city.

UAW Local 180 and the fight against
Corporate Conservatism and Anti-Unionism

A fierce battle between Case and UAW Local 180 during most of 1960 reinforced the ongoing political and legal debate over the relationship among unions, capitalists, and government generated by the Kohler strike. Questions over collective bargaining, management paternalism and prerogative, and union leadership raised in the 1930s, revisited during the 1946 strike, and throughout the struggles at Kohler and Case in the 1950s, had yet to be resolved. The six-month strike kept the ideals established in the postwar period concerning workers' rights to organize, collectively bargain, and choose their bargaining agent without duress, at the forefront of the Racine labor community's outlook. As we have seen, Case workers tried to improve their contract with Case starting right after World War II. While activists pointed to Local 180 members' nearly thirty-year history of organizing and battles for better wages and working conditions as an example, the contract with Case was one of the worst in the agricultural implements industry. As the largest union in Racine whose nearly 3,000 members played a very active role in organizing other workers, civic engagement, and political action, Local 180 activists felt that 1960 marked a crucial moment in their relationship with Case.

From the start, the Local 180 executive board, led by President Tony Valeo, framed the union's demands as necessary advancements for the Case plants and the agricultural implements industry in Racine. In correspondence with membership and the public, Local 180 leaders stressed the old-fashioned nature of the paternalism and tactics of Case's management team. The executive board explained, "we feel compelled to insist that the Company also make a genuine attempt to modernize our labor agreement to bring it in line with contracts currently existing between the UAW and their Competitors in the Agricultural Implement Industry" in a letter to members announcing the beginning of contract negotiations in January.[3] The bargaining committee presented an 18-point list of contract changes including a union shop clause, dues checkoff, supplemental unemployment insurance, arbitration procedures, and new seniority rules—all generally standard items in collective bargaining agreements throughout the industry. After a month of failed negotiations, workers voted to go on strike to force Case to bargain.[4] As Morris Fields, UAW Farm Implement Department Assistant Director explained, "We are not asking Case to break new ground, merely to come up near the other contracts in the industry."[5]

As with the Kohler strike, which had entered its sixth year, both labor and management saw the Case strike as one of major importance for labor relations not only locally but across the nation. The Case management team maintained their attitude that the labor union was encroaching on management's prerogative and that the whole notion of collective bargaining was un-American. They refused to participate in any forms of arbitration and sought to limit what they saw as outside influence in management decisions. The company also continued a long history of sending letters directly to all employees and using local media in an attempt to influence public opinion while refusing to sit down at the bargaining table with union representatives. Company correspondence attacked UAW representatives as seeking their own interests at the expense of workers. Management went so far as to label Harvey Kitzman an "outsider" even though he was a former employee, had helped start the union at Case, and still lived in the city. Case President William Grede also went on television and threatened to move the plants out of Racine, which would have had a major impact on the local economy. One letter argued that union members should attend the next Local 180 meeting and "protect your human rights" because Detroit outsiders were attempting to gain undue power.[6] The reference to human rights illustrates how the idea of a postwar accord between labor and management did not exist in Racine; management tried to coopt the language of the liberal coalition and twist it against the labor movement.

Despite these tensions, Local 180 members defied the company's back-to-work campaign in June. Tony Valeo answered the company's boast that workers had lost their insurance coverage because of the ongoing strike by reiterating that premium payments were part of the strike benefits workers received from the International Union.[7] Union leaders also gave update reports on WRJN. In one radio report toward the end of the strike in August, Sam Rizzo, a Racine native and international representative for UAW, spoke to "Mr. & Mrs. Racine Businessman . . . Mr. & Mrs. Racine Citizen more so than to the members of Local 180" and asked them to encourage Case management, their social and business associates, "to engage in good faith collective bargaining. Insist that this strike be settled."[8]

Racine's labor roundtable group decided to hold a public meeting to detail the history of the strike and Case's unwillingness to bargain fairly when the company refused to sit down with the bargaining team in August. Valeo detailed the union's original list of demands and explained how they were whittled down in an effort to get Case to negotiate. Leaders from the community spoke in favor of continuing the strike, promised the full support of the UAW international offices, told of Governor Nelson's factfinding team, and asked for more donations to the Local 180 strike fund.[9] Labor activists worked hard to keep public opinion on the side of the Case workers out on strike. These actions by Valeo and other union leaders during the strike illustrate the ways in which many union activists made an effort to keep the whole community involved in labor disputes and offered opportunities for more democratic decision-making and rank-and-file involvement in the strategies and directions unions took during major disputes. This rally and others like it went a long way in crafting a political narrative showing the strength of the community, beyond a simple struggle between one employer and one union local.

While local leaders worked hard to counter negative messaging from Case, their efforts highlighted the gender tensions related to women's work in the local foundries within the evolving labor community. Early in the strike, the executive board sent a letter to "the wives of striking members" inviting them to attend a meeting at the Racine Labor Center so they could "hear the facts and ask questions on our current labor dispute." Wives were invited to "ask husbands to babysit" so that women would be free to attend.[10] No suggestions were offered for husbands of Case's working women. The willingness to engage with workers' families demonstrated union leaders' commitment to maintaining the momentum of the strike and eliminating family pressure for individual workers to return to work. However, the focus on workers' wives belied the fact that women were also out on strike and perpetuated a notion of the male as breadwinner and woman as homemaker. In fact, Local 180 had resisted the company's efforts to hire women, in part because they felt that it would give management justification for keeping the wages low at Case.[11] The language and ideas it reproduced about gender roles illustrated that some labor leaders had not fully adapted to changes in the workforce and the demands of labor feminists.

Union leaders also worked to sustain strikers' commitment to staying on the picket line despite the economic hardship and some members' defections. For the first time in over ten years, some workers crossed picket lines.[12] To counter claims that leaders were benefiting from the strike to the determinant of rank and file members, representatives reminded workers that "it is all of us in Local 180 rank-and-file members, stewards, committeemen, and Executive Board members who have to work in the shop under a contract that doesn't come close to any other contract in the agricultural implement industry."[13] Workers were invited to come to the strike headquarters at the Racine Labor Center at any time to speak with union leaders or UAW international representatives. The Labor Center also served as the pickup point for strike benefits payments. The Polish Center, closer to the Case plants and a familiar location where union meetings had been held before the Labor Center was built, served as picketing headquarters. Informational meetings for workers were held by department and across several days so all could find time to attend. The value of establishing headquarters and holding meetings in different parts of the city went beyond strategic convenience for Case strikers. It also kept the workers interacting with the larger working-class community and maintaining networks of solidarity.

Racine's labor community, and labor communities across the nation, rallied to the aid of the Case strikers. UAW locals from Milwaukee, Madison, and Detroit made contributions to the Case strikers' fund. Brewery, steel, and meatpacking workers from the Milwaukee area also made contributions.[14] By early June, other workers had donated $13,705.18 to aid Local 180's strike effort.[15] Workers in Racine, Kenosha, and at Allis-Chalmers near Milwaukee held food drives to help support the Case strike.[16] *Racine Labor* ran informational stories and editorials throughout the six-month strike. In one issue, the labor paper listed the contract provisions the workers wanted and compared them to similar contracts at other agricultural implement plants including Allis-Chalmers, Caterpillar, International Harvester, and John Deere. In each instance, Case management refused to budge on issues already agreed on at other plants including union security, dues checkoff, and supplemental unemployment benefit plans.[17] Various rank-and-file and union leaders from Local 180 were featured in the "Who's Who in Labor" weekly column in the newspaper as well. For example, the 3 June column featured Moises Diaz, originally from San Antonio, Texas, who had joined Local 180 in 1958. The article pointed out that Diaz had served as a steward and as a member of the Fair Practices Committee and rose to prominence in the union due to his tireless efforts working as a picket captain.[18]

The Mexican American population had just started to grow in Racine and would only reach the 5,000 mark in the 1970s. Yet, Mexican American workers like Diaz found jobs in industrial settings, mostly working in Racine's foundries at Case and Belle City Malleable. Like Black workers, Mexican Americans worked within Racine's unions to improve their economic positions and served as active members, despite their limited advancement within the international union hierarchy and upward job mobility in the plants.[19] By featuring Diaz in the *Racine Labor* weekly "Who's Who" column, the editors showed their willingness to highlight the diversity of Local 180's members to the labor community.

The paper also participated in public shaming by publishing "The Dishonor Roll: Scabs of the Week" report on the first page.[20] It listed the names and addresses of workers who crossed the picket line. Again, it was an opportunity for the paper's editor to display the nature of the Racine labor community, this time by showing those who had stepped out of bounds of the community. Some workers may have crossed the picket lines because plant closings and restructuring limited their ability to find short-term employment during work stoppages. The use of the term "scab" to describe strikebreakers and the frequent listing of actual individuals who decided to cross the picket lines reinforced the community boundaries. Those who did not support the strikers' cause would not get community support.

As can be expected in a strike like this, with twenty-four-hour picket lines, with some union members crossing as strikebreakers, and with the company's refusal to bargain, tensions remained high. This tension erupted into violence on the picket lines. On 23 March, just a few weeks into the strike, a worker crossing the picket line hit Tony DeLaat, one of the union's picket captains, with his vehicle.[21] DeLaat suffered a fractured kneecap and other injuries. However, he said as soon as he was given permission to move around, he hoped "the boys can fix me up with a wheelchair at strike headquarters so I can at least be around."[22] In June, four other picketers were hit by strikebreakers. One driver had his window broken by one of his victims. Case used this incident to leave the bargaining table. The Local 180 executive board sent a letter to members detailing the events that led up to the attack and condemning both the strikebreakers and managements' actions.[23] While *Racine Labor* had run a few small articles about worker solidarity and the value of supporting strikes, in July the paper ran a two-page article, "Strikebreaking Really Doesn't Pay Very Well," which detailed all the reasons for not crossing picket lines. Included in this column was the contrast between short-term paychecks compared to long-term better wages and working conditions. The column also discussed typical company tactics during a strike and how they were designed to cripple unions and local economies.[24] When workers started twenty-four-hour picketing and non-Case workers joined the lines, management filed charges of mass picketing against the union with the NLRB.

Local union leaders took a public stand in support of UAW Local 180 and its strike efforts, recognizing the serious impact a lost strike would have on the Racine community. Indeed, as the largest union in the city, Local 180 served as a model for other union locals, provided key civic services in the community, and helped organize workers throughout the agricultural implement industry and in other employment sectors alike. The fact that Case workers had one of the least progressive employment contracts in the city spurned continued action on the part of labor activists. The Racine County Industrial Union Council met and pledged to offer "financial, moral, and whatever other support needed."[25] Union presidents from the area held regular meetings and formed a committee to aid in the

70   CHAPTER 3

strike and stay abreast of events. This committee reported to area unions providing updates and collecting strike assistance funds, spoke at rallies for the workers, and organized food drives.[26]

In July, as the strike seemed no closer to resolution, UAW Local 553 members from Belle City Malleable Foundry voted to increase their monthly union dues by one dollar to increase their donations to the Case workers' strike fund. When asked about his union's contribution efforts, local secretary Jim Rizzo replied, "We hear a lot of talk about cooperating to make Racine a better town and how management and labor should work together but if Grede and [company] have their way in crushing the union, which seems to be their goal, Racine might as well forget about any future progress."[27] While not taking a public stand to support UAW Local 180, Governor Gaylord Nelson denied Grede's request that he restore "law and order" in Racine and admonished Case to sit down at the bargaining table with the union and sign a "mutually agreed upon contract."[28]

Best known for his environmental and consumer protection politics, as we saw in chapter 1, as governor and senator, Nelson relied on the support of labor activists and was known for his commitment to labor-friendly policies and legislation. Scholars have pointed to Democrats like Nelson, William Proxmire, and Eugene McCarthy, as a new breed of liberals, influenced by postwar liberalism but with fewer ties to strict party politics, and "imbued with a sense of activism," ready to step outside of tradition and use pragmatic solutions to social and economic problems of the 1960s.[29] Nelson had been elected as the first Democratic governor in over twenty years during the 1958 election by upsetting the incumbent Republican, Vernon Thomson. Leading up to the election, Nelson delivered over 200 speeches, many in local union halls. He would show up at plant gates to talk with workers as they came and left work. As a young party organization newly reorganized in the postwar period, the Wisconsin Democrats needed strong grassroots support. Through clear discussion of issues important to workers in the state, Nelson, along with other Democrats, were able to get the urban and labor votes that had been going to the Progressive Party during the New Deal period.[30]

In the Senate, Nelson was a member of the Labor and Public Welfare Committee and often supported policies related to workers' rights and antipoverty initiatives. Bill Cherkasky, who worked closely with the Wisconsin Democratic Party throughout the 1950s and 1960s and served as Nelson's chief of staff in the Senate starting in 1968, recalled that Nelson "was a hundred percent down the line on labor." He remembered that Nelson always had the backing of labor organizations and that the Nelson administration "relied on labor to a great extent to be the backbone of our

UAW Local 180 and the Attack on New Deal Liberalism 71

campaigns."[31] In a 1960 speech on civil rights, Nelson linked the history of trade union organization to social justice campaigns which would help serve as a model for civil rights protections for all.[32] *Racine Labor* would often accept columns written by Nelson and offered editorial support for his legislative agenda throughout his term as governor and during his Senate career.[33] Nelson demonstrated his support of workers' rights during the strike by urging Case management to bargain fairly with Local 180 instead of aligning with management's call for state intervention.

Even with public support and Governor Nelson's admonishment to go to the bargaining table, Case president Grede and his management team withstood the pressure and continued to refuse to bargain. This left workers with few options. The union filed a complaint with the National Labor Relations Board detailing managements' unwillingness to bargain, but the process of hearings did not force Case immediately to the bargaining table.[34] By August, the Local 180 bargaining team had dropped many of the eighteen original points in an effort to get management back to the table.[35] While a few workers crossed picket lines (the union named at least twelve by name), a large contingent of the workers continued to push for remaining on strike. At a July union meeting with over 1000 members in attendance, workers voted to "continue our strike against the J. I. Case [Company] and that all of us stand united in our fight to win a fair share of dignity and justice—by the negotiation of a just and honorable contract for our members."[36] While many workers sought to stay the course, management's refusal to bargain left few options.

With negotiations at a standstill, Governor Gaylord Nelson sent in a factfinding committee that succeeded in resuming talks between Local 180 and Case. Throughout August, labor leaders held public meetings, wrote editorials, and found every avenue available to argue for the value of collective bargaining and the need for Case to negotiate. UAW Vice President Pat Greenhouse participated in the governor's commission. He publicly stated that the strike would end if Case recognized the union's right to collectively bargain.[37] While the company had consistently challenged the union's right to collectively bargain since members gained recognition in 1934, it was hard for current workers to accept the removal of the original eighteen points from the negotiation table. They and union leaders maintained that their requests were fair and necessary in order "to break out of the bonds of second-class citizenship and take their place alongside other workers in Racine who have long enjoyed [these] rights."[38] However, the strike was taking a heavy toll on Local 180. Finally, members voted on 18 September, by a margin of 816 to 360, to accept the negotiated agreement mediated by Governor Nelson's team. The strike did not win workers a union shop or dues checkoff, but it did get improvements in insurance benefits, better piecework payments, and seniority. The company maintained its wage increases at its initial offering from four to seventeen cents, depending on department and seniority.[39] Despite the failure to win a union shop and dues checkoff, union leaders focused on the wins they did receive and Governor Nelson's ability to force management back to the bargaining table.[40]

The memory of this 1960 strike between Case and UAW Local 180 remained an important element in the continued militant activism within the Racine labor community. Immediately after the strike ended, Local 180 leaders and activists in the community started a campaign to rebuild the union and to educate members on the value of remaining committed to unionization. This illustrates just one way in which the Racine story complicates scholars' claim that unions sacrificed internal and external organizing in favor of top-down leadership and business services. Fifty stewards attended a two-day institute in November where they went over the new contract, learned strategies for dealing with grievances, and planned to grow membership.[41] The local's education committee was reinstituted, and its stated goals were to inform members about current events, increase attendance at union meetings, eliminate discrimination, and increase voter registration and political participation.[42] But it was not until 1962 that Local 180 negotiated a contract that included a pension plan, a clear arbitration agreement, and leave of absences.[43] *Racine Labor* ran a banner headline in January of the next year declaring, "CHECKOFF WON BY 180," speculating that it represented a step toward a new era at the Case Company. President Valeo reported, "We seem to detect a new attitude on the part of the company and we look to the future with some measure of optimism."[44] The union was able to negotiate a settlement with the company for vacation pay withheld from workers during the 1960 strike so 1,648 workers received checks totaling over $340,000 in July 1963.[45] These long-term payoffs from the strike vindicated the union's position to fight against management resistance and supported the idea of worker solidarity not only at Case but in the whole community.

Political Use of Labor History for Organizing

The hard-fought 1960 Case strike motivated the labor community in Racine to continue to fight for the interests of working people in the city. When William Jenkins was asked why Racine had a good record with progressive unions, he attributed it to "the strife that we've had here—the labor strife," particularly against the Case Company. He maintained that because workers at the largest industrial plant in town had to fight repeatedly to reaffirm their right to collectively bargain, it kept Racine's working-class activists determined to push even harder to gain full economic democracy. While the 1960 strike was going on at Case, workers across Racine kept up their efforts to improve the economic and civic conditions of the city. New organizing drives continued in industrial plants. For example, maintenance and miscellaneous-classified workers at Western Printing and Lithographers voted to affiliate with the UAW and formed Local 1007. They signed a three-year agreement with the company that improved wages, added a cost-of-living adjustment to the contract, and a union shop. When the Wisconsin Employment Relations Commission (WERC) held their election by secret ballot the next month, workers voted overwhelmingly (279–17) to approve the contract clause for a union shop.[46] The lithographers' (Local 54) collective bargaining agreement expired in August 1959, but negotiations dragged on and they threatened to strike in February 1960 for better wage increases. The strike authorization vote got management to open negotiations again, and they signed a new contract in April with a "terrific" wage package and improvements across the board.[47] In 1959, the mostly female employees of Rae Motor Company, manufacturers of fractional horsepower motors for small electronics, affiliated with UAW as Local 1296 and signed their first agreement. In 1960, they voted overwhelmingly for a union shop by a vote of 87–1 out of ninety-nine possible votes.[48] These new organizing drives strengthened the labor community and boosted their collective power to initiate economic, political, and social changes in Racine.

Employers kept up the pressure. The Walker Manufacturing Company, a supplier of exhaust systems for the automobile industry, tried to force all workers over the age of sixty to retire in 1962. After going through the grievance procedure with Walker Manufacturing for two years, UAW Local 85 took their case to the fair practices division of the State Industrial Commission in 1964. This was the first case of age discrimination since age had been added to fair practices legislation in 1959.[49] To the union, it seemed as if the company was forcing older workers with more seniority and earning potential out of work and replacing them with young, cheaper, less experienced employees. The men who were forced out of their jobs still wanted and needed to work to support themselves and their families. One worker wrote a letter to the editor using the familiar labor-liberal rhetoric: "We live in the good old U.S.A., a land of freedom, liberty and justice for all. Let's all of us uphold that thought and lineup to these ideals . . . Let's fight for our rights!"[50] Three workers filed an injunction against the company to keep their jobs until the dispute was settled. When the Industrial Commission ruled that the retirement policy violated the state's

74 CHAPTER 3

Fair Employment law because it discriminated against older workers, the company took the case to the Wisconsin Supreme Court. The Court eventually reversed the Industrial Commission's ruling because Walker's retirement benefits to those workers laid off was greater than what they would have received with voluntary retirement benefits.[51]

"Total Person Unionism"

Racine's labor activists did not limit their activities to the shop floor or legal battles but also focused on the needs of all working people in Racine. As historian Robert Bussel details in 1930s and 1940s St. Louis, in Racine, labor leaders understood that collective bargaining was only one tool in gaining full citizenship for working people. Activists pushed the concept of "total person unionism" to transform the community to address all aspects of workers' lives including access to good housing, education for their children, public services, and local decision-making power.[52] This civic involvement was one of the things that made Harvey Kitzman excited about his work with the UAW. He reflected, "We also believe that every single member of our union ... ought to make a contribution to his community ... and make whatever contribution he can. He owes that to his community."[53] Racine's activists led the way in the labor community's efforts to maintain the civic health of the city and exemplified the engaged citizen.

So, for example, the teachers' union, Racine Education Association (REA), reached out to local organizations and citizens' groups to advertise a national campaign centered on strengthening schools in the coming years. Union leaders invited groups like the NAACP, which was working on school integration strategies, to send representatives to area schools to learn more about funding, enrollment, and staffing issues, and they initiated a publicity campaign to highlight their concerns and ideas about improving Racine's schools through integration, improved funding, and full staffing.[54]

The labor community's civic engagement included funding mutual aid initiatives and oversight of community resources. Annual Christmas parties generated funds to donate to area organizations, including the mental hospital and orphanage. Funds also went to provide gifts for workers' children and to hold a party for retired workers at the Racine Labor Center.[55] The county labor council voted to work with the Red Cross to institute a citywide blood bank program, expanding their existing agreements that were organized by union locals. For example, William Jenkins started a vision and prescription drug program when he was president of the labor council.[56] The board also continued its campaign to have a labor staff representative on the board of the United Fund. Working-class activists collected donations during the annual fundraising drive and felt that the organizers needed better communication within workplaces. Activists also felt that workers used the services of the organizations funded by the United Fund and should have a voice on the board. However, the power struggle between business and labor leaders that was evident in the interwar period in city politics emerged during midcentury on the boards of public and private charitable organizations.[57]

Community involvement also included education and lobbying against corporate plans to turn back labor's economic and political gains. Labor activists and their allies fought corporate efforts to reduce business taxes. Companies would lobby for lower tax rates and force communities into bidding wars for the lowest rates. *Racine Labor* reprinted a study prepared for the Wisconsin Committee for Fair Taxes showing that despite some business leaders' claims, University of Wisconsin scholars had found that economic growth had not been affected by higher tax rates for manufacturing firms in the state.[58] The labor community also lobbied against legislation that limited workers' ability to collectively bargain.[59] For example, working-class activists sought to change a state law that required a two-thirds majority vote to approve a labor agreement's union shop clause, whereby all eligible members of the bargaining unit were required to become union members. Manny Brown, the State Assembly representative from Racine, brought legislation to change the two-thirds majority to a simple majority during successive legislation sessions in response to local activist lobbying. In 1965 and 1967, the law passed in the Assembly but failed in the State Senate.[60] Both of these issues represented tactics conservative business leaders used to offset strong labor communities by attacking local economies and workers' rights.

The built environment union members inhabited also shaped Racine's labor community and played a valuable role in activists' efforts to remain active in the local political economy. So, in early 1960 when the city parking department approached the Union Hall board of directors to replace the building with a parking ramp they fought to keep the space. Located downtown on Wisconsin Avenue, Union Hall was home to many of the original AFL locals in Racine, and at the time had twenty-four member unions. A landmark of the city's labor community since 1912, the building held a special place for many workers. Along with the Teamsters Hall and the Labor Center, it represented the labor community's commitment to the welfare of all working people in the region.[61] The delegates looked around for another site to relocate in the area but found none that would accommodate the meeting space needs and recreation facilities the current building contained. The parking department approached the Common Council to condemn the whole block of Wisconsin Avenue, including Union Hall. The labor community rallied together, attended the public hearings, and successfully fought the parking department's move.[62]

By 1968, the Union Hall Association had accumulated the necessary funds to build a new building and purchased land on the outskirts of the city. When workers removed the cornerstone, it revealed a copper box containing materials from the early-twentieth century, including newspapers, correspondence between members of the building committee, and histories of the original twenty unions involved. William Sommers, past president of the Union Hall building committee enclosed a brief note, "I hope the day is not far away when the workers will come into their own. May this building be a lasting monument of Labor." The old cornerstone was placed in the new building during a special ceremony commemorating the history of the Racine Trades and Labor Association and Union Hall.[63] David Harvey has shown that union halls and other sites where union members congregated, and the memories associated with them, affect people's lived experience. They are part of the labor community's collective memory, political identity, representing notions of working-class solidarity.[64] Keeping the original Union Hall until the unions purchased more land and built a new site allowed the labor community to maintain its power over the built environment and shape the city's image as a labor town.

Another key factor in reaffirming and shaping working-class history was the use of family history, history of struggles successful or not, and the idea that improving the city had always been an important element of working peoples' activism. The "Who's Who" column in *Racine Labor* illustrated the history of activism with Racine's families. The sons, daughters, siblings, and family histories all confirmed the notion of the labor community as a family of activists. For example, in the column about Bob Mathieus, the newly elected Local 180 Vice President, readers learned that his father also worked at Case and was a shop steward for the union.[65]

Racine Labor also played a key role in highlighting working-class activists' efforts and the ways whole families participated in sustaining the community. For example, the obituary for Edrie Kitzman, wife of Harvey Kitzman, detailed her long history of political and labor activism. Harold Thompson used his weekly column to commemorate Edrie Kitzman's service to the Racine labor community, including her early years working at Case and helping develop leadership education programs for local unions.[66] Retirements also offered a way to celebrate the history of activism within the labor community. Loretta Christensen retired after forty-five years of active union and community work. She was one of the first women hired by Western Publishing, worked on the RTLC board for twenty-five years in various roles, and was one of the leading women in the labor community. The list of her service activities for the community illustrated a long history of engaged activism.[67] When Russ Johnson retired from the city, the labor paper's story focused on his whole family. Both he and his wife, Roma, served as past presidents of Local 67. His son Russell was a union steward at Hamilton-Beach and son Robert was president of UAW Local 72 at Greene Manufacturing. Tom Faucett retired at the same time as Johnson and was at the city because he took a job during the Case strike in 1946 when Mayor Wendt provided public works jobs for the strikers.[68] The stories of individuals' service on behalf of local unions and the larger community worked together with the physical landscape, labor organizing, strike activities, civic involvement, and social activities, to make and reaffirm the working-class identity in Racine.

For Racine's labor community, total person unionism also included maintaining their efforts at cross-sector solidarity. Racine's labor leaders had supported organizing in all employment sectors since the immediate postwar years. Racine's firefighters had been organized since the early-twentieth century and counted on AFL unions' support when presenting demands to the Common Council.[69] County employees had been members of the Racine Trades and Labor Council since at least the early 1930s.[70] City workers had a regular column in *Racine Labor* and participated in the CIO union council.[71] By the mid-1960s, changes in employment law at the state and national level opened the door to even greater organizing efforts. By 1964, nearly 1.5 million workers belonged to public sector unions across the United States, largely through the efforts of AFSCME, which was headquartered in Madison, Wisconsin.[72] As part of the effort to grant these workers the right to strike and improve workers' ability to bargain effectively, Racine local union delegates to the 1964 Wisconsin AFL-CIO convention supported the removal of the no-strike clause from the Public Employee Bargaining Act.[73] In 1966, Racine locals across industries stood together in support of mandatory factfinding, conciliation, or mediation, to force municipalities to bargain faithfully with public employees as another way to strengthen MERA.[74] These resolutions submitted to the Wisconsin AFL-CIO conventions demonstrate the broad-based nature of issues concerning Racine's labor community as well as their understanding of state and national-level economic and political changes.

Once changes at the state level helped improve bargaining rights for public employees even further in 1962, Building Service Employees International Union (BSEIU) Local 152 started organizing school janitors in the area, and the union signed an agreement with the Racine School Board.[75] BSEIU started as an organization of janitorial unions in Chicago and expanded to include elevator operators and other nontrade workers in public and private buildings. In the early years, the union was mainly a collection of autonomous local unions but started to streamline and organize more formally in the 1940s under the leadership of William McFetridge. He also recognized the potential of organizing all sorts of service workers, including office workers and hospital workers.[76] Racine's industrial and trade unions sought to actively support the service employees in the area. When BSEIU Local 152 met resistance in their 1964 bargaining sessions with the school board, the local AFL-CIO council voted to support the union and sent a delegate to bargaining meetings on the local's behalf, as they had done on behalf of police, firefighters and other city and county employees since the Depression era.[77]

Labor activists continued to organize workers in new employment sectors despite management hostility and their weakened position within the labor-management relationship. The 1960s saw a tremendous increase in low-wage service, public sector, and office workers in the city. Across Wisconsin, BSEIU locals consolidated to meet new requirements to hold a union charter. Many locals had dwindling memberships or all retired members as building owners moved to automatic elevators and outsourced janitorial services, and over the early part of the 1960s, most of these locals were subsumed by Local 150, based in Milwaukee. While many members complained about the lack of follow-through by Local 150 President Don Beatty, his ability to organize workers and get contracts signed helped fuel consolidation of locals across the state. At the same time, Beatty used the pooled resources and additional funds from the International to start organizing drives and increase the statewide membership of Local 150.[78]

Legal changes also opened the door for increased organizing campaigns. Labor union feminists had worked to amend the Fair Labor Standards Act (FLSA) since its passage in 1935. For example, garment workers' unions had sought to include the mostly female workers under the minimum wage protections of the law throughout the 1940s. Labor and civil rights groups forged coalitions to push for expansion of FLSA concurrently with the passage of the Civil Rights Act. And as William P. Jones details, Black working women and their allies pushed the debate around the Civil Rights Act to address gender discrimination more directly. For example Pauli Murray's memorandum detailing the ways protection from sex discrimination would help Black women convinced President Johnson to keep sex as a protected category.[79]

In 1966, at its annual conference, the AFL-CIO made expansion of FLSA one of its top priorities. This concerted effort paid off as Secretary of Labor Willard Wirtz acknowledged that policy makers had not considered the impact on so many women and nonwhite male workers. He admitted, "This apparent objectivity has tended not to ensure equal treatment but to camouflage unequal treatment."[80] Following changes to the Fair Labor Standards Act in 1966, which incorporated nearly a million and a half new hospital and nursing home workers under the minimum wage requirements and allowed workers previously excluded from the National Labor Relations Act to join unions, labor activists intensified organizing efforts in the industry. The new amendments brought an estimated 84 percent of the nonsupervisory workforce under the protection of federal law. Only domestic workers remained unprotected.[81] In Racine, BSEIU started organizing campaigns in the healthcare industry under the direction of Local 150. They focused on service employees—nurses' aides, dietitians, food service workers, and janitors—at hospitals and nursing homes.

As part of the BSEIU healthcare campaign, Local 150 started organizing efforts at St. Luke's Hospital in 1966, which employed many Black and brown women workers in low-wage service positions. After a concerted organizing effort, Local 150 asked WERC to hold a union representation election. In a letter urging employees at St. Luke's to vote "yes" to accept BSEIU Local 150 as their bargaining agent, Charles Heymanns, regional director for the AFL-CIO and former head of the Kohler union, wrote, "Hospital Employees, like all other groups of American wage-earners, have the legal, moral, and American right to join Unions and be represented."[82] Not-for-profit institutions like St. Luke's Hospital had served as employers for new immigrants, Latine, and southern Black migrants to northern cities for many years. Like other jobs available to nonwhite workers, these were often the lowest paid in the area. Exempt from provisions of the National Labor Relations Act until 1974—the rights of workers to organize a union of their choice, bargain collectively, strike, boycott, and picket, and the prohibition of employers from intimidating, firing, or blacklisting employees for union activities—these hospitals could keep workers' wages below those in other industries. At the same time, the life-support function of hospitals, their centrality to the healthcare system of cities, and the role of local and federal governments in sustaining them, led to the involvement of government officials, the press, organized pressure groups, and the general public in labor-management disputes.[83]

Holding to his promise to focus on a strong win at St. Luke's Hospital, Local 150 President Don Beatty continued to work closely with the 250 employees throughout the successful representation election and

80 CHAPTER 3

the appeal by St. Luke's. When the election was upheld by WERC, Beatty appointed a bargaining committee and opened negotiations with the hospital. When management refused to negotiate an acceptable agreement, Beatty asked for and received strike authorization sanctions against the hospital. However, when the registered nurses threatened to walk out in support of the service employees—a clear example of class solidarity—hospital management raised their offer. Finally, in February 1967, members voted in favor of a one-year contract providing for wage increases going up to twenty cents an hour, ten-minute breaks, seniority for promotions and vacancies, and six paid holidays.[84] When the contract came up for negotiation again the next year, members focused on adding a union shop clause to the contract. When writing to the international union again for strike sanctions against St. Luke's, Beatty explained, "The big stumbling block is Union Shop, which seems to be more important to the employees than even wages."[85] While Beatty was surprised by the militancy of the St. Luke's service workers, the tradition in Racine of local unions working together to protect the rights of workers regardless of union affiliation or employment sector most probably helped spur the employees at St. Luke's Hospital.

Automation, Corporate Restructuring, and Deindustrialization

While the Racine labor community welcomed the newly organized hospital workers into the group, they also remained aware of technological changes that could negatively impact the growth and strength of the community. The effect of technological changes and automation remained a topic of concern. Activists focused on three key areas related to technology and automation, and they made efforts to educate workers and to train new workers on the latest technology. Importantly, labor activists kept the relationship between automation and unemployment in the public conversation so that business and government policymakers would address this issue. Finally, activists sought to improve retirement plans and social security laws in order to move older workers out of the workforce earlier without economic hardship on their families.

New sources of education and job training were needed to improve workers' economic opportunities. In the early 1960s, union officials worked with the Racine Vocational and Adult School to participate in a program to train recent high school graduates in technological and administrative fields while also receiving on-the-job training. Leaders hoped the program would serve to provide options for young people who could not afford college or who needed to work and also attend school. They also hoped to keep newly trained workers in the area to boost the local economy.[86] Workers were encouraged to continue education through programs offered by the School for Workers and union councils financed special classes at the local vocational school to that end. The vocational school also had a program designed for workers whose jobs required advanced training to keep up with new technology.[87] Unemployed workers could take a ten-week course designed to improve their skills to get back into the labor force. This course was held in the evenings, so that if workers were called back to their previous jobs, they could continue their skills training.[88] Professor Jack Barbish, an economics professor from the University of Wisconsin School for Workers, taught several different classes in Racine. His classes included Economics for Labor, which explained economic policy as it related to working-class people.[89]

Worker education also took place at the national level. For example, BSEIU initiated several social justice campaigns in conjunction with efforts to organize office workers and hospital workers, sometimes seen as "unorganizable." These social justice campaigns increased with the election of George Sullivan to the presidency. Under Sullivan's leadership, the union started focusing on national issues like automation, unemployment, and civil rights.[90] BSEIU started a scholarship program for members and their children in the 1960s. Arthur Heitzer, the son of Local 150 member Michael Heitzer, was chosen to receive one such award in 1965.[91] Heitzer went on to become a lawyer and represented BSEIU Local 150 members when they were unjustly fired from St. Luke's Hospital in the late 1970s.[92]

Political work never abated, as local activists sought to keep the needs of working people on the minds of local, state, and national politicians in relation to the effects of automation. *Racine Labor* published articles throughout the decade that demonstrated the labor community's continuing efforts to keep abreast of technological changes as well as lobby for effective means to cope with unemployment caused by automation. Early in 1960, James B. Carey, secretary-treasurer for the AFL-CIO's industrial union department, reported that the combination of record high levels of industrial output combined with steady to rising unemployment should be seen as a warning of upcoming economic trouble.[93] The paper also reprinted segments of a speech by David J. McDonald, United Steel Workers of America President, at a conference of governors, where McDonald suggested reducing the work week to offset worker displacement caused by automation. He also declared "Bold action and cooperation between many forces, primarily, labor, management and government" was needed to resolve unemployment.[94] *Racine Labor* published excerpts from a letter

82   CHAPTER 3

from Walter Reuther, President of UAW, to industry leaders outlining a seven-point program to train industrial workers for white-collar work. Reuther called for company policies to promote from within, aptitude tests for production workers to determine other positions they may be capable of pursuing, and training programs.[95] Union members in Racine kept abreast of these national conversations as they hoped to work locally to minimize the negative impact on the Racine job market.

Finally, local labor activists sought to influence legislation at the local, state, and national levels to minimize economic problems related to automation. Labor activists participated in the Committee on Aging of the Community Service council, which advocated for city services for elderly citizens.[96] Harold J. Thompson, UAW Secretary, advocated for the Forand bill (H.R. 4700) to provide better health coverage for retired workers in his weekly "The Secretary Says" column in *Racine Labor*. He urged readers, unions, and social justice groups to write letters and telegrams to their elected representatives to support this legislation.[97] Thompson often wrote articles related to broad-based economic and social policies to keep residents informed of important issues of the day.

In response to job loss resulting from technological and corporate restructuring changes, local activists hailed Governor Nelson's plan to expand unemployment benefits in the state. Wisconsin had led the way in unemployment laws across the nation, and the Racine labor community had participated in the call for more extensive unemployment benefits for workers due to the seasonal nature of foundry and agricultural implement work in the city. Companies like Case laid off workers each year as demand within the agricultural industry rose and fell. In 1960, Governor Nelson signed a new law that increased the minimum and maximum weekly payments and extended benefits from twenty-six and a half weeks to thirty-four weeks. Over 50,000 unemployed workers on the brink of reaching the maximum time limit found relief with this new law.[98] Racine unions also supported an early retirement program and benefits coupled with training and hiring young workers to gain experience and seniority at the 1964 and 1966 Wisconsin AFL-CIO state conventions.[99] The activism, education programs, and outreach by labor activists during the 1960s demonstrate their efforts to improve the economic prospects of all working people.

Unfortunately, labor community efforts to respond to and counteract economic and political changes did not stop the tide of plant closings, corporate restructurings, and layoffs that increased pace in the late 1960s. A partial list shows the increase in transfers of ownership and plant closings. The Sunbeam Corporation purchased John Oster Manufacturing Company, manufacturer of hair clippers, and moved the Racine operations to

Florida in 1964. B. D. Eisendrath Tanning was sold in 1965 and closed the next year, the last tannery in the city. The Horlick malted milk company lost local ownership in the 1940s, and in 1969, Beecham, a British-owned firm acquired the company. Hartmann Luggage closed in 1962 after being purchased in 1955 by an outside management company, and the operations moved to Tennessee. Both Case and Walker Manufacturing were purchased by Kern County Land Company in the mid-1960s, which was then purchased by Tenneco in 1967. Jacobsen Manufacturing became a subsidiary of Allegheny Ludlum Industries in 1969.[100]

The biggest transfer occurred with the Hamilton-Beach Company, the largest electrical machinery manufacturer in the city. Founded in 1910, the company produced fractional horsepower motors for electrical appliances. In 1962, the company started moving operations to plants outside of Racine. In 1968, Hamilton-Beach announced it was closing all Racine operations and laid off the few remaining members of UAW Local 577—down from 1,300 to 300 members and over one hundred nonunion clerical and office workers.[101]

A close look at the events surrounding the closing of Hamilton-Beach in Racine reveals the ways in which plant closing involved the whole community and not just the lost jobs of the workers at the plant. It demonstrates some of the ways unions and working-class activists sought to fight back against such closings and the uneven power relationships among corporations, local governments, and workers. Hamilton-Beach started moving production lines to facilities in North Carolina in 1966. When the union's bargaining committee, led by UAW Local 577 President George Iverson, could get no clear answer about the fate of the Racine operations, they asked for help from Sam Rizzo, UAW Sub-Regional Director. In response to Rizzo's letter, the company's general manager sent a statement explaining that rapid growth in blender production forced the company to move mixer production out of Racine. He said rumors that the company planned to move were false but cautioned, "I have also stated very clearly to union people that we, like any other business are in no position to guarantee long-range projection of employment levels."[102] A year and a half later, the company was still dismantling equipment and laying off workers.

George Iverson, a Hamilton-Beach employee for nearly twenty years with fourteen years' experience serving in leadership positions in the union, felt overwhelmed and frustrated with the lack of communication and the lack of recourse. In May 1967, Iverson convinced Racine Mayor William Beyer to contact corporate headquarters asking for information on the Racine operations, but the mayor's requests went unanswered. In September, the union filed unfair labor practices charges against the company with the National Labor Relations Board claiming refusal to bargain per the contract clause on department closings and transfer of work. Iverson gave hours of testimony in the case, sat for what amounted to a 19-page deposition, and went to Detroit to get UAW International lawyers to amend the charges and present additional evidence. However, the case was still pending as employment at Hamilton-Beach dropped from over 1,000 to about 300.[103]

Workers and union officials were lost as to how to proceed. They tried every avenue available as far as using the grievance procedure in the contract, filing charges through the NLRB, appealing to management for clear plans, yet they were at a distinct disadvantage. The company kept quiet on plans to close until the workforce had dropped below 300 and most of the production lines were shut down. The union recognized that the company held all the cards. Older workers and women faced the most uncertainty; many workers with long years of service felt cheated out of their seniority, pensions, and ability to support their families based on what became a useless labor agreement with Hamilton-Beach. As late as January 1968, Employment Relations Manager H. C. Scheible told bargaining members that "nothing is definite yet," in a meeting where all in attendance could see workers dismantling and removing a machine. He also argued that layoffs were normal during that part of the year and claimed workers were overreacting to "wild rumors."[104] Yet, the inability to plan paralyzed union efforts to protect members and stifled workers' new job searches.

The union blamed management policy and federal and state tax policy for the dismantling of the Racine plants and transfer of operations to North Carolina. The union charged Hamilton-Beach with inflating expenses in Racine to make it appear unprofitable by charging plant expenses for the North Carolina facilities and the salary of at least one company official that did not actually work in Racine. Activists also expressed frustration at federal and state policies that allowed the free movement of capital across the nation. As Iverson explained, "this whole setup stinks . . . Our taxes help make up the difference when these southern states offer tax-free land or other bonuses to companies to lure them there."[105] Politicians recognized this as well. When U.S. Senator Gaylord Nelson introduced legislation to prevent states and municipalities from using tax-free bonds to induce businesses to move to their regions and to limit corporations' ability to write off building expenditures from income taxes, he referenced an example similar to the Hamilton-Beach situation that happened in Milwaukee.[106] Yet, the need for revenue and the appearance of job creation forced many municipalities to continue this practice and ultimately continued to tip the power away from governments and workers and toward corporations.

Most Hamilton-Beach workers found jobs in other plants in the area, but women had a hard time finding new employment. Pauline Partach wrote a long letter to *Racine Labor* detailing her frustration with the job market in Racine, the constant advice she received to go on welfare, and her inability to qualify for education programs to improve her typing speed. Partach, the forty-five-year-old widow of a former Case employee, a single mother with over three years at Hamilton-Beach, spent almost a year looking for work. She had worked in the clerical office for Hamilton-Beach but her typing skills kept her out of similar positions, and she reported that no one would hire a middle-aged unskilled woman for factory work. She was finally offered a dishwashing job at $1.25 per hour, which did not cover her expenses, and another part-time position that did not guarantee more than five hours a week. After the plant closed, workers waited another seven months for a severance and pension package to be negotiated. With the company gone, there was little pressure to place on management to come to terms. In March 1968, Local 577 filed charges with WERC arguing that the company could not leave before August 1969 when the contract expired, and they filed an injunction in Circuit Court to prevent the company from moving any more equipment until the case was settled. However, that failed, and the plant officially closed in June.[107]

Although workers felt helpless to prevent the lost jobs and security associated with losing another plant from the city, the union helped maintain the social connections among workers. The Local 577 recreation department held a Valentine's dance the week after the company officially announced it was closing operations. The bowling and dartball tournaments continued throughout the season. The Hamilton-Beach Credit Union Board of Directors moved quickly to discuss options for shareholders and those with loans, and they held meetings to explain options to all involved. The credit union was formed in May 1950 with company backing. After members heard all their options, they voted 887 to 2 to dissolve the credit union's assets and reinvest. They voted to dissolve the credit union even before the company would confirm they were leaving and made arrangements to liquidate all the funds and deposit them with a central credit union service. The union paid for newspaper subscriptions to *Racine Labor* for all members until March 1969 so that everyone could stay current with the pension and severance bargaining situation.[108] The former members of UAW Local 577 held annual Christmas parties for many years after the plant closed, maintaining the social ties and connections built over the years in the plant. As this first tide of plant closings illustrates, the impact of deindustrialization would have a heavy toll on industrial communities. The Racine case supports scholarship that points to early signs of the transformation of the U.S. capitalist system.[109] It demonstrates the unequal power between capital and labor and underscores the need for government intervention to balance the scale.

Conclusion

Throughout the turbulent 1960s, Racine's labor activists successfully mobilized the labor community around the Case strike, using it and the Kohler strike to reinforce the narrative of the valuable role of working-class solidarity and politics for economic democracy. A strategic use of labor's history in the city also played a key role in sustaining a sense of working-class consciousness and collectivism, even as racial and gendered critiques helped broaden and diversify the members, as we will see in chapter 4. Successful organizational drives, the changes at Case, and new public employees and service workers fueled the growth and solidarity of Racine's labor movement in the 1960s. Despite continuing issues surrounding corporate restructuring and plant closings, labor liberals' successful efforts to incorporate more workers into the labor movement and to support a broad notion of economic and social justice prevailed in Racine. Women workers and working-class women's organizing as seen in BSEIU also expanded the vision of Racine's labor community. The continued growth of public sector and low-wage service unions strengthened the ranks of labor. This solidarity proved invaluable in the coming decade, especially as public sector and healthcare workers looked for organizing and strike support in a hostile political environment.

CHAPTER 4

Race and Shifting Class Boundaries in Racine

Corinne Reid-Owens moved to Racine in 1946 with her husband, Burse, from Mississippi. She came to work as a teacher, like she had been doing for the past thirteen years. However, she was told that Black people did not teach in Racine's schools. Reid-Owens spent the rest of her time in Racine breaking down housing, education, and employment barriers for Black people in the city, where she is known as the "Rosa Parks of Racine." Along with William Jenkins and others, Corinne Reid-Owens helped build the Racine chapter of the National Association for the Advancement of Colored People (NAACP). She organized community improvement groups, led the fight for fair housing in the city, and worked to get Black teachers and police officers hired in the area. In a 2002 interview, when looking back on her activism in the postwar period she recalled, "you had to fight for everything back then. You'd fight and fight, and eventually you'd win."[1]

Reid-Owens worked as a janitor for twenty years until completing teacher certification requirements and becoming a teacher again in 1971. Like other Black women, she was denied access to most jobs outside of low-wage service work. During this time, she led several committees for the Racine NAACP, where she served as president in 1953, and was a member of Mayor Humble's Commission on Human Rights. She organized the South Lafayette Neighborhood Group and Community Women's Club, and also helped establish the Dr. John Bryant Neighborhood Center. She worked to bring hot lunches to Racine's schools and continued to volunteer in local schools into her nineties. She was active with the YWCA and received numerous awards and recognitions from the NAACP, Racine PTA, YWCA, and the city. The local public transportation center is named in her honor and when she died in 2012, President Barack Obama was one of the political leaders who sent dedications and remembrances.[2] Corinne Reid-Owens's work in Racine is indicative of the work Black women did to improve the economic and social conditions of their communities.[3]

This chapter details the ways Black workers like Corinne Reid-Owens and William Jenkins fought for economic and social citizenship rights through demands for fair housing, access to jobs, and class solidarity across racial lines in their unions. In Racine, Black workers used their UAW locals and the local NAACP chapter, as well as the Urban League, state and local human rights committees, and other labor and social institutions, to demand a greater voice in the local political economy. Building on the momentum of the 1963 March on Washington for Jobs and Freedom, they formed cross-union racial alliances to help fight employment discrimination.[4] Frustration boiled over into rebellion in Black neighborhoods and helped galvanize welfare rights activists and county social workers to demand change. As we will see, the Racine labor community continued to focus on a class politics that was informed by racial analyses to organize workers, maintain economic stability, and implement social reforms in the city throughout the 1960s.

Intersectional struggles for race and gender equality expanded the labor community's demographics as labor activists responded to and participated in these same struggles. Throughout the decade, organizations connected to social movements—the NAACP, the Urban League, and the League of Women Voters—maintained close relationships with Racine's labor community. Despite internal social tensions, the Racine labor community built on the foundation established in the postwar period, shaped a public narrative that legitimated working-class politics, and garnered widespread public support for labor issues, all the while adapting to the influx of new workers into the community.

Black Workers in Racine: Reshaping Class Politics in the City

William Jenkins served as an important figure in bridging the Racine labor and Black working-class communities. As president of the Racine NAACP, he had worked closely with the UAW in establishing a UAW Fair Labor Practices Committee in the city in the late 1950s.[5] His ardent criticism of local union leaders' failure to adequately respond to racial discrimination within workplaces and union locals demonstrated his willingness to lead the UAW's antidiscrimination campaign in Racine.[6] Jenkins also placed heavy demands on the "leadership, if you can call it that" of the Black community. He expected all leaders to actively work to improve the Black and working-class communities in the city.[7] Internal politics within the Black community shaped the various ways workers used unions, civil rights organizations, and community groups to address racial discrimination in the city and to bring a racial analysis to the class struggle.

Efforts to address racism were complicated by class and political differences among Black residents. Joe William Trotter, Jr. shows how the Black working-class community in Milwaukee often put class issues before race as middle-class Black reformers focused on integration and equal access.[8] Some of this tension can also be seen in Racine's Black community politics during the 1960s. By the mid-1960s, leaders in the NAACP branch started to focus on building alliances with local government, business, and religious leaders instead of relying solely on the close alliance with the local labor community of the previous decade. The efforts to place Black candidates into leadership positions in private industry and local government throughout the 1960s gives some proof of this shifting focus. More importantly, the Racine NAACP branch presidents built close ties with city officials and sat on multiple advisory boards related to human rights, housing, and educational issues. While these issues concerned all members of the Black community, the focus on political lobbying limited the amount of organizing and community building needed to relate to many of the working-class Black residents. However, local Black leaders also spent a significant amount of time in the decade working on perceptions of the Black community. They collaborated with the Kiwanis Club to remove images of Aunt Jemima from their annual Pancake Day, sponsored by the Quaker Oats Company. The NAACP argued that the images and the actor that usually represented the character, dressed in the attire of a domestic slave, perpetuated racial stereotypes, which reinforced notions of racial inferiority and prejudice.[9] NAACP representatives also spoke with industry leaders about hiring more Black workers at city plants. Yet, most of their efforts to improve Black community life in Racine were conducted through political lobbying and court cases, signaling a shift in strategy.

Middle-class leadership limited the Racine NAACP's approach to certain problems. So, when Black and Latine residents complained about police harassment and brutality in public spaces, the NAACP's solution was to work to keep Black people from gathering outside of local clubs and bars, relying on respectability politics. In a letter to the recently formed Urban League of Racine, NAACP President Julian Thomas wrote that the executive board was concerned "about the problem of loitering in front of Taverns, and the explosive situations which could result between offenders and policemen."[10] Scholars have noted that in the postwar period a trend

90   CHAPTER 4

started across the nation to police urban spaces in new ways that made public behavior by Black people suddenly illegal.[11] By calling for an effort to eliminate loitering, and even by seeing loitering as the problem, the NAACP response reaffirmed what local residents saw as another attempt to blame the victim. Instead of concrete efforts to increase employment opportunities, solve overcrowding issues through a fair housing policy, and educating the police force, most efforts by city and civic leaders offered policies that put the weight back onto the residents themselves. Thomas's actions reaffirmed some residents' belief that his notions of middle-class respectability colored his leadership of the NAACP.

By 1969, a serious class divide existed within the NAACP and in the community. Thomas called a special meeting of the executive board to address claims that low membership in the Racine branch "stems from the fact that my leadership has been too *MIDDLE CLASS* and, that as President, my action or lack of action is interpreted as local branch policy."[12] These complaints against Thomas came from the labor community as well. For example, Loren Norman, *Racine Labor* editor, criticized Thomas's approach in dealing with the mayor's poverty committee. When Thomas demanded that poor people or people qualified to speak for poor people should have seats on the committee, Norman took offense because he perceived Thomas's approach to community problems as out of touch with Black and Latine working poor in the city.[13]

During the controversy, Thomas hoped to create a new leadership and organizational structure that would make the Racine NAACP "the type of branch that all people concerned with social justice will want to be a part of." Thomas recognized that his strong personality may have interfered with the work of the organization, and he offered an open dialogue to make needed changes.[14] On the other hand, when LeRoy Wooley kicked off his 1968 campaign for alderman, he promoted himself as clearly aligned with working-class issues, as the only Black skilled trade worker at Case, and as an active member of both labor and civil rights organizations. His campaign team was made up of a diverse group of labor activists as well.[15] While both external and internal racial tensions impacted community life, working-class citizens sought both labor and social justice organizational aid in their struggle for economic and social justice during the 1960s. This tension highlights the centrality of working-class politics in Racine's Black community, even within the context of the civil rights movement's demands for political rights based on racial identity.

A 1963 case of rental discrimination fueled the NAACP calls for local legislation. A new Black teacher, Obry Moss, came to Racine, but the rental agent denied his rental application. The bank agent overseeing the property agreed to rent the unit through the Racine Education Association (REA) teachers' union, which was arranging housing for new teachers moving to the area. However, when the agent discovered Moss was Black, the bank backtracked. The agent suggested that Moss meet the property owner, a local doctor, and have the owner decide if he should rent the property. When REA leaders tried to intercede on Moss's behalf, the owner said he would not be coerced into renting to anyone. REA contacted the Racine NAACP for assistance. A contingent of NAACP members began picketing both the doctor's office and the bank in August 1963. Sloan Williams used the opportunity to press the mayor and Common Council to open more discussion for proposed antidiscrimination legislation.[16] The city's Commission on Human Rights agreed that the incident was a case of discrimination and went on record supporting the NAACP's proposed legislation.[17] The Racine AFL-CIO council adopted a resolution stating "that the Racine AFL-CIO council protest and condemn this act of racial discrimination, and wholeheartedly joins, supports and commits itself to actively aid the Racine branch, NAACP, in its fight against such discrimination by all moral and physical means available."[18] This concerted effort by civil rights and labor activists illustrated the Racine community's broad social justice politics. It also highlights that without legal structures and enforcement, justice is too easily denied.

Black and other workers of color also sought the aid of the NAACP during the 1960s. Representatives often took workers' complaints to union leaders, to company human resource and management offices, and wrote job recommendations for various employment openings in both white- and blue-collar positions. For example, in 1966, a worker approached the NAACP to speak on his behalf about employment opportunities and equal employment practices of the American Motor Company in Kenosha, instead of going through UAW Local 72, possibly due to tensions within the union and between management and the union. Through Jenkins and Julian Thomas, the Racine NAACP had close ties with UAW locals in the city. Local UAW Fair Practices Committees, the NAACP, and after 1963, the Urban League, often worked in alliance to address social issues in Racine. The Racine AFL-CIO council worked closely with the NAACP on local political issues as seen with the local civil rights legislation. They also coordinated political campaigns.[19] The AFL-CIO council sent a delegate to the Urban League of Racine's monthly meetings.[20] The 1960s also brought alliances between the NAACP and local women's social and political organizations. As president of the chapter, William Sloan II joined the Women's Civic Council of Racine. The NAACP and League of Women Voters members participated in joint voter registration drives,

92   CHAPTER 4

and NAACP representatives corresponded with local church officials at Holy Communion Lutheran Church, St. Lucy Catholic Church, and St. Paul's Baptist Church on issues related to the Racine Black community and more broadly on general social welfare issues.

Hiring Discrimination in Racine

By 1960, Black and women workers were more adamant than ever about the need for greater roles in union management and greater efforts on the part of unions to protect the rights of all workers. In Racine, labor activists concerned with issues of race and gender sought various means to improve unions' ability to meet their needs. William Jenkins organized a UAW Parley on Human Relations and Civil Rights at the Labor Center and invited members of the NAACP, Jewish organizations, the mayor's committee on human rights, and members of local union fair practices committees to come and discuss related issues and interests.[21] At the November 1960 AFL-CIO national conference on civil rights in Chicago, the delegates passed resolutions calling on union groups to hire staff to address civil rights issues and improve enforcement of existing guidelines related to antidiscrimination in union bylaws and union contracts.[22] The first AFL-CIO national conference on women held in 1961 demonstrated "a new, more tumultuous relationship between labor women and the established male leadership." The theme focused on the problems of women workers, and over three days of meetings, delegates outlined the issues related to their roles as women and workers. Women labor activists had "sounded a challenge to the male leaders of their movement and to society at large."[23] This challenge would be reinforced by women in the civil rights movement and the New Left later in the decade.

Worker activists and their liberal allies brought even greater attention to the problem of employment discrimination during the decade. In 1962, labor and civil rights activists criticized the mayor's Commission on Human Rights for its failure to make any significant progress in eliminating hiring discrimination in the city. LeRoy Wooley, an active member of UAW 553 at Belle City, and the first Black man to be apprenticed in a skilled trade in Racine, spoke on the subject in Milwaukee on behalf of the NAACP. Racine Mayor Humble expressed anger at the statements printed in the *Milwaukee Sentinel* but William Jenkins came to Wooley's defense. Jenkins issued a statement asserting, "Mayor Humble must face the fact that when it comes to assisting Negroes gain employment in the white- and blue-collar brackets, his organization is a nonentity." Jenkins criticized the Commission for failing to act on reports that the Racine

State Employment Office was administering aptitude tests to Black and Mexican unskilled workers, but not to white unskilled applicants. He also charged the Commission with ignoring complaints about industry hiring practices in the city.[24] Black and Brown workers continued to struggle to find jobs while only a handful of Racine businesses had more than a few nonwhite employees.

As scholars and activists have observed, the labor movement was one of the best placed institutions to address the needs of Black and poor workers, both those inside and outside of labor unions.[25] Bayard Rustin made this argument in *Harper's Magazine* in 1971 and pointed to the ways in which the labor movement offered a comprehensive program to meet the economic needs of urban Black workers and their families. This was especially true of the AFL-CIO's Committee on Political Education and the UAW's Political Action Committee, both of which led the way in Racine's efforts to end discrimination in hiring and housing throughout the decade. Rustin saw the labor movement as the most progressive it had been in its history as demonstrated by a "commitment to broad, long-term social reform in addition to immediate objectives of improving wages and working conditions."[26] This happened because of Black workers' efforts within their unions during the postwar and into the civil rights era. By the end of the 1960s, the percentage of Black workers in unions exceeded their percentage of the larger US society, and Rustin called on liberal journalists and activists to see the progressive nature of the labor movement and recognize labor unions as a legitimate avenue for improving the social lives and economic situations of urban Black families.[27]

Black workers had slowly worked their way into leadership positions within the UAW, and to a lesser degree, the AFL-CIO leadership. For example, A. Philip Randolph used his membership on the executive board of the AFL-CIO to continue his fight against employment discrimination.[28] This gave Black union activists the ability to demand better hiring practices from employers and to negotiate better contracts that would benefit the low-wage and unskilled workers joining the labor force. In Racine, while Black union members met with continued resistance within the building trades, an outreach program started in the late 1960s added a significant percentage of nonwhite workers to apprenticeship programs. Black workers formed the UAW South Lakeshore Area Fair Practices Committee (representing Racine and Kenosha) to support continued efforts by the International to address hiring discrimination and other issues related to systemic racism in the United States. The local chapter aimed to work with civil rights groups, private companies, and other union groups to improve conditions in the area.[29]

Nationally, Black workers' efforts paid off. Walter Reuther, president of the UAW, one of several progressive international unions, sought to join civil rights coalitions during the early 1960s and worked closely with the Johnson administration to expand and strengthen Great Society programs. Reuther sought to link civil rights with economic justice from his leadership position in the labor movement.[30] Black trade union activists working through the Negro American Labor Council expanded their efforts beyond economic reforms to include antidiscrimination and voting rights as they organized workers and community groups to participate in the 1963 March on Washington. These Black activists maintained their commitment to equal access to stable employment for Black workers as they gathered support from local unions and civil rights groups. They helped people like Reuther and liberal civil rights leaders to recognize the need for broad-based demands for economic security. While the national coalition formed around the March on Washington did not last beyond the mid-1960s, at the local level many powerful coalitions brought significant change. New York, Chicago, Detroit, and St. Louis all saw powerful coalitions built between labor activists and civil rights organizations.[31] Union activists also helped facilitate a sea change in Black female employment in the postwar period. For example, the United Packing Workers union, known for its progressive agenda, formed coalitions with community-based groups to fight racial discrimination and provide workers of color access to jobs in Chicago and other locations.[32] Working-class activism in labor and civil rights movements during the 1960s expanded the boundaries of working-class identity, focused on social and economic justice for all, and created a sense of sustained activity that lasted throughout the decade and beyond.

While union bureaucracy expanded, those filling new staff positions often came from ranks of engaged rank-and-file and local union leadership. Harvey Kitzman, Sam Rizzo, and Tony Valeo are only three of the many Racine labor activists who moved into full-time staff positions, either in the UAW or the Democratic Party, from their local union leadership positions. Despite their failure to gain leadership positions in international union hierarchies, Black male and white female union activists did move through the local ranks of union leadership in Racine. For example, William Jenkins felt that although he repeatedly ran for leadership positions in the UAW infrastructure he was never selected because of his outspoken critique of the UAW's International leadership. However, in the local community, his fellow union activists voted him president of the AFL-CIO council, and he sat on various other labor and community boards. Jenkins also remained active in the county Democratic Party infrastructure.[33] Loretta

Christensen also never moved up the ranks of the bookbinder's union but did serve for many years on the Racine Trades and Labor Council, and she was the only woman on the board of *Racine Labor* for many years. Racine's labor community built on their momentum from the postwar period and broadened their demographics and social consciousness throughout the decade without losing sight of the value of collective class politics. As the careers of Christensen and Jenkins illustrate, class politics in Racine created greater space for racial and, to a lesser degree, gendered participation than the labor movement in general.

At the national level, efforts by Black leaders within the UAW and Walter Reuther's efforts to strengthen the coalition between civil rights activists and the labor movement led to union policy initiatives to improve minority hiring, urban renewal, and full employment policies. While the UAW had mobilized workers to vote for John F. Kennedy, the union's hopes for a strong domestic economic agenda did not materialize during his presidency. Reuther instituted internal structural changes and worker-education programs to revamp the International and open the door to better collaboration with civil rights activists who had pressured the union to address the racial conservativism within its ranks. In his speech at the August 1963 March on Washington for Jobs and Justice, Reuther declared that "we will not solve education or housing or public accommodations as long as millions of American Negroes are treated as second-class economic citizens and denied jobs." In his 1963 Labor Day speech, Reuther linked economic justice and civil rights declaring, "Without a job and a regular paycheck . . . the right to sit at a lunch counter is a mocking mirage."[34] Nonwhite worker activists and their allies in the labor community sought to capitalize on the national debate around economic citizenship rights for all to improve hiring practices and job promotions in Racine.

When the Wisconsin Industrial Commission held statewide hearings on racial hiring practices in 1964, the nineteen Racine firms that participated had 904 nonwhite workers out of a combined 15,615 employees. Belle City Malleable had over 400 Black and Latine workers, while most firms only had two or three, all of whom had just been hired a few weeks before the hearings took place. This demonstrated what Black working-class activists had charged about discriminatory practices of local firms. While there were several Black union members serving in leadership roles in local unions, there remained little concerted effort to bring in and train nonwhite workers across the city's diverse manufacturing industries. A guest speaker at a local NAACP event commented on the city's racial issues including hiring practices a few months after the Racine hearings were held and exclaimed in shock that "the Negro [is] so severely proscribed in where he can work."[35] Black labor activists continued to push for changes in Racine.

With the aid of activists in Milwaukee and Chicago, local Black union members formed a Racine-Kenosha chapter of the Negro American Labor Council (NALC) in 1965 to address employment discrimination in the city. Formed in 1960 by A. Philip Randolph and other Black union activists, NALC councils sought to address the economic justice issues of racial discrimination within the labor movement, workplaces, and the nation. Randolph had continued to push the fight against employment discrimination as a critical battle in racial justice for most of the twentieth century. Local NALC councils recruited members from labor unions to study problems of nonwhite workers and to look for solutions to those problems.[36]

Augusta Hill, UAW Local 72 member at American Motors Company in Kenosha, was elected first president of the council and urged all unions to actively participate in NALC. At civil rights labor conferences, Black activists also urged union members to fight against discrimination in the workplace. At the 1965 UAW Region 10 Conference, for one, Harvey Kitzman pushed the unions to back efforts to force management to hire Black workers. Similarly, at the AFL-CIO conference on civil rights held that same weekend, Black activists charged that union leaders were not doing enough to give all workers equal access to jobs. Delegates passed resolutions calling for the state AFL-CIO council to take the lead on giving civil rights groups information on how Black workers could qualify, apply for, and find information on building trades apprenticeships. The building trades unions were almost 100 percent white at the time.[37] Black workers and their allies in Racine and the surrounding area continued to work on expanding the economic and social citizenship rights that grew out of the labor movement and New Deal liberalism of the earlier period.

In Racine, organizing by Jenkins, Kitzman, and other activists concerned with biennial conventions of the Wisconsin AFL-CIO led to Racine locals cosponsoring or jointly offering resolutions to submit to the main body on issues of civil rights. In 1964, workers across industries, including foundries, publishing, garment making, and teaching, all supported the hiring of a permanent staff person solely concerned with managing a Fair Employment Practices (FEP) committee at the state AFL-CIO as called for at the Chicago conference. Each participating union from Racine submitted separate but identical resolutions calling for "the immediate appointment by the Executive Board of a new staff position with sole duties confined to working with the Fair Employment Practices program and problems within the State of Wisconsin."[38] The push for fair employment, and organizational support to help enforce federal regulations through union bargaining contracts, continued throughout the 1960s as workers demanded equal access to full economic citizenship. As we have seen, local unions' FEP committees had been active since the 1950s. As William Jenkins moved up the ranks of the labor community leadership, he took the opportunity to merge the labor council's political action and education committees and spearheaded a campaign to increase the participation of Black and women workers in Racine's labor activities through political action at the city and state level as well as within their local unions. Although frustrated with the lack of opportunity for Black union activists to move through the ranks of the UAW, Jenkins continued to push for greater education within the labor movement and created local programs to get more Black and female rank-and-file workers involved in union activities. He also worked, with limited results, on improving the local trade union members' commitment to civil rights issues.[39]

Housing Discrimination, Urban Rebellions, and Labor Politics

Access to affordable, quality housing remained an issue in Racine for non-white residents. The NAACP, Urban League, union FEP committees, and other organizations responded to deteriorating conditions within the non-white neighborhoods in Racine. Due to ongoing housing shortages, Black and other people of color were trapped in older, poorly-maintained rental units mostly in the Franklin neighborhood area, but also in several smaller areas located on the northern and southern edges of the city limits. For those Black residents who could afford to buy homes, few were available. As Jenkins recalled, he and his wife spent several years trying to buy a home for his family. If his wife, who was very light skinned, went to look at possible homes, she would have success, but when Jenkins showed up, suddenly, the real estate agent would be unable to make a deal. He remembered how one of his white friends offered to broker a deal on behalf of his family, but he refused because his dignity and manhood would not allow him to accept such aid.[40] Black residents had fought for two decades to improve housing conditions through city and state legislation. As we have seen, the real estate lobby was able to mount a campaign against the housing legislation of the 1950s, which sought to alleviate deteriorating conditions in rental units. In the 1960s, when an antidiscrimination housing code still could not make it past a city council vote, it mixed with frustrations of

98   CHAPTER 4

poor employment opportunities, segregated and inadequate schools, lack of city services, and frustration over poverty to mobilize various segments of the Black, labor, and civil rights communities.

In his 1966 "State of the City" address, Mayor William H. Beyer made improving neglected neighborhoods a priority. He blamed the city's decreasing tax base, increasing social problems, and "flight to suburbia" on the failure to implement sanitation codes and fair housing laws. In response to Black residents' demands for antidiscrimination housing laws, the mayor formed the Hill-Kidd Committee to find a solution to Racine's housing problem. A year later, the committee's plan called for a nine-month education campaign for fair housing. Some programs for neighborhood improvement were implemented, but they did little to resolve issues of overcrowding, deteriorating buildings, and the lack of city services. The failure to pass a fair housing code prevented Racine from applying for federal urban renewal aid, yet the Racine real estate association and building trades' council advocated against federal funds as a threat to their industries. However, private enterprise did little to alleviate the continual housing shortage in the city. Racial discrimination also severely limited the options of nonwhite residents. The mayor's 1967 address again stressed the need for better race relations, housing, and urban renewal.[41]

Tensions surrounding race relations remained high in the city. Threats and rumors of riots in August 1967 led to emergency meetings with city, religious, labor, and civil rights leaders. Community centers in Black and Latine neighborhoods stayed open into the evenings with events designed to keep young adults off the streets, while job service agents offered job referrals in underserved neighborhoods, and groups organized public meetings. The Franklin Community Center and the Southside Community Center opened in the early 1960s to provide space for neighborhood children to play, to give residents more opportunities to meet with social service organizations that would hold office hours several days a week, and to provide job training and employment resource information. The centers opened during the early push for better community service in underserved neighborhoods. By the mid-1960s two-thirds of the Franklin neighborhood residents were Black and Brown.[42] Over the next several months, services at the Spanish Center increased: job, financial planning, and language courses were offered. Local activists ran for city offices to improve representation in Racine's First Ward. Local labor unions were encouraged to talk with members about pushing for an open housing bill in the city. Finally, in June 1968, the city's efforts culminated in a Race Unity Week that included a picnic and panel discussions on race relations, education, and religion. However, tensions remained high, and residents felt betrayed by the lack of actual improvements.

In the first week of August, a fight at a party spread into the streets and turned into a neighborhood-wide disturbance in the Washington Park area. A few people were seriously injured in fights and one from a gunshot wound. People broke windows in neighborhood businesses, some stores were looted, and about thirty people were arrested for a range of offenses including disorderly conduct. Residents felt that the disturbance (called a riot by media and city officials) had its roots in the failure of the larger community to act on Black and Brown residents' grievances. In response to the disturbance, a group of residents formed the Concerned Minority Citizens association and submitted a list of recommendations to the mayor including hiring diverse applicants for police and fire departments, as teachers, administrators, and social service workers, and a call for a minimum housing code. As Julian Thomas explained on the WRJN "UAW Speaks" radio broadcast the next week, young people had become disillusioned because "they see us beat at the doors of city hall, the welfare office and other agencies and come away empty handed."[43]

A sociological study of Racine conducted over the decade demonstrated that the increased concentration of Mexican American and Black residents in Racine's inner city left them in "isolated ghettos." Surveys revealed that residents felt isolated and hoped for better integration into the city's economy and society. For example, 63 percent of Black residents felt that housing discrimination limited their ability to secure better employment opportunities and education opportunities for their children.[44] These conditions fueled the anger and frustration demonstrated by the uprising. Racine was not unique. Government policies at the national and state levels shifted funding to the suburbs and away from urban centers. Riots occurred in the late 1960s in Milwaukee, Tampa, Cincinnati, Chicago, Baltimore, and Detroit. The Kerner Commission, charged with studying areas hit by riots, pointed to unemployment, underemployment, police practices, and housing issues that led to what has been termed the urban crisis. The Kerner Commission report called for national action to combat "discrimination, create jobs, renew urban areas, and build more public housing" outside of ghettos.[45]

Another disturbance caused newly elected Mayor Kenneth L. Huck to institute a twenty-four-hour curfew for the city. Heated council meetings that followed pitted residents against each other as some white residents felt that aldermen should not give in to Black demands through riots, and Black residents demanded action on housing, access to good jobs, and recreation centers. In their continued support for the right of decent housing for all, *Racine Labor* ran a frontpage series of photos depicting some of the housing conditions in the city called "Shame of Racine: Indecent Housing." Civil rights activists and residents kept pressure on city officials to make concrete changes to local conditions.

In August, thirty welfare recipients held a sit-in at the county social services office and presented a letter containing thirty-one demands to the director. Most demands called for better treatment by case workers, more access to services, and a training program for caseworkers. This list of demands led to an investigation and recommendations for changes within city and county services that played a role in the social workers' strike. The Milwaukee priest, civil rights activist, and NAACP youth branch leader Father Groppi came to Racine and led a young people's march for better social and economic services. Groppi was known nationwide as a supporter of better housing and social services for minorities in Wisconsin.[46] Race relations, equal access to city services, and discrimination in housing and employment plagued Racine throughout the decade. The heightened visibility of racial upheaval that played out in the city and across the nation also highlighted frictions within the local Black community.

These tensions between race relations, housing discrimination, and segregation played out in the 1969 county social workers' strike. The International Association of Machinists (IAM) Lodge 437 represented the Racine County social workers. Social workers felt dissatisfied with pay rates, training and promotion procedures, and the lack of some level of institutional authority in dealing with individual cases brought to the department. Turnover in the department was high and many suspected it was due to low wages. High turnover limited case workers' ability to help applicants. When negotiations failed to produce any changes in policy from the County Board of Supervisors, social workers started an informational picketing campaign in December 1968. In the announcement calling for the strike on 2 January 1969, union attorney, Jay Schwartz (whose father represented AFL unions for over thirty years in city) said the primary demand was binding arbitration by a locally appointed committee to hear their case against the county board.[47]

The strike was a volatile issue in the community, due to recent unrest in the city stemming from poverty issues and housing. After a street protest started in response to police action after a fight outside a party in August 1968, a group of Black citizens formed the Concerned Minority Citizens Group and demanded neighborhood improvements from the mayor's office. The city still had not passed a housing code, and rental homes in these areas remained in substandard condition despite plans that had been under discussion for three years. Officials authorized a study designed to rate the efficiency of area welfare organizations after residents demanded changes. The study called for public aid recipients to sit on a community board that helped make administrative decisions, a consolidation of the county and city public welfare departments, and better training of case workers to address citizen needs. Social workers received the support of residents because the strikers' demands mirrored some of the changes suggested by the welfare services study.[48]

The strike also caused concern in the city because of opposition to the social workers' right to join a union and to go on strike. Some social workers in the area condemned the County Welfare Department workers for joining a union and then going on strike as unprofessional. During one of the county meetings to discuss the social worker situation, someone called in a bomb threat. Yet, the Racine labor community supported the social workers. The building trades' council publicly supported the social workers' strike. The Executive Director of Racine's United Fund (the charitable aid umbrella organization) asked all supervisors and staff to support the social workers by not crossing the picket lines to get to their offices inside the county building. This shows how activists' efforts in the postwar period to add more working-class voices to the United Fund board paid off.[49] The Racine-Kenosha chapter of the National Association of Social Workers issued a public statement supporting the aims of the county workers as well. After six weeks of negotiations, the county switched bargaining teams and a final settlement was reached granting a new merit system, increase in personnel, wage increases, a new salary schedule, and union dues checkoff.[50] This was an important strike for the Racine labor community. While city and county workers had gone on strike several times during the postwar period, this strike by social workers opened conversations about the rights of teachers, police officers, and hospital workers to use strikes as a tool for gaining their economic and workplace demands. It also highlighted the link between the working poor and labor unions as an avenue for gaining economic security and social capital. Public debate around the strike also highlighted the labor community's continued commitment to the broad-based notion of the postwar liberal idea of economic and social citizenship rights.

Black workers' civil rights activism helped extend this postwar liberal agenda within the local political economy of the city. Internal tensions still existed. Racial conservatism among white workers in the community limited labor's response to housing discrimination problems, a more proactive approach to hiring more nonwhite workers in the city's industries, and especially in opening apprenticeships within the building trades. The traditional AFL locals, with their long history of narrow organizing goals and conservative approach to political and social issues that would further democratize society, also caused tensions within the labor community during the decade. In Racine's Black community, intraclass conflict flared in the decade as well. Black workers' commitment to class politics conflicted with the more middle-class approach of new leaders within the NAACP to community problems. Yet, Black workers' intersectional activism played off in Racine. By the 1970s, the Racine labor community had a broad class politics that incorporated antiracism and was broad enough to include all working people in the city. This would prove valuable for key political and economic battles of the 1970s.

CHAPTER 5

Cross-Sector Solidarity
Amid a Shifting Landscape

Ellen Kovac was married with three children and had worked at St. Luke's Hospital for two years when she and her coworkers voted to go on strike in May 1976. Kovac was a shop steward and vociferous supporter of her fellow Service Employees International Union (SEIU) Local 150 members during contract negotiations. When talks stalled, Kovac led her colleagues on the picket lines in front of St. Luke's Hospital. The 250 men and women who worked as janitorial staff, nursing assistants, and food service workers called a strike to demand higher wages for the lowest-paid members of the bargaining unit, who worked full-time and still qualified for public assistance. They also included demands for better staffing for support services and more dignity at work. Kovac's husband, a member of UAW Local 82 at Modine Manufacturing, supported her decision to go on strike. The SEIU members at St. Luke's received support from the UAW locals and other unionized workers in the city.

UAW members joined the picket lines in the second week of the strike, after a police car hit two women. Support from the broad Racine labor community opened the door for these multiracial, mostly women SEIU members to see themselves as part of a larger collective. Despite not winning most of their demands, SEIU Local 150 became more active in the city's labor community and reorganized themselves for the next round of contract negotiations. The solidarity displayed by UAW members to these low-wage service workers demonstrates the effectiveness of Black worker activists' efforts to expand the boundaries of working-class identity in the 1960s. Together with the community's commitment to the ideals of postwar labor liberalism, this created a multiracial, gender inclusive,

104 CHAPTER 5

cross-sector community intent on expanding economic citizenship into the turbulent times of the 1970s.

By the 1970s, Racine had a long history of manufacturing, financial, and personal services, including a great diversity of industries such as auto parts, small engines, cooling systems, household goods, and financial and healthcare institutions. In 1972, a few years after the height of industrial employment in the late 1960s, Racine's 262 manufacturing firms employed over 10,000 workers. Construction and skilled trade workers, garment industry employees, white-collar office workers, city employees, and low-wage service workers added to the unionized presence as fifty union locals had a combined total of 17,000 members. The unionized sector represented some 26 percent of the city's workforce.[1] The expansion of AFSCME and SEIU increased the numbers of unionized private and public service workers in the city, especially in the realm of the healthcare industry. Working people in Racine faced challenges on multiple fronts. But, unlike the challenges from within, such as expanding access to jobs and unions for Black and female workers in earlier decades, new outside forces—political conservatives in the region, plant closings, and labor leaders from outside the city—presented new obstacles to the labor community's goals of expanded economic citizenship and dignity at work. The community's adaptive and responsive class politics allowed them to overcome internal challenges and face external pressure with solidarity and conviction.

This chapter begins with the Racine labor community working in coalition with a community group to push back against a conservative takeover of the Common Council and Unified School Board. While dealing with the impact of deindustrialization, fighting plant closings and concession demands, industrial workers in the private sector joined forces with public workers to shift local politics. The decade saw an intensification of the plant closings and downsizing that began in the 1950s in Racine. Industrial workers relied on a long history of labor solidarity and militancy as they sought to hold on to economic stability and workplace democracy, despite overwhelming odds. Even late in the decade, when it seemed as if economic decline and political conservatism would overwhelm the city, the labor community actively supported workers at St. Luke's Hospital and in other service jobs as they went on strike for better wages and working conditions and to obtain a sense of dignity and power at work. The Racine labor community rallied behind public workers and inspired low-wage service workers to push back against both management resistance and union bureaucracy to improve their wages and working conditions. Worker activists leveraged their power to elect workers to key seats on the school board. The labor militancy and cross-racial class commitment to expanding economic and social citizenship to more of Racine's working class created an atmosphere of working-class solidarity and commitment to common goals in the city.

Fighting Backlash Politics
while Supporting Public Workers

Municipal governments in the United States struggled to maintain sufficient resources during the inflationary 1970s to cover infrastructure, education, and other expenses. Shrinking tax bases due to deindustrialization and suburbanization severely limited cities' ability to justify expenditures on social services to a resistant and distant public. As scholars have detailed, cities' efforts to remain attractive to an increasingly mobile industrial capital severely impacted both city budgets and taxpayers' wallets.[2] Working-class families felt the impact of reduced local spending for the public good. A group of citizens from the rural area of the county, for example, formed a group called Stop Outlandish Spending (SOS) in the late 1960s to protest rising county taxes to cover expenditures in the city. The push against government spending raised real concerns for city employees, who feared cuts to schools and other social services in the inner-city. SOS campaigning led to voters rejecting a school bond proposal in 1969, even after an inner-city elementary school was forced to close in the middle of the school year due to deteriorating building conditions.[3] SOS candidates gained two seats on the Unified School Board and helped conservative Kenneth Huck defeat the labor-backed incumbent William H. Beyer in the 1969 mayoral election. Pressure from taxpayers to lower municipal expenditures also led the Common Council to walk a tough line with unions representing city employees.[4]

The movement of families to the suburbs, facilitated by New Deal postwar policies, reshaped the political alignment of urban areas and affected local decision-making. As white, middle-class families moved outside the city, city and county budgets became stretched due to shrinking tax bases. The workers who moved held on to most of the well-paying jobs and positions of power in the city, which directed even more funds to providing services for these developing suburbs while leaving older, central city services and public works projects without the needed funds to make improvements. While the labor movement and liberal agenda that supported unions during the high tide of postwar prosperity opened the door for many workers, the ways in which they reshaped society privileged those who held the best union jobs (white, male, suburbanites) in growth industries. By the 1970s, a growing social divide existed.[5]

106   CHAPTER 5

For example, in cities like Oakland and Detroit, the decline of urban areas coupled with the growth of nearby suburbs allowed postwar white homeowners to prosper from low taxes and government subsidized loans (e.g., G I Bill/FHA mortgages) while excluding racial minorities and limiting tax dollars to fund improvements to the inner-city public services. White, male suburbanites failed to acknowledge the ways that government expenditures contributed to their growing wealth and instead took up a narrative of independence and self-help that political conservatives embraced, fraying their ties to the postwar liberal agenda of expanding economic citizenship and social justice.[6] This realignment of power structures and political sensibilities, which occurred across the nation, created new challenges for Racine's labor community in the 1970s as they increasingly battled rural conservatives for seats on the common council, county council, and school board. Activists had to counter developing narratives that elided labor's important role in bringing prosperity to so many more Americans and delegitimized continuing efforts to expand economic citizenship.

The 1970 contract negotiations between Racine Common Council members and the city's firefighters' union exemplified challenges public workers faced in this new political and economic environment. The year started with firefighters in deadlocked contract negotiations with the city. SOS members were determined to use city-employee contracts to reduce spending. In this instance, public employees fought back. Firefighters were frustrated particularly because the city failed to pay them at a level like police officers. In response, thirty-one firefighters called in sick on Tuesday, 6 January, forcing one fire station to close for the day and bringing the parties back to the bargaining table. The gambit worked. After an all-day bargaining meeting two days later, firefighters and city negotiators reached an agreement for a series of pay raises over the course of the year, an increase in the clothing allowance, and better insurance benefits.[7]

Soon after, however, the city council voted for pay increases to police officers and other city employees, excluding firefighters. Racine firefighters went out on strike for seventy-one hours in protest. The city immediately filed an injunction against their union, Local 321, because Wisconsin's public sector laws prohibited strikes.[8] But after an emergency Common Council meeting, aldermen agreed to what amounted to binding arbitration: a "blue ribbon" committee would determine wages and fringe benefits for the firefighters. The council also agreed not to discipline striking workers. In the court decision regarding the injunction, Racine County Judge Richard Harvey dismissed the city's suit, but issued a written judgment condemning the firefighters and the "rash of illegal strikes by public employees" as a warning to Wisconsin's public workers.[9] Judge Harvey's reaction was typical of much of the judicial response to public sector strikes in the early 1970s. Public workers across the country received minimal support from public officials and the judiciary, and they often faced injunctions or arrests when leveraging for better wages or working conditions.[10]

Racine's firefighters rallied again in July when aldermen attempted to remove forty captains and lieutenants from the bargaining unit for Local 321. Teamsters, machinists, and other union members from around the city came to the council meeting to support firefighters. Robert Tighe, Racine AFL-CIO president, also spoke at the council meeting. With this public display of support from other unions in the city, firefighters argued that the city would be in breach of contract if they broke up the bargaining unit. Firefighters also brought letters from thirty-nine of the forty members in question affirming their desire to stay in Local 321.[11] Continued support from other members of the Racine labor community, and the commitment by most of the Local 321 members to take a stand for their group interests, allowed the firefighters to challenge the efforts of SOS members of the Racine Common Council.

Public employees in Racine did not back down. Over the course of the 1970s, teachers, janitors, and other public workers joined firefighters and police in demanding better working conditions, increased wages and benefits, and a voice in decision-making. Indeed, workers flocked to public sector unions across the United States. Strike activities were also impressive. Public workers' strikes increased significantly in the late 1960s and into the early 1970s, from an average of about 375 in the 1970s, and 478 strikes in 1975 alone.[12] In Racine, public workers had a broad network of support, empowering them to take action even when deemed unlawful.

Racine activists organized community organizations as well as unions. In response to the attack on public schools by the SOS committee, a new community group, the Support Excellence in Education (SEE) committee, formed to reframe issues related to public schools and to advocate for funding and policies that members felt would benefit all of Racine's school-aged children. While SEE did not have any formal connections to the Racine labor community, the organization shared similar goals. Like organized labor, it opposed the SOS agenda and battled for more efficient and equitable school funding. A showdown developed between the two community groups during the 1970 school board elections, in which the three SOS candidates elected in 1969 were replaced by SEE- and labor-backed candidates. SEE followed up its victory by endorsing a $16.2 million bond issue to fund new buildings and better management of elementary

108   CHAPTER 5

school busing. Labor unions endorsed school board candidates backed by SEE and labor activists ran for city council seats. Leroy Worley, the only Black skilled trade worker in the city, won an alderman seat during the election that swept SOS candidates out of office.[13]

Education remained a hot-button issue, and teachers were often caught between advocacy groups and budget cuts. While Racine's teachers had started to bargain for wages in the 1960s after the passage of the Municipal Employee Relations Act (MERA), they became more active in city political and social issues after their affiliation with the National Education Association (NEA) in 1970. Like other public workers across the nation, their activism gained momentum in the 1970s as they went on strike and advocated for higher wages, greater authority in their workplaces, and better schools. In January 1970, Racine Education Association (REA) Local 325 released its bargaining proposals for the upcoming year. In their statement, teachers aligned themselves with the labor movement, both locally and nationally. While emphasizing the need to have a say in class sizes, workloads, and salaries, the statement also criticized the county for ignoring inner-city schools and demanded that funds be allocated to build a replacement for Howell School. The teachers also acknowledged support of labor's boycott of GE products, showing their worker solidarity across industry lines. Local 325 President Michael Margosian said, "It is absolutely necessary for solidarity among unions to utilize maximum strength. Our local heartily endorses and supports the boycott of GE products," in explanation of why this was included in their proposals for the year. Their actions in 1970 represented a major turning point for Racine's teachers, who had been previously criticized within the labor community for not taking an active role in working-class issues.[14] This continued push by labor activists to fight against conservative influence in Racine's public offices demonstrates the level of confidence the working-class community held in its voice in local affairs as well as the continued necessity of pushing their class agenda.

Yet the school budget cuts implemented by SOS members, the shrinking state aid to local governments, and officials' slow move to integrate public schools in the county continued to negatively affect Racine's schools especially in terms of racial justice. School desegregation and quality of education issues were at the heart of Racine's NAACP activities in the 1970s. Branch president Julian Thomas, Corrine Reid-Owens, and Keith Mack, a Black educator and civil rights activist, worked throughout the period to improve educational resources. The Unified School District started a program that entailed massive busing and the closing of area schools in Racine with large Black enrollments. Once these schools were closed, NAACP leaders demanded that the hot lunch program expand to all the new schools to cover eligible students. Although the school board responded within a few months to the request for hot lunches, the Racine NAACP asked for federal intervention to improve education standards for the city's students of color.[15] The closing of Howell Elementary intensified the segregation of poor students, mostly Black and Latine, in a few inner-city schools. This segregation severely limited their opportunities to compete in the larger society.[16]

Local parents and other community groups organized to support Racine's children. Parents of elementary students from Howell School initially started carpool services to get their students to Fratt School when the county failed to provide transportation to the young children who had to walk up to a mile and a half to their new school. Parents then formed the Back Our Youth Organization as a fundraising group to purchase a school bus for the displaced students. When parents of Howell Elementary students could not sustain the carpool services to get young students to their new school, county unions, including SEIU Local 152 members, contributed to their fundraising campaign. Continuing the broad-based support from the postwar period, community and labor allies paid to provide bus service for these students.[17]

Teachers and students were not the only ones affected by the reduced school budgets. SEIU Local 152, representing the janitors and food service workers for the Racine Unified School District, went on strike in January 1971 mainly over cost-of-living increases. The 270 members felt that the 7 percent cost-of-living adjustments offered by the board were insufficient because other district employees received 9 percent increases and the operating budget increased by 11 percent. Although Local 152 members voted to strike over the weekend, union leaders asked members to wait until Tuesday to give the school board an opportunity to reopen negotiations. However, when the board did not offer to restart negotiations, janitors started picketing the school board on Wednesday, January 13th, in subzero temperatures. School janitors and other service employees issued a statement aligning themselves with Racine County taxpayers against administrators who received 25 percent raises and used state and federal funds to supplement wages for cafeteria workers and other district personnel while local taxes had recently been increased.[18] This tactic represented a clever attempt to gain the support of rural residents who had been protesting increased taxation, while also securing economic benefits for the lowest-paid county workers.

The union also linked the recent closing of Howell School to the school board's refusal to put children's safety first. The closing illustrated the lack of public funding for inner-city schools which mostly served non-white students. The school board's failure to budget for and make building renovations led the fire department to close the school right before Christmas break in 1971 due to code violations. SEIU Local 152 labeled this failure the result of the school board's refusal to put children's safety first.[19] Members also fought the reclassification of engineers to lower pay grades by removing license requirements for those positions. The strike brought the Unified School Board back to the bargaining table and schools went down to part-time schedules during the eight-day strike. After a week of additional negotiations, the union and school board agreed to wage increases for most of the employees covered by Local 152's bargaining unit, which included a boost to cost-of-living raises and a lump sum payment. The union also stopped the school's attempt to downgrade engineers and secured promises to upgrade workers in food service.[20] The public debate and strike paid off for Local 152 in a much-improved labor contract in 1971.

The struggle continued, however. On 25 September 1972, for example, about 1,500 teachers in Racine went on strike and picketed all forty-seven schools in the county district (representing 32,000 students), making it the sixth teachers' strike in Wisconsin that year.[21] Negotiations that started in May moved slowly, and the Unified School Board unilaterally implemented work rules that the bargaining committee rejected concerning elementary school teacher planning time. In late August, at a union meeting of over 1100 teachers, members voted seven-to-one to authorize a strike. At the meeting, teachers expressed concerns about the school board members' willingness to disregard the bargaining table and enact arbitrary administrative rules. For teachers, these acts of bad faith on the part of the school board were regarded as a sign of disrespect for hardworking educators and for collective bargaining. Local 325 set up headquarters in the Labor Center. The week before the strike, teachers engaged in informational picketing at a few schools and spent the weekend distributing brochures detailing their goals at shopping centers in the area. Union officials kept negotiations open and sought mediation to resolve the bargaining standstill. Teachers returned to work seventeen days later on 11 Oct 1972 when workers voted 1031 to 108 to accept a proposal by the court to supervise negotiations between REA and the school district. As usual, union officials reached out to the AFL-CIO labor council for support, and the Alliance for Labor also voted to support REA Local 325 in their contract negotiations.[22] A big concern for labor activists centered on the resistance of the school board during the months of bargaining between the teachers and Unified School District board members. This tension would last throughout the decade.

Sustaining Community during
Hard Economic Times

Public employees were not the only workers at odds with management in Racine during the early 1970s. Worker activists recognized that both public and private sector employers were attempting to limit workplace democracy. Workers in industrial plants in the city also fought back against plant closings, concession bargaining, and other assaults on their economic security. It was clear that the tide of plant closings, which began in the late 1960s, had not abated. While Local 180 members were encouraged by a change in management at Case, negotiations were still slow, and worries of massive layoffs led them to seek the aid of federal mediators. After months of rumors and failed negotiations, Case finally announced it was closing the Rockford, Illinois plant in July 1970. Five hundred workers faced layoffs, while production from Rockford moved to plants in Racine and Bettendorf, Iowa. Rockford employees had priority in moving to other Case locations and keeping their seniority, but of course for workers with over twenty years at a plant, moving between 90 and 120 miles away was not as easy as it was for the company to switch facilities. Standard Foundry workers, members of UAW Local 60, also learned their plant was closing in 1970. The foundry, purchased by Motor Castings Company in nearby West Allis, Wisconsin, closed after only three years under new management. Most workers were able to find employment at Belle City Malleable in Racine or other plants in the Racine and Milwaukee areas, but the loss of the facility did limit opportunities for those seeking work.[23] Meanwhile, workers in Racine and throughout the agricultural implements industry sought to increase cost-of-living adjustments and improve grievance procedures.[24]

It seemed that well-paying factory jobs were getting harder and harder to find. Modine Manufacturing, for instance, maintained its headquarters in Racine, but it started shifting production out of the city in the 1970s. Started in Racine in 1916 to produce radiators for automobiles and tractors, the company opened a plant in Indiana in 1934 and another in Kentucky in 1947. After it opened yet another facility in Ohio in 1970, it started laying off workers in Racine. Under a special agreement, twenty-three workers, represented by UAW Local 82, retired in November 1970, and over thirty workers were moved to new positions, while the company estimated that less than forty-five people would be laid off at that time. The company shifted from a focus on production and instead housed its research and development center in Racine.[25] This was indicative of the shift from unskilled to skilled labor that accompanied some corporate restructuring during the period. The shift to high-skilled jobs impacted young workers and nonwhite workers who had not had the opportunity to receive the skills needed for these new positions.

In the most devastating case of a plant closing in the early 1970s, Howard Industries closed its Racine operations, giving workers only a fifteen-minute notice. UAW Local 841 found itself scrambling to gather information to bargain for pension, severance packages, and insurance coverage for the nearly two hundred employees in the bargaining unit. On Monday, 14 February 1972, in what was supposed to be a resumption of bargaining agreement talks, the company announced to the union that the plant was closing and terminated 110 workers on the spot. Despite the announcement during contract negotiations, management claimed the decision was based on obsolete plant facilities. Seventy workers would remain on the payroll until production ceased. Howard Industries had manufactured fractional motors for small electronics in Racine since World War II, but was sold in 1965 to a holding company, MSL Industries.[26]

In August 1970, just a few months after battles between firefighters and the Common Council were resolved, members of UAW Local 642 went on the first strike since 1935 against the Dumore Company. Opened in 1913 by Louis Hamilton of the Hamilton-Beach Company, Dumore produced small motor-operated electronics for the automobile industry and home and light-industrial products. The members of Local 642 wanted to add a strike clause as the final step in the grievance procedure, but when the company refused, they decided to go on strike. The following week, over one thousand UAW Local 553 members went on strike against Belle City Malleable, one of the largest foundries in the Midwest. Belle City employees protested the company's attempt to change how incentive workers were paid for non-piece work. Union officials argued that the company wanted to intimidate individual workers and to keep these employees in a part-time status for incentive pay. Workers wanted to keep the existing contract language that called for an average of their normal incentive pay scale while doing other duties.[27] In an ironic twist of fate, Belle City members of Local 553 used the closed Standard Foundry site as a base for picketing during the strike that started just two months after operations ended at Standard. These two strikes illustrate employers' continuing efforts to maximize profits at the expense of employees' wages and to maintain greater power in employment relations.

Like public workers, UAW strikers received a broad level of support among the Racine labor community. Local bowling alleys opened their doors to the strikers and, as usual, area unions contributed to the strike funds of each striking local. The Dumore and Belle City workers even held a solidarity strikers' slow-pitch softball game. SEIU Local 152 issued a public statement of support for the UAW strikers and promised "moral and financial support." UAW Local 642 President Paul Kozlik published a public letter in *Racine Labor* in response to Case workers' show of support: "I remember when we were miles ahead of Local 180 in about 10 categories … Now if Dumore would give us the language of the Case contract on cost of living [and] right to strike on grievances … we'd be most of the way home toward settlement."[28] The local support encouraged strikers to stand firm. On three separate occasions, over 800 Belle City strikers returned letters the company sent to workers' homes, attempting to intimidate or entice them into returning to work. Such acts of defiance demonstrated their solidarity with each other and their firmness in refusing to compromise on incentive pay changes.[29]

Kozlik also accused Dumore and Belle City management teams of using the same tactics that the Case Company used in the 1960 strike to intimidate workers and force unfair settlements.[30] This reference back to the Case strike was a key part of the working-class identity in the labor community. Workers and labor activists used past union activities and workers' struggles in the city not only as inspiration but also as explanation of what kept people engaged in working-class issues. During strikes, organizing drives, public rallies, and annual Labor Day celebrations, activists traced the history of struggles for economic and social justice in the city as evidence of the continued importance of thinking, acting, and mobilizing around working-class issues. Looking back, William Jenkins linked the continued success of organized labor in the city to the hard-fought gains of the UAW local that represented the workers at J. I. Case Company. He maintained that because workers at the largest industrial plant in town had to fight repeatedly to reaffirm their right to collectively bargain, Racine's working-class activists became determined to push even harder to gain full economic and social citizenship rights for all workers. Jenkins recalled, "Racine's always been a union town, you know, progressive as far as labor's concerned." He also emphasized that, "The strife that we've had here—the labor strife" was the motivating factor keeping union activists engaged in maintaining an active labor community.[31] Linking the struggles at Dumore and Belle City to what happened at Case in the 1960s was a call to action for the broader labor community.

The local labor community rose together in outrage in response to a county official's comments in the local paper in late August saying Belle City Malleable strikers were engaged in thievery by applying for welfare benefits. Workers from across industries, including Sam Rizzo in his role as UAW International Representative, converged on a county board meeting to protest the statements and called for the firing of Robert Hess, head of the surplus foods division of the Racine County Welfare Board. At the meeting, another Welfare Department representative assured citizens that Belle City employees and any family could use the resources of the Welfare Department, reminding that many families with full-time workers still qualified for various benefits.[32] These acts of solidarity and financial contributions from other unions went a long way in helping workers maintain their course during a period of tough negotiations. Racine's working-class activists recognized that more and more employers in Racine and across the nation were taking hardline approaches to collective bargaining, and the support for strikers across industries proved valuable in stemming this tide of push backs in the city. This exemplifies the success Racine's activists had in shaping the local political economy. While local and state governments around the country were cutting back social services in the late 1970s, in Racine, the labor community's ability to center the needs of working people paid off in public debates.[33]

Employers felt the pressure. Federal mediators in both the Dumore and Belle City cases moved negotiations to Chicago to escape the tensions in Racine. However, both unions and companies refused to compromise. The Dumore strike lasted for eighty-two days and ended with a three-to-one vote in favor of a new three-year contract that included major improvements in the cost-of-living assessments, higher wages for lower paid employees, and better pension agreements.[34] The Belle City workers felt that they had given the company so many concessions over the previous ten years of negotiations that they could no longer claim to have the best contract or wage agreement in the city. Local 553 members ratified a three-year agreement after a twelve-week strike. While union leaders hailed the contract as the best one in over ten years, with substantial wage increases and a 6 percent yearly cost-of-living adjustment, it came at a high price. The company closed the malleable iron casting operation, affecting about 500 workers, leaving only the steel casting operations in business. A week after the new contract was signed, only 300 of the original 1050 strikers had been called back to work. Union officials acknowledged the loss of jobs and made efforts to find new positions for those workers who would not be recalled to Belle City. As the largest concentration of nonwhite workers, these most vulnerable employees had to find new employment, lost the seniority they had achieved at the foundries, and would carry the brunt of the economic instability that occurred over the next two decades. While labor leaders praised the new agreement, it was clear to activists that better negotiation strategies were needed.

Again, race mattered. Black and Brown workers were the first laid off as those most often with the least seniority. As we have seen, as late as 1963, many industrial plants in Racine had no nonwhite workers. Apprentice training in skilled trades was still all-white in the city despite a half-decade of organizing by Black workers. Despite the hard work by Black activists within and without the labor movement, in a 1971 survey of Racine residents, 76 percent of Black respondents felt that there were not equal job opportunities for all people. While 72 percent of Mexican Americans in the study felt that job opportunities were equal for all people, data collected as late as 1990 for Racine County suggests that Black and Latine workers remained marginalized from the skilled jobs available in the city.[35]

While looking to their unions for workplace issues, many nonwhite workers sought assistance through local social safety net and War on Poverty programs. Yet, poor staffing and budget restraints stood in the way. A group of Black and Latine residents, working through the Spanish Center and Project Breakthru, petitioned the Wisconsin State Employment Service (WSES) office in Racine to hire Spanish-speaking full-time staff and to offer better services for marginalized job seekers and those looking for job training.[36] In response, the WSES office issued a statement listing the advances made in the previous two years toward helping disadvantaged workers gain the skills needed to join the workforce and find job placement. The Racine office also highlighted its efforts to reach all areas of the city by holding extended hours in local neighborhood centers and its current recruitment efforts for Spanish-speaking staff.[37] However, the continued demands for more services illustrated the high level of unemployment in these historically excluded populations in the city and the inability of those with limited skills to find employment in increasingly technical fields within the context of layoffs due to plant closings and relocations.

Industrial union leaders had actively participated in War on Poverty programs, and during the changing economy of the 1970s, they continued to build alliances with liberal groups seeking to improve social and economic equality.[38] The Spanish Center also continued its programs of language instruction, financial assistance, and job services for Mexican Americans and other Latine people. While the services helped many residents, debate over center management led to high turnover in many positions. In 1972, the nonprofit Jobs for Progress's Service Employment Redevelopment (SER) program came to Wisconsin to help the Chicano population in Racine, Kenosha, and Milwaukee find better employment opportunities and combat the 12 to 15 percent unemployment rate. By the early 1970s, there were 10,000 Chicanos in Racine County. The local office offered education, vocation, and on-the-job training for residents, and initiated an employer-education program and sought to improve public school services for Spanish-speaking children.[39]

116   CHAPTER 5

The Spanish Center, SER, and the neighborhood centers that popped up in Racine's Black and Latine neighborhoods were all products of Johnson's War on Poverty programs. Robert Tighe, Racine AFL-CIO President, participated in a union leadership training program to help unions participate more fully in War on Poverty programs.[40] The War on Poverty came out of Johnson's Great Society agenda and included job training for youth and the unemployed, community action programs for urban renewal, and small business development. Yet, these domestic programs suffered due to budget expenses for the Vietnam War. The programs also reflected the postwar liberal shift away from direct government involvement and toward favoring private-sector solutions to social and economic concerns at the community level. The underfunding and the lack of government oversight severely limited the effectiveness of these programs on relieving inner-city poverty and unemployment. War on Poverty programs were also attacked by liberal and conservative policymakers from the beginning.[41] In the face of these challenges, these social safety net programs provided only minimal aid to the most vulnerable workers during the increased job scarcity due to deindustrialization.

Union leaders continued to rely on public support as tensions mounted because of plant closing and concession demands from employers. In 1972, UAW International Representative Sam Rizzo brought contract negotiations between UAW Local 1007 and Western Printing Company to the public to fight against a local company's refusal to bargain in good faith. While workers were not out on strike, negotiations became deadlocked in July. After several frustrating rounds of failed negotiations and public statements by managers against the union, Rizzo held a public meeting where he justified the union's position. In Rizzo's speech, he reiterated that more importantly than pay raises or additional benefits, the workers demanded respect and real recognition of the union as a bargaining agent. The mayor, a county board member, and several journalists were present in the audience. When the union president and another organizer spoke, they likened Western Publishing to the Case Company of the 1930s and 1940s, once again using the history of labor activism and worker solidarity against management intransigence to justify current activities. Just two days after the public meeting, management requested a return to the bargaining table, and members overwhelmingly accepted the new agreement, which included many of their original demands.[42] While this represents another example of management's pushback against unions in the 1970s, it is also evidence of the power of a vibrant labor community to influence public opinion and pressure employers to bargain.

Labor Solidarity Radicalizes
SEIU Local 150

This environment of working-class activism and labor-community coalition building helped shape the decision of Ellen Kovac and the other members of SEIU Local 150 to go on strike against St. Luke's Hospital in 1976. Not-for-profit institutions like St. Luke's Hospital had served as low-wage employers for new immigrants, Latine, and southern Black migrants to northern cities for many years. Wage injustices by sex lowered income for women even more. For example, the mostly male maintenance department received an average of $2.00 more per hour than did the female-dominated housekeeping department at St. Luke's.[43] Exempt from provisions of the National Labor Relations Act until 1974—the rights of workers to organize a union of their choice, bargain collectively, strike, boycott, and picket, and the prohibition of employers from intimidating, firing, or blacklisting employees for union activities—these hospitals could keep workers' wages below those in other industries. At the same time, as Leon Fink points out, the life-support function of hospitals, their centrality to the healthcare system of cities, and the role of local and federal governments in sustaining them, led to the involvement of government officials, the press, and organized pressure groups—i.e., the public—in labor-management disputes.[44]

SEIU Local 150 members had to carefully negotiate their role with the public. Service workers at St. Luke's Hospital recognized that their wages fell far below industrial union wages in the county but, at the same time, they understood the possible danger of taking their wage demands to the public arena.[45] They knew they needed to marshal a broad range of support. The workers' activism and the local labor community's solidarity inspired action when the opportunity to demand better wages and benefits came on 30 April 1976 at the end of the existing labor agreement between the 250 members of SEIU Local 150 and St. Luke's.[46] Jay Schwartz, a local lawyer hired as lead negotiator, and newly elected Chief Steward Art Burdick sought this opportunity to increase the wages of the service workers who made up one-third of St. Luke's staff. But negotiations did not go well.

Both the hospital management and the union bargaining committee moved quickly to declare their positions to the media and demonstrate their unwillingness to compromise. In the local daily newspaper, Personnel Director Herbert Scheible (former human relations director for Hamilton-Beach during the plant closing in 1968) announced that the pay raises and other benefits offered in contract negotiations would go into effect for non-striking workers. Employers often used this tactic to break worker solidarity. In fact, with the shift in national political will away from supporting labor in workplace democracy, employers found it increasingly beneficial to engage in unfair labor practices. Enforcement was lax and companies were willing to pay fines to break worker solidarity and limit labor's power.[47] Chief negotiator Schwartz outlined the union's complaints: St. Luke's was unable to maintain basic housekeeping chores because of understaffing, and the hospital paid part-time employees sub-union wages, while many full-time union workers could not support their families on their hospital pay.[48]

Three weeks later, when negotiations reached an impasse, Local 150 members set up a picket line at the hospital's front door. By occupying this public space, workers altered social relations within the city. Hospital staff not involved in the strike, as well as patients, strikebreakers, and visitors had to engage with the picketers as they entered St. Luke's. The women strikers actively claimed the sidewalk in front of the hospital, which instantly became a contested space. Police cars struck several strikers, requiring at least one woman to stay overnight at a nearby hospital. While the strikers protested the harsh treatment by security guards and police officers, hospital management claimed that officers did not properly control the picketers. Hospital security guards had two women arrested for slashing car tires while on strike duty.[49] These public acts of violence signified the strikers' willingness to claim this space to present their grievances to the public and hospital management. Their picket signs conveyed these demands: "Wages not Welfare," "Your Loved Ones Are Cared for by Poverty Level Wages," and "St. Luke's Management Hates Labor."[50]

Strong support from the labor community showed how committed industrial workers were to a broad notion of who counted as a worker. Very early in the negotiation process, the Racine labor community demonstrated its support for members of Local 150. Volunteers from other unions joined the picket lines in a show of solidarity and as a means of protection for women strikers as they had for industrial workers over the years. The UAW subregional director issued a statement in support of the hospital workers, declaring, "Like all of us, hospital workers deserve a decent contract."[51] Local unions also contributed financial aid through the "Friends of St. Luke's Strikers" fund. *Racine Labor* often carried frontpage articles or images updating readers on the progress of contract negotiations and strike activities. The paper printed multiple articles featuring profiles and comments of rank-and-file union members and those on the bargaining committee. Several regular *Racine Labor* contributors used their columns to support the strike effort to improve wages at St. Luke's Hospital. For example, Dean Pettit, in his REA column, objected to the hospital's use of strikebreakers and praised other local union members who helped with picketing duty at St. Luke's in the 4 June 1976 edition.[52]

Surprisingly for Racine, hospital workers faced opposition from their own union leadership. Based in Milwaukee, Local 150 was a statewide local representing 7,000 members at the time of the St. Luke's strike. The 250 members at the hospital did not have the support of Union President Don Beatty. In fact, Beatty negotiated a contract agreement with St. Luke's management without the knowledge or support of the local bargaining committee. On 24 May 1976, Beatty mailed a letter to the members urging them to accept the deal, which offered five cents more than the previous agreement the workers rejected on 13 May. The members rejected the agreement offered by Beatty by a vote of 140–7. As reported in *Racine Labor*, Beatty's letter urged workers to go back to work because the climate was not right for a protracted strike against the hospital; he noted that several other strikes in the area (Milwaukee, Burlington, and Kenosha) had proved unsuccessful.

St. Luke's workers decided to push forward with the support of the Racine labor community and their hired negotiator, Jay Schwartz. The workers felt empowered by the activism and radicalism of these local leaders, which encouraged them to continue to struggle against heavy-handed practices by hospital management and Local 150 union leadership based in Milwaukee. The legacy of local labor radicalism and the gains Schwartz achieved for other unions in the area also boosted the workers' confidence. Don Beatty did not fit into the Racine labor community's idea of an engaged, militant union leader. His unwillingness to adapt to Racine's ideals put the statewide Local 150 outside the bounds of community. Instead, the community embraced the Racine-based members, supported their strike effort, and educated members on how to reshape internal union culture and politics.

Active union members continued to support local representatives despite internal union politics and the backroom deals by President Beatty. In interviews with *Racine Labor*, local bargaining committee members reemphasized their support for Schwartz and Burdick and urged the labor community to remember that the strike at St. Luke's was initiated to improve workers' wages and to focus on that result rather than the internal union disputes. The interviews revealed the longstanding tensions between local members and the Milwaukee leadership, especially President Don Beatty. Workers felt that having a local lawyer (Schwartz) on the negotiating team gave them more authority at the bargaining table, and they resented Beatty's attempt to keep them out of the negotiating process.[53] The comments of the workers and their refusal to accept the

120   CHAPTER 5

contracts Beatty negotiated demonstrated the ways in which rank-and-file workers sought alternate means to improve their wages and job security, even against union leadership's direction. Racine's militant labor community created the space for St. Luke's workers to remain determined despite the resistance from Beatty and hospital management.

Although union members continued to picket St. Luke's Hospital, on 24 June, Don Beatty and hospital administrators signed an agreement previously rejected by members. Left with few options, the local bargaining committee voted to recall the strikers on 1 July 1976 after personnel director Scheible threatened to fire all workers who did not report for duty on 2 July 1976. The new contract contained slightly less than a dollar an hour wage increase spread over three years, which represented six cents more than the first offer that led to the walkout and strike in May. The most active union members felt betrayed by their local yet they were determined to continue to work together to effect change at St. Luke's.

Despite the strike defeat, SEIU hospital workers in Racine continued to fight against management's heavy-handed practices and used community support and available legal means to effect changes within their workplace. They brought charges against union leadership with SEIU International headquarters, used the National Labor Relations Board (NLRB) process to address the illegal firing of strikers, and worked to build a stronger steward system in the hospital. Workers remained committed to the idea of working-class solidarity based on the support they received from the local community and Racine's labor activists.

The workers felt empowered by the activism and radicalism of their local leaders, which encouraged them to continue to struggle against heavy-handed practices by hospital management and union leadership. Typically, when local labor leaders address workers' needs for dignity at work as well as bread and butter issues, they are more effective. For example, the history of the Hospital Workers' Union Local 1199, from its beginnings in the late 1950s New York to a powerful nationwide service union just over a decade later, relied on grassroots activism, a radical union leadership, and aggressive organizing to garner significant gains within the health care industry. Fink and Greenberg detail the high expectations yet stifled progress of Local 1199's organizing and bargaining activities on the national level in the 1970s, but they also highlight key factors for success. Analyzing the results of organizing at New York's Columbia-Presbyterian Medical Center, the largest nonprofit hospital in the nation, leads them to conclude, "By aggressively responding to workers' feelings of powerlessness and to their demands for respect rather than by just meeting their economic needs, however real, Local 1199 continued to invest union campaigns with the 'sense of liberation'."[54] This sentiment helps explain why workers in Racine at St. Luke's continued to support Burdick and Schwartz even after Beatty stepped in and took over negotiations. The legacy of local labor radicalism and the gains Schwartz achieved for other unions in the area help explain members' support.

Jay Schwartz had a long history of providing legal counsel and supporting the labor community. Born and raised in Racine, Schwartz attended Horlick High School, received a bachelor's degree in Industrial Relations from Cornell University, and graduated from the University of Chicago's Law School in 1957. He provided legal counsel and negotiation services for most of the public workers in Racine County, for firefighters in Walworth County, and for firefighters and police officers in Kenosha County. He constantly advocated for worker solidarity and helped build a coalition between the different public workers unions, which were represented by the machinists, AFSCME, and SEIU. Schwartz was also active in local politics; he ran unsuccessfully for the Democratic congressional seat in 1962 and for the Attorney General of Wisconsin in 1968. During his political campaigns, he received constant support from the labor community and received endorsements from the Machinists and Building Trades Council for both his election campaigns. He served for several years as an assistant district attorney and successfully advocated for changes to local law, for instance, making jury selection in Racine County more representative of the local population. Schwartz had a fraught reputation as a union negotiator because many in the labor community felt he personalized each struggle.[55]

Others saw this personalization as a strength, which infused a sense of passion into his demands for economic security and human rights for all workers. Some unions would threaten to bring Schwartz to the bargaining table because of his reputation as a fierce supporter of workers against management and his frequent public appearances on behalf of local unions. He worked actively with the Democratic Party and pushed the state party to adopt a more forceful civil rights platform in the 1968 election. He demanded a local judge step down after a Black police officer accused him of racial bias in his case against the Racine police department. When SEIU Local 150 President Don Beatty published a public rebuke for Schwartz's actions in the strike at St. Luke's, the local labor community came out in full support of Schwartz, labeling Beatty as a traitor to St. Luke's workers. The labor community's actions inspired workers to keep fighting against management's tactics and against the leadership of Local 150. When Schwartz died in 1978, Dick Olson, the *Racine Labor* editor, described him as "a loyal ally, a compatriot, a fighter and a leader."

He served in all those roles for the workers at St. Luke's, advised them of their options, kept them connected to the larger labor community, spoke on their behalf with management, and after they were forced to return to work, vowed to help them maintain their local union activities.[56]

In the aftermath of the strike, hospital management fired four employees, including Chief Steward Art Burdick, bargaining committee member Ellen Kovac, and two sisters, Barbara DeRosier and Beverly Smith.[57] The firings took a toll on the activist workers' leadership. Burdick had been chief steward for five months when the hospital fired him. During that period, he worked diligently to protect union members' rights, filing 100 grievances between February and May 1976. The hospital fired and then rehired Burdick on several occasions for his aggressive performance of union duties. The militant Burdick had a tumultuous relationship with Union President Beatty and with some members of the maintenance department at St. Luke's. These workers, mostly men, and among the highest paid in the hospital, did not like Burdick's radicalism. During the strike, Kovac, Smith, and DeRosier had been among the most militant. Kovac provided a constant, energizing presence on the picket line. She was very vocal and yelled encouragement to the other strikers. A single mother with five children at home, Smith went on strike so she could afford to support her family without working overtime or finding another job to supplement her income. She worked as a central services aide with a salary of $2.73 an hour.[58] The failed negotiations, lack of union leadership support, and firings dealt a severe blow to Local 150 members.

The immediate issues centered on the firings and the disagreements with Local 150 management. Hospital management alleged that Burdick had instigated a work stoppage on 7 May 1976, charged Kovac with an illegal work stoppage on 22 May, and blamed DeRosier and Smith for picket-line misconduct, all causes for dismissal. Smith also faced criminal charges related to strike activity. In a meeting with hospital workers, Schwartz outlined the available legal options. Members could file a lawsuit over the legality of the labor agreement, continue to strike against the hospital and risk a mass firing, support the efforts to rehire the fired workers, or any combination of those options. Most of the workers voted not to file a lawsuit over the disputed labor agreement because of the additional expense and time involved. But many workers expressed frustration and regret over their options. One worker spoke out, saying: "We're chicken from the word go if we let them fire our leadership. We're back in the frying pan where we've been for nine years." While many agreed with this sentiment, at the same time, the majority felt that despite their respect for Burdick and approval of his behavior as chief steward, they could not afford to continue the fight.[59] In the end, members enlisted Schwartz's aid to have the fired workers reinstated in their previous positions at St. Luke's.

Management at St. Luke's Hospital, mostly represented by Scheible, refused to give any concessions to the fired workers and took the issue all the way to the US Court of Appeals. A local judge dismissed charges of tire slashing against Smith, but the hospital still refused to drop its effort to prevent her and Kovac from receiving unemployment compensation.[60] Scheible and hospital lawyers continued to fight the unemployment claims of Kovac and Smith and the grievance procedures for Burdick throughout the rest of 1976 and 1977. Finally, Burdick and Kovac turned to the NLRB for resolution with the assistance of a new attorney, Arthur Heitzer. An arbitrator upheld the firings in April 1977. Concurrently, the fired employees filed suit in small claims court to receive the vacation pay denied them when they were fired. In July, the NLRB ruled that Burdick's firing was illegal, but upheld Kovac's dismissal. The hospital also paid Burdick and DeRosier the vacation pay withheld at their firings. However, the battle over unemployment compensation for Smith and Kovac continued.[61] Under appeal, Kovac's case was resubmitted to the NLRB.[62] After Schwartz became ill, the case was handled by Arthur Heitzer, who fittingly had received a four-year scholarship in 1965 as part of an SEIU program which granted $500 each year to a SEIU member's collegebound child. Heitzer's father had been a member of SEIU Local 150 when he received the award.[63]

Two years after their dismissals, Burdick and Kovac received news that an NLRB administrative law judge ruled their dismissals illegal and ordered St. Luke's Hospital to reinstate them both with full back pay and interest. Yet, the hospital immediately challenged the ruling.[64] In a show of continued union solidarity, an editorial in *Racine Labor* called on the state review commission to deny St. Luke's request to raise patient charges because the hospital was using valuable funds to continue a "futile battle to avoid obeying the law."[65] Finally, on 21 May 1980, the United States Court of Appeals, Seventh Circuit, ruled that the NLRB could disregard the arbitration award and pursue the case because the proceeding did not fully decide the unfair labor practices charge against St. Luke's Hospital. The court also ruled that the discharge of Burdick and Kovac violated two sections of the NLRA. The ruling indicated that Burdick had filed 100 grievances during his first four months as chief steward and that management fired Kovac for her union activities. By firing these two active, militant union members just four days after the strike, the NLRB concluded, the hospital demonstrated that its actions were in retaliation for the workers' union activities.[66]

Though they finally received vindication, the process for Burdick and Kovac proved long, expensive, and emotionally draining. In an interview after the court ruling, Kovac indicated that the four-year battle had strained her and her family. She was glad to have her name finally cleared, felt relieved that the ordeal was over, and thanked all those who supported her financially and emotionally during the process.[67] Yet just five months later, Kovac no longer wanted her name associated with the strike. A frontpage article in *Racine Labor* reported that St. Luke's made the largest back pay settlement in Wisconsin's history but referred only to Burdick and "another worker (who asked that her name not be used . . .)." The hospital paid a combined $80,000 to both workers for back wages and interest.[68] Employers like St. Luke's willingness to use unfair labor practices and extend these legal fights with the NLRB really dealt a blow to workers' ability to use their labor power to hold on to workplace democracy and economic security for their communities. The shifting US political economy, with local and federal power brokers unwilling to level the labor relations playing field, really hampered labor's power in this period.[69]

The support received by Local 150 members at St. Luke's demonstrates the continued effectiveness of working-class solidarity in the city, despite the economic, political, and social uncertainty and loss of numbers in industrial unions. Instead of retreating from active engagement, union members inspired workers in low-wage service positions in the healthcare industry to get the fullest economic and political power from organizing as possible. The solidarity and continued activism of industrial workers also benefited teachers during this period.

Supporting Teachers through Political and Community Activism

By the mid-1970s, Racine's teachers faced a school board intent on cutting every possible expense. In the spring of 1976, the board unilaterally stopped paying teachers' health insurance premiums, prompting REA to take them to court to force them to honor the existing agreement. As the August contract deadline fast approached, the board refused to bargain, called an impasse, and then implemented new administrative guidelines. REA officials again took the board to court, asked the teachers to work under the rules, and follow the Wisconsin Employment Relations Commission (WERC) and court decisions. However, when the board still refused to bargain in good faith, teachers decided their only option was to go on strike on 27 January 1977. The union was asking for written administrative codes, cost-of-living increases, an end to merit pay, and health insurance benefits.[70]

The Racine community came out in support of the striking teachers. SEIU Local 152, who served as custodians and other service employees in the school district, voted to honor the picket lines. Carpenters in Local 91 refused jobs for the Unified School District. Local 180, still the largest union in the city, also came out in support of the teachers and custodians. The UAW locals in Racine asked union families to keep their children out of school so that they would not have to cross picket lines. One student interviewed by the daily paper told a reporter, "My dad's a teacher at Starbuck and he said I wasn't gonna cross any picket lines."[71] Father Anthony Dorn of St. Mary's Church gave a sermon condemning the school board for union busting and allowed the sermon to be published in *Racine Labor*. Editors of the *Racine Journal Times*, the local daily paper, came out in strong opposition to the strike. The *Journal Times* placed a box on the first page of each issue, counting the days of the "illegal strike." However, the unionized clerical workers and copy editors at the paper picketed the office with signs in support of the striking teachers. One teacher, Gerald Kongstvedt, sent an editorial to *Racine Labor* expressing his determination to continue to disobey the law and face firing after a judge issued an injunction demanding the teachers return to work. Kongstvedt explained that he would tell his students that he disobeyed the judge and participated in an illegal strike because of the example of Martin Luther King, Jr. In a sample lesson plan, he used Martin Luther King Jr.'s "Letter from a Birmingham Jail" to "explain why some civil disobedience is called for when morality is on your side." State Senator Dorman also issued a statement condemning the Unified School District's board for bad faith bargaining.[72]

The strike ended fifty days after it started, on 15 March 1977, when teachers tentatively agreed to a new contract. The contract called for an end to merit pay, a one-time increase in insurance premiums, new cost-of-living adjustments, and some improvements in seniority rules. The teachers received partial fair share considerations wherein newly hired teachers would either join the union or pay fair share dues. However, fair share was not applied to teachers already working and not part of the union. The teachers were forced to accept the board's decision to discipline eleven employees for strike activities but voted to reimburse their lost wages. Teachers waited to approve the agreement until Local 152, representing the janitors and food service workers, finished their last round of negotiations with the Unified School District on the same night. While the teachers' strike, like others over the years, did not garner a complete victory, the working-class community in Racine continued to see the value in collective class action. The language, strategies, and tactics demonstrated a continuation of the labor activism as well as a continued commitment to broad-based economic and social issues.

The working-class solidarity in the community led to an all-out effort to resolve many of the remaining issues within the county's Unified School District by campaigning to replace recalcitrant board members with labor-endorsed candidates. During the teachers' strike, both REA members and other labor activists pointed to individual school board members who they felt mishandled both contract negotiations and the county's school administration. Reverend Howard Stanton received most of the negative publicity. *Racine Labor* ran several articles detailing his poor attendance record at board meetings and his legal troubles after hitting several teachers on picket lines during the strike with his vehicle. At the same time, activists praised board member Howard McClennan for his efforts to end the strike, his resistance to having striking teachers arrested, and his commitment to fair bargaining. Both the AFL-CIO and the UAW Political Action Committee put considerable effort into campaigning for new school board members between the February primary and the April election. William Jenkins, now retired from his active role in the UAW and serving on neighborhood improvement committees, decided to enter the school board race to protect public education in the county. He campaigned against what he considered the bloated school administration, calling, for instance, for less regulation of teachers' lesson plans. The other labor-supported candidate was UW-Parkside Assistant Professor of Education Marv Happel. He also campaigned against top-heavy administration positions and advocated for building a better relationship between administration and teachers to improve teacher morale in the school system.[73]

The AFL-CIO and UAW PAC committees treated the Racine County school board election like a presidential campaign. They organized phone banks, sent out widespread political mailings, handed out literature in front of local industrial plants (Case management refused to allow hand-billing outside of its gates), and provided transportation to the polls on Election Day. The hard campaigning paid off as Jenkins and Happel received about 10,000 additional votes between the primary and the election, moving into the second and third slots and ousting their main rivals to fill the four open school board seats. The most significant result was Stanton's fall from first to fifth position in the election. Both Stanton and Lowell McNeil, the antagonistic negotiating committee member, were ousted from the school board. A *Racine Labor* editorial argued that Jenkins's and Happel's victory added "balance and reason to a board that for too long has operated without much of either."[74]

Although still outnumbered on the school board, the two new members kept pressure on the school board and demanded transparency and fair labor practices. In June, both Happel and Jenkins walked out of a hastily scheduled closed meeting of the board because they said it violated Wisconsin's open meetings law as it did not allow public participation. The board held the closed meeting to vote on appealing a recent state decision that forced Unified to pay disability payments to two local teachers who took time off after their pregnancies. During the next bargaining period that began in July, Happel publicly attacked a subcommittee of the board for spending over $1000 on negative campaign ads published in two local papers.[75] As the school board election shows, the Racine labor community demonstrated a clear example of working-class solidarity and actively embraced public school teachers. Echoing the political battles in the post–World War II period, local activists ran for public office to keep working-class voices alive in city debates. The community came together to support their candidates, and while they did not have a majority on city and county boards, their interests were represented.

Across the nation, teacher strikes in this period met a different response. As Jon Shelton shows, when teachers sought to fight back against austerity measures in places like Pittsburgh and New York City, they were met with fierce pushback and a further dismantling of the liberal agenda. Teacher and other public-sector worker strikes in deindustrializing cities fueled political backlash.[76] In Racine however, the labor community mitigated this response. The continued broad-based coalition of public and private sector unions, the ability to impact local elections, the example of engaged worker activists like Jenkins, and combined efforts of the labor community kept labor liberalism on the table.

Racine's labor community backed public workers outside of the city as well. When Wisconsin state employees organized rallies and eventually went on strike in the summer of 1977, the Racine labor community offered their full support. Led by AFSCME Council 24, representing fifty-two locals across the state, including clerical workers, prison guards, state troopers, institution aids, job service workers, and parole officers, the strike sought to bring greater wages to the lowest-paid state workers. The unions wanted flat wage increases across the board while the state negotiators insisted on percentage increases. Labor activists argued that percentage increases gave the bulk of the funds to the highest paid workers leaving the lowest paid still below the national poverty line and below what other public workers received across the state. State workers in Racine and surrounding areas picketed state offices and UW-Parkside during the strike with support from the local labor community.[77] Racine's labor community rallied to protect their city's economic environment and that of the whole state. This broad, militant outlook existed because of the long history of working-class politics to advance a more equitable society for all workers.

The strong sense of cross-sector labor solidarity and the commitment by local activists to support broad-based economic and social justice despite economic downturns, rhetoric against public spending, and antilabor management tactics, proved critical to the successes garnered by public employees and low-wage service workers in Racine during the 1970s. This support expanded beyond the early years of the decade when public workers' militancy was at its strongest and into the period of economic stagnation and management pushbacks. The long history of expanding and nurturing working-class identity, the continued efforts to build a strong support base in the community by collaborating with other social justice organizations, and the sense of working-class political power, put the Racine labor community in a position to resist the decline of labor solidarity and class politics seen in some other areas in this period. While workers still suffered the effects of divestment by industrial corporations, the economic downturns that resulted in high unemployment and stagnant wages, and the inability or unwillingness of public officials to close the gaps in the social and economic security nets, they did not retreat from class politics or lose confidence in their combined efforts to impact the lives of working people in Racine. As we will see in the next chapter, the 1980s saw Racine's labor community rallying around immigrant workers, working to ease rising unemployment, and organizing across the growing private service sector.

CHAPTER 6

Racine's Labor Community and Deindustrialization

The situation in Racine was dire in the 1980s, same as it was in Rust Belt urban areas across the nation. The accelerated decline of manufacturing meant a sharp reduction of better-paying union jobs and an increase of less unionized, low-wage service work. The increasing power of corporate managers and the accompanying free movement of capital allowed companies to demand rollbacks from workers in labor agreements across industries. New adherence to free market principles also shifted the relationship between the government and private interests, whereby deregulation and defunded social programs eroded protections for workers and widened the holes in the social safety net. The unemployment rate in Racine reached 14 percent in the early 1980s and would remain higher than the national average throughout the decade. Applications for welfare programs increased 79 percent in the county during the first half of 1980. The rate of home foreclosures was rising almost uncontrollably, changes in federal law threatened nearly 1,000 people's unemployment benefits, and state and local budget cuts slashed typical resources that workers had come to rely on in dire economic situations.[1]

The economic recession had been pushing the unemployment rate up since the late 1970s, real wages continued to drop, and volatile interest rates added to uncertainty as people lost their jobs and homes at an ever-increasing rate. Racine's workers took a heavy toll. At the same time, Wisconsin Governor Lee Dreyfus cut state spending through the Department of Health and Social Services for welfare and medical assistance programs, placing families in an even greater state of instability. By early 1981, over 600 workers at Case were laid off with no news of when they would be recalled due to the downturn in the agricultural implements industry.[2]

The political and economic landscape had shifted in Racine and around the country. Racine's labor activists faced these changes by gathering their remaining resources to protect as many jobs as possible through strikes, rallies, legal maneuvers, political appeals, and negotiations during plant closings or threats of plant closings. They addressed the needs of nonwhite workers—those most severely impacted by the recession—by intensifying the fight for more equitable hiring practices, improving the community's social service programs to deal with a diversified clientele, and protesting raids by the Immigration and Naturalization Service (INS). The labor community continued to organize new workers and welcome them to the community. Activists and the workers they represented showed a militant resistance to corporate push backs throughout the decade, despite losing many battles. As they had over the previous years, the labor community adapted their tactics, sought new political allies, and maintained a strong commitment to a broad view of who belonged in the labor community and how they should fight for economic and social justice. This chapter details these events to illustrate the ways in which Racine's workers continued to think of themselves as members of an active, engaged labor movement that could garner its resources and fight back. By the end of the decade, the labor community held on to the hope of a resurgence of labor power and celebrated key local political victories that seemed to make such hopes realistic.

Political Landscape of Deindustrialization

Activists in Racine's labor community faced overwhelming economic and political challenges but rallied in an effort to offset their weakened position in bargaining with managers. When a local Burger King franchise hired a nonunion contractor from outside the county to build a new restaurant in Racine, a delegation of skilled trade workers attempted to convince the contractor to use local union labor instead. When negotiations failed, members of Ironworkers Local 8 started picketing the construction site. The rest of the labor community provided needed support. Teamsters from Local 43 refused to drive concrete trucks across the informational picket line. *Racine Labor*'s cartoonist Gary Huck drew a series of cartoons condemning Burger King. One such cartoon showed a man wearing a hard hat walking with a woman carrying a picket sign that read, "Unions are 'Our Way,'" in a play on the company's popular advertising campaign.[3]

In response to the picketing, the franchise and contractor appealed for and received an injunction against the protestors. This injunction points to one of the ways in which Taft-Hartley weakened workers' ability to support each other during conflicts. The law made secondary boycotts illegal, meaning workers could not boycott another company involved in a labor dispute.[4] This opened the door for companies to file suits against unions for supporting other workers outside their individual work sites. Failing to persuade the local franchise, area unions voted to boycott all Burger Kings in Racine and Kenosha Counties to protect union jobs. As the open letter from the Racine County Building and Construction Trades Council explained, "the only way to persuade Burger King to stop insulting the union members in Wisconsin is to refrain from patronizing Burger King." The public pressure finally paid off when Burger King corporate management stepped in and required franchise owners in the area to use union labor where available. And the boycott ended after a construction site broke ground just north of Racine and the contractor hired union workers.[5] Economic conditions demanded that workers insist on the higher wages and protections offered by union jobs. This Burger King incident shows how the Racine labor community continued to be able to rally its forces. They believed that all workers belong in the labor community, and they effectively adapted to changing circumstances.

Although unemployment was high and management had a clear advantage in contract negotiations, workers at Young Radiator decided to go on strike on 1 July 1981 after they were unable to come to terms with the company. Local 37 represented 290 active employees and 170 laid-off members who manufactured heat exchangers for industrial equipment and heavy-duty radiators. The union previously accepted a wage cut in exchange for the promise to keep jobs in Racine during the 1972 contract negotiations. Young Radiator followed through by opening a newly built facility in 1975, but then started moving production to other plants in Iowa and Illinois soon after. The members of UAW Local 37 wanted a severance pay clause in their contract to protect workers who lost their jobs as the company moved production to a nonunion plant in Iowa. However, management would not negotiate on any terms until the union's bargaining committee agreed to a new incentive pay plan that workers felt significantly cut their wages.[6]

Union members felt they had to strike because accepting wage concessions had not brought them any job security. After two months of picketing, the company finally agreed to negotiate on all the terms that employees hoped to bring to the bargaining table. The strike lasted thirteen weeks and finally ended when workers ratified the new three-year agreement without the job security provision, but with changes to the company's incentive plan that reduced the lost wages to two dollars an hour unless productivity increased. Although Local 37 President Richard "Red" Johnson called the new contract "one of the best" in the last few years because of the wage increases for non-incentive workers, new fringe benefits, and cost-of-living increases, the inability to secure job security was a big blow to the union. Workers ratified the new agreement because they felt the changes to the incentive pay plan would help boost productivity, yet they were still at the mercy of the company's decision to move production at will. Striking workers received letters from the company demanding acceptance of the incentive plan along with threats to move all production to Iowa, which pressured acceptance of the contract.[7] While the strike did not pay off as well as the workers hoped, they felt strongly enough to stay on the picket lines for three months and showed a willingness to fight even with the weakened union position. This continual push to get all they could on behalf of all workers is what kept the community vibrant in hard times.

As well-paid union jobs continued to disappear, Black and Latine workers sought entry into better-paying public service jobs and joined forces with labor activists to address hiring discrimination that kept marginalized workers out of all but the lowest paid positions. Growing numbers of Black and Latine workers in the city and their demands for equal access to jobs and services had continued to rise since the late 1960s. The work of Corinne Reid-Owens, Keith Mack, and Julian Thomas to get Black teachers and school administrators hired in Racine County and throughout city and county government offices did lead to a few new hires in the school system. All three held leadership positions in the Racine NAACP and other social justice organizations in the city. Thomas worked his way up at Case, eventually becoming director of their minority relations department, served on the mayor's human rights council, and participated in state-level efforts to enforce equal opportunity hiring practices. Mack and Reid-Owens worked in the Racine United School system and struggled to make sure Racine's poorest students received a quality education. Owens also sat on the local vocational education board.[8]

As the Black and Brown workforce continued to grow in Racine and across the state, union leaders sought to better incorporate nonwhite workers into union activities. In 1979 members of the Wisconsin Education Association formed the Ad Hoc Minority Involvement Committee (MIC) to increase engagement in local teacher unions and in area professional associations. Robert Ware, a Black teacher at Horlick High School, served as the first chair of MIC and helped organize a statewide meeting in Racine, in February 1981. Representatives from the Racine Education Association (REA) Black Caucus and others around the state met to participate in leadership building, planning sessions, and in-depth workshops on collective bargaining and current contract bargaining agreements. The

Racine Black Caucus had been active for a few years after organizing to improve the educational experiences of the working-class students in the county. Through dances at the Racine Labor Center, the group raised funds for a scholarship in 1980 for a graduating senior to attend Yale University.[9] Union and community involvement played a large role in gaining members' active participation and sustaining public goodwill.

Black and other nonwhite workers continued to demand access to jobs and fair treatment in those jobs. The American Civil Liberties Union of Racine and Kenosha hosted a forum on racial and sexual discrimination in June 1981 at the Unitarian Church. These organizations had long histories of working with labor and civil rights activists to address social and economic issues in the area.[10] Organized around the firing of a Black police officer, Sam Jones, the forum extended to a general discussion of discrimination in the city and possible solutions. Speakers highlighted the extremely low level of Black and Latine employment at the city and county levels, segregation of Black and Latine neighborhoods and uneven municipal services to those areas, problems in the school system concerning bilingual learning opportunities, and unequal treatment in the criminal justice system. While focused on these existing problems, speakers also provided information on services and programs to assist with discrimination cases, hiring programs, and several union and community activists focused on building coalitions to improve both access to jobs and better education for children in the community.[11] To emphasize the low level of employment and promotion of marginalized workers in city jobs, sanitation worker Thomas Love filed a class action lawsuit in federal court against the city for failure to hire and promote these workers under the same procedure as white applicants. As late as 1981, no Black or Latine workers held supervisory positions in city employment. The lack of opportunity for nonwhite workers to escape declining employment sectors and secure more stable positions led to their higher unemployment levels and the economic and social problems this entailed.

UAW Local 553 at Racine Steel Castings (formerly Bell City Malleable) had the highest numbers of Black and Latine workers in the city and continued the union's long history of improving all aspects of people's lives in Racine, total person unionism. The community services division of Local 553 often led the effort in demanding equal services from community agencies for union members and residents. As layoffs and other economic setbacks took its toll on the city, Local 553 members pushed for the A-Center—a social services agency serving alcoholics in the community—to hire Black counselors. Black workers went to their Local 553 stewards to say that they could not relate to the counselors and would not continue to seek treatment. Administrators at the A-Center claimed that there were no Black applicants for the social worker positions and that race was not a factor in providing services. However, after continual pressure by the union and community allies, the center hired two Black and one Latine counselor in August 1981.[12] Labor activists recognized the need to provide services to workers beyond the shop floor and to improve the quality of life for all in Racine. Solving the issues of racial justice, equality, and discrimination, went a long way to strengthening rank-and-file commitment to working-class solidarity as jobs became even scarcer and those just getting a foothold started to lose ground in their struggles for economic security. Worker activists understood that they needed to continue to look beyond the shop floor and address community concerns.

The Fight against Deindustrialization

Workers' determination to fight against the odds to save their jobs and some sense of economic stability for the city is best exemplified in the long battle to keep Massey-Ferguson operating in Racine. The story of how the members of Local 244, with the support and encouragement of the labor community and their political allies, fought to keep the Massey-Ferguson warehouse in Racine reflects a broader pattern of militant resistance to plant closings in the 1980s. Massey-Ferguson had stopped production of tractors in the city in the late 1950s and, by the 1980s, the only operation in Racine was the replacement parts warehouse where 330 workers did some repair and maintenance work and another sixty-eight worked in clerical positions. UAW Local 244 signed a new three-year agreement with the company in March 1980 that improved wages and started a series of step increases to bring workers' pay rates up to the level of other plants in the United States. At the same time, over sixty workers in Racine had been laid off since March, and in April, the company announced it was laying off an additional 1500 workers in Detroit and Des Moines the following month. The Canada-based chain was facing severe financial difficulties and appealed to workers in both countries and the Canadian government for assistance to continue operating and reduce its debt burden. By June, the Racine replacement parts warehouse employed 375 members of Local 244. In November, the union agreed to open the contract and accept economic concessions. Local President Ron Thomas explained that the workers were taking a gamble to see if it would save the company from complete collapse. The company agreed to continue business in the United States, to include management-level employees in any proposed layoff plans, and workers agreed to defer the 3 percent annual wage increases they previously negotiated in the contract earlier that year.[13]

Despite the new agreement, the company laid off over one hundred unionized workers the following year, while keeping its entire supervisory staff. Relations continued to deteriorate between the company and the union as layoffs disproportionately impacted the union members, while nonunion workers retained their jobs at the warehouse. Short notice of layoffs also angered union members. Despite their frustrations, workers again agreed to wage concessions in April 1982. The new agreement also took away one week of vacation and froze pension levels. When workers heard later that year that the company was negotiating with business leaders in Des Moines, Iowa, to move the warehouse facilities from Racine, they felt betrayed. Although the company promised they had no immediate plans to move, workers in Racine remembered that when plants in Des Moines and Detroit closed, workers received less than a week's notice. The union vowed to fight against Massey-Ferguson moving the Racine facility and disregarded the company's reassurances. Despite no news of a move, workers organized a rally in December to start generating support for a campaign to keep the 400 jobs at the Racine Warehouse.[14] When workers at Massey-Ferguson realized that agreeing to wage cuts and contract concessions did not provide them with any reasonable amount of job security, they voted to reject contract concessions in the August 1983 contract talks. Faced with massive layoffs, workers decided to stop negotiating even as the company was packing up to move operations from Racine to Des Moines.[15]

Across the country, hundreds of thousands of workers in the steel and auto industries lost their jobs due to plant closings from the late 1970s to the early 1980s. Workers and their unions formed coalitions with community groups, appealed to companies to honor their perceived commitments to local areas, sought legal injunctions, tried to take over production at individual plants, and, in general, did everything they could to save their communities. Industrial communities responded to deindustrialization in ways determined by local labor movement strength, community social and cultural heritage, and political involvement. For example, in Connecticut, unions, community activists, organizers, and religious leaders formed the Naugatuck Valley Project to combine forces in the region to fight against plant closings, build democratic economic institutions to support area communities, and to exert more power over local businesses. In Youngstown, Ohio's steel industry activists argued that companies had a responsibility to the community, meaning that decisions to close the plants were not private corporate managers' alone, but because of the long history of workers and governments supporting the steel plants, managers had no right to arbitrarily shut down plants. Workers launched a legal battle to wrest control of a local steel plant and keep it from closing. While the effort proved only partially successful for a short time, it did empower workers across industrial North America to fight plant closings more vigorously.[16]

In Racine, activists did not establish new community coalitions because the local labor community was already intricately tied to other social justice organizations. It was never one union against one company fighting plant closings. Workers, their political allies, and other social justice organizations rallied together to stem the tide of closings. Members of Local 244 knew they had the support of the community when they decided to fight the warehouse move.

While the tactics are similar, collective identity and memory often shape community responses to the threat or reality of plant closings.[17] In Racine, workers thought of themselves as members of an active, engaged labor movement that could garner its resources and fight back. By the early 1980s, workers were angry and uncertain but determined. Mitch Blada, a laid-off machinist from Case, called for the whole labor movement to combine resources to help transform the economy. "If we got together the heads of the UAW, the Teamsters, the AFL-CIO, we could shut it all down ... It would have to be a complete banding together to make it work, but something needs to be done."[18] An older worker at Massey-Ferguson who had gone through two plant closings before moving to his warehouse job decided that the best thing for the union to do was fight vigorously against the proposed warehouse move. He said, "I didn't fight at the two other plants where I worked when they closed down, but I'm going to fight like hell this time."[19] Workers recognized the need to combine the strength of the whole labor movement and their allies to fight the battle against capital flight. Local 244 members repeatedly refused to accept any concessions, and the company announced in November 1983 that it was moving most of the warehousing facilities to Memphis, Tennessee. In a statement published in the *Racine Journal Times*, General Manager James Wimpress said the company was leaving because workers refused to give $1 million in concessions to retool the Racine factory.[20] While some workers thought another round of concessions would convince management to leave at least some jobs for the remaining 170 employees, most union members voted to stop negotiating on concessions. They did successfully bargain to do the labor of dismantling the machinery for shipment to Memphis after the company initially made plans to hire outside contractors, but this temporary assignment added insult to injury.

As workers and labor activists sought ways to reduce the impact of closings like the Massey-Ferguson case, they continued to push for job security at other job sites, participate in community-sustaining activities, and made connections with those outside the labor community to address issues of social and economic security in Racine and beyond. The workers at Jacobsen Manufacturing, represented by UAW Local 556, voted 294 to 54 to reject the company's "final offer" and went on strike on Tuesday, 3 May 1983 because they were concerned with the lack of job protection in the current contract. As Local 556 President Ed Buhler told members at a meeting that morning at the Racine Labor Center, "If they're going to take our jobs, let them try to take them past us on the picket line, instead of asking us to help them load the trucks with our jobs."[21] The company's proposal granted them the right to shift production of certain lawn tractors to North Carolina at the company's discretion.

Along with the transfer of jobs, management also sought to circumvent the existing seniority system in job transfers. Jacobsen management hoped to persuade workers to accept the contract with a very lucrative financial pay package. However, workers felt that the company asked them to give up more rights than they felt justified in doing; instead they chose to go on strike and push the issue. Buhler explained, "They've seen what's happening in the entire community—Massey-Ferguson, McGraw-Edison, and lots of others"—referring to the shutdowns and threatened moves by manufacturing firms out of the city. The strike lasted one week, and Local 556 successfully bargained to a set limit of job transfers to North Carolina of twenty-two positions and kept the existing seniority system. Union members voted 304 to 34 to accept the new agreement. Buhler was optimistic about the successful strike and contract negotiations and looked at the win at Jacobsen as the start of a promising trend in Racine.[22] Workers recognized their weakened bargaining position yet continued to fight for every step forward they could achieve.

Union activists also fought against political assaults on workers' rights in the community. In June 1984, the US INS started a series of raids at Racine Steel Castings. Often at the behest of companies, the INS would come into workplaces, round up Latine workers, and detain them until they could provide documentation of their right to work in the United States. The INS would also ask for employee records from companies and pick up workers whose documentation seemed suspect. Over the next several months, INS agents arrested nineteen Racine Steel Castings workers and charged them with being in the country without proper documentation. Of the nineteen arrested, eighteen were born in Mexico and one in Jamaica. UAW Local 553 President Dick Fought stood behind the workers who all

138   CHAPTER 6

had over five years of seniority at the foundry. He argued that the raids were politically motivated to induce resentment of immigrant workers at a time of high unemployment and to turn the attention away from the impact of the Reagan administration's role in the country's economic crisis. The INS had completed its investigation into employment at Racine Steel Castings two years earlier but waited until the summer before elections to initiate the raids.

Immigration and immigration reform were hotly debated in the 1980s, fueled in part by the continuing economic instability in the United States, the rise of cultural conservatism, and nationalist rhetoric that intensified with Reagan's Cold War policies and his 1984 reelection campaign. Although many undocumented workers filled an economic need as more and more jobs became deskilled and paid lower wages, political and popular rhetoric by legislators, journalists, and public protestors against immigration and integration in the 1980s and 1990s declared that there was an increasing "Mexican menace."[23] This menace painted Latine immigrants as burdens on US society, unwilling and unable to integrate into American society. Politicians and popular culture lamented the inability of the nation to control its borders and prevent penetration by "undesirable illegal aliens."[24] At the same time, political conservatives attacked affirmative action programs designed to aid previously-excluded workers or offer equal opportunities by promoting the idea of "reverse discrimination."[25] The idea that undocumented workers stole jobs that native workers needed led to a national debate around removing and preventing undocumented immigrants from finding employment in the United States. This narrative was countered by the continuing need for workers to fill the lowest paid positions in industrial, service, and domestic industries. Employers continued to hire undocumented workers and often recruited undocumented workers in a continuing strategy of reducing wages and fomenting dissent within their workforce. Despite the rhetoric around nonwhite workers stealing jobs and opportunities for the more deserving white workers to achieve the economic and social benefits of moving into the middle class, Black and Latine workers suffered increased economic hardship during the 1980s and 1990s. Yet, employers and policymakers used the immigration debate to intensify the attack on undocumented workers through raids and other INS initiatives. This scenario played out repeatedly in the workplaces between Chicago, Racine, and Milwaukee during the mid-1980s and into the 1990s.[26]

As in other Midwestern communities like St. Paul and Chicago, in Racine, union and Latine community activists worked together to provide legal aid for the detained workers at Racine Steel Castings. The local

Catholic parish raised funds to provide bond for one worker being held in Chicago, and the community came together to help workers provide the needed paperwork to stay in the country. Union president Dick Fought also refused to endorse the firing of the nineteen workers. The union successfully argued that Racine Steel Castings could not fire the workers until they were actually deported and got seventeen of the nineteen union members reinstated to work. Fought also challenged the notion that undocumented workers were stealing jobs from the Racine community. As he pointed out, the foundry work at Racine Steel Castings was hot and dirty, and native-born workers who could afford to do so shunned those jobs, which is why so many Black and Latine workers filled the slots in the postwar period and into the 1980s. Fought also argued that the current legislation going through Congress would have granted all workers in question amnesty based on their years in the country. The Immigration Reform and Control Act finally passed in 1986, granting amnesty to 2.7 million undocumented immigrants.[27] The INS continued to target Racine Steel Castings workers, but the union stood behind all its members and actively fought to save their jobs. This case demonstrates the multiple ways in which labor activists in the city sought to build connections with all workers, even in hard political times, to improve the sense of class solidarity that would strengthen their efforts in the long run.

Even as unions lost power on the shop floor, workers throughout the area kept seeking to organize and work within labor organizations to mitigate the economic uncertainty of the times. As plants laid off workers or closed altogether, other local businesses felt the impact. Grocery stores in Racine closed locations because of declining population during the late 1970s and into the 1980s. Similar events occurred across the Midwestern industrial sector. In Gary, Indiana, more than one-third of all retail stores closed as 20,000 steelworkers lost their jobs.[28]

Sustaining Labor Politics with Organizing and Community Engagement

At the same time, workers in the retail industry continued to unionize and sign labor agreements with grocery stores. When a local franchise of Sentry Foods closed, it was several months before a new location opened. The store only rehired a few of the old employees, but the new workers decided to organize with the United Food and Commercial Workers. The workers at Randall's Country Market, located down the street from Sentry, ratified their first agreement and received substantial wage increases, which brought them up to line with other unionized grocery store workers in the city. Workers also received holiday and vacation pay and a slight wage increase for any hours worked on Sundays. Because of the poor economic climate, Piggly Wiggly's unionized workers agreed to defer their upcoming pay raises to keep stores from closing in Racine and Kenosha. Paul Whiteside, Jr., business representative for UFCW Local 1444, represented the grocery store workers in bargaining negotiations and oversaw the successful union election through WERC for the Sentry workers. The Retail Clerk locals and Meatcutter locals in Racine and Kenosha merged into the Milwaukee Local 1444 to increase their organizing capabilities and negotiating power.[29] Whiteside followed the path of his father, a longtime labor and political activist in Kenosha, as a labor organizer in the region. The continuity of activists and their families that carried over from generation to generation in Racine and surrounding areas helped sustain the sense of labor solidarity and the history of both cities as union towns.

This continuity is also illustrated by the ways the Racine labor community continued to help workers who were falling through ever-increasing gaps in the economic system. During the decade, activists and the social justice and charity organizations that they worked with and within provided laid-off and underemployed workers in the city with the means to provide for themselves and their families as they had since the postwar period.[30] Al Hartog, a member of Local 180 at Case, and other members of the Labor Advisory Board to the United Way, organized a Labor Run to kick off the 1980 campaign drive. Hartog explained, "It will be a demonstration of solidarity and commitment to our community."[31] Union members had made the United Way yearly fund drive an integral part of the labor community's activities since they had successfully fought for the creation of the Labor Advisory Board in the 1960s. In the weekly "United Organized Labor Activities" column in *Racine Labor*, representatives advertised United Way organizations, suggested services for workers, and kept the labor community informed of events and activities throughout the decades. Workers joined forces with Project Racine and Project Kenosha and brought unions together from both cities for a community party and dance to raise funds and supplies for area food banks. This event in March 1983 raised over $5,000 for organizations in the area. Postal workers set up collections during the organizing drive leading up to the party and delivered twenty boxes of food from the National Association of Letter Carriers local.[32] With the unemployment rate almost to the double digits in Racine and Kenosha, union members recognized that most families could use additional help and that service providers were straining to meet current needs. They also publicized the role of the labor community in addressing community needs. This kept the movement relevant even with declining power.

Racine's labor activists recognized the need to push back against the existing national political climate to help improve local economic and social conditions. In 1981, the national AFL-CIO organized "Solidarity Day" as a march and rally to protest President Ronald Reagan's attacks on the social and economic programs of the 1960s. Reagan ran his 1980 presidential campaign on a combination of nostalgia for an idealized vision of postwar America—flush from government largesse—and the role of liberals' overindulgence of radical demands on the government as the destruction of true freedom. Many of Reagan's domestic policy makers and their supporters looked at his 1980 victory as the perfect opportunity to roll back progressive social and economic policies associated with postwar liberal efforts to expand economic and social citizenship rights.[33] But labor activists and their allies were determined to push against Reagan's promised spending cuts for social programs and economic policies that would limit growth for the poorest Americans. The rally included a broad section of those fighting for social justice, including union members, environmentalists, civil rights activists, and feminists, led by AFL-CIO President Lane Kirkland in his efforts to attack Reagan's overtures to white rank-and-file workers. Organizers also took the opportunity to show their support and solidarity with the striking PATCO workers to counter Reagan's insistence that public workers had no right to strike. About thirty-five workers from Racine took a chartered bus to Washington, DC. Seven local NAACP members rented a van, and some families drove down together. Bruce Burman, a UW-Parkside employee, thought it was an important event for the labor movement. He explained, "It brought labor factions together, ethnic groups, Blacks, whites, Chicano, and the elderly . . . It was a tiring bus ride, 40 hours, but it was worth the inconvenience. If they want to do it again next weekend, I'd do it."[34]

Burman's statements illustrate the continuing saliency of building broad-based coalitions centered on working-class issues to effect change in US society despite the notion that identity politics delegitimized class-based identity formation. Cookie DeBruin, a Local 556 member at Jacobsen who drove down with her husband and children, felt that Reagan did not care or respond to the events but that it was good for people to push back against his policies. Scott Zierten, a Local 180 member at Case, felt inspired that the rally brought out around 250,000 people, and he wanted to organize a similar rally in Madison to protest unemployment cuts in the state.[35] Despite declining political power, workers evidently saw the need to combine forces and participate in public debate.

142   CHAPTER 6

Locally, activists sought to create or join coalitions that would help provide some level of economic security for the city, region, and state. In 1981, the Racine County AFL-CIO voted to join the Citizen/Labor Energy Coalition. This statewide group of labor, community, and senior citizen groups hoped to lobby the state to impose higher taxes on oil companies operating in Wisconsin. When longtime labor activist Tony Valeo was elected to the Citizens Utility Board's (CUB) leadership, he went around to local union meetings explaining the organization's aim to represent the interests of utility consumers in the area and to recruit new members. CUB was enacted into state law in 1979 to serve as a counterweight to the utility lobby and better represent citizens within the Wisconsin Public Service Commission.

Organizations like CUB came out of the consumer movement of the 1970s and 1980s most often associated with Ralph Nader's activism and supporters. In Wisconsin, Senators Gaylord Nelson and William Proxmire also promoted consumer action groups to combat corporate power and to protect natural resources in the state. CUB was legislated to provide consumer education and lobbying at all levels of Wisconsin government. The legislation did not provide any funding; instead funds came entirely by donations and any citizen over eighteen could become a member with a three-dollar membership contribution. While funding came from CUB, the law also stipulated that Wisconsin public utility providers had to send CUB's informational mailings with billing notices to customers.[36] One of CUB's first actions was to fight a proposed $141 million rate increase by Wisconsin Electric, the state's largest utility company that served customers in Milwaukee, Racine, Kenosha, and surrounding areas. The proposed change would raise residential rates by 23 percent.[37] CUB lobbyists and their allies successfully reduced the proposed rate increases and put the greater burden for the increase on large corporations instead of small business and residential customers.[38]

Tony Valeo's involvement in CUB is illustrative of the ways in which Racine's labor activists embodied total-person unionism and extended their civic activism beyond the labor movement. Labor activists like Valeo also joined forces with community groups and area politicians to provide aid and support to laid-off workers in Racine. Organizers formed a Citizen-Labor Coalition for Jobs to lobby for and arrange congressional hearings on plant closings and joblessness in the area to be led by Congressman Les Aspin (D-Wisconsin) and Congressman Richard Gephardt (D-Missouri). The Citizen-Labor Coalition was made up of members of the Racine AFL-CIO Council, the UAW political action committee, Machinists unions, and the United Electrical workers union locals. They were joined by nuns from the Dominican Sisters of the Siena Center and members of the Racine Urban League. The group publicized the hearings to put plant closings and the resultant job loss on the national political agenda. They hoped to draw participants for the local hearings mainly from Racine and Kenosha but also Milwaukee and Janesville.[39]

Labor activists continued to reach out to their allies in public office, despite the resistance of the Reagan administration. Congressman Aspin supported legislation at the national level to limit plant closings and to extend unemployment compensation benefits for the long-term unemployed during the early 1980s. Local labor leaders also sought to rally workers together for Labor Day events and planned a march and rally with Democratic candidates for governor and other local offices to protest joblessness and gather momentum for upcoming elections to change the political landscape at the state and local level.[40] Labor activists continued to demand answers and action from political leaders and actively sought to push the needs of working people to the forefront of political debate. While they recognized the landscape had changed, they did not abandon their efforts to keep working-class issues as part of the public debate and to continue to press for full economic citizenship for all.

Racine labor activists worked hard to provide relief for laid-off and underemployed workers through job creation and training programs. Local 180 members laid off from Case made up a large contingent of the rising ranks of the unemployed. Union leaders sought to alleviate some of the layoffs through contract negotiations but also looked outside of the collective bargaining system. Union leaders collaborated with the local technical school, Gateway Technical Institute, and the Racine Job Service office and won a $627,000 grant to train laid-off workers from Case and help them find employment that offered at least 75 percent of their former pay rate. The program, called RESTORE, also provided education on community service programs, classes on budgeting, and job search clubs to alleviate the sense of isolation laid-off workers experienced. Paul Smedegaard, a laid-off Local 180 steward at Case, served as coordinator, in a role he found similar to his steward duties. He steered workers toward the agencies and training that would serve each individual best. Instituted in August 1984, the funds for the program ran out in June 1986, but the program did provide jobs averaging $11.12 an hour for many workers on permanent layoff at Case.[41]

William Jenkins served as manager for a similar program called REC Industries and provided training and guidance to young, unemployed men seeking jobs.[42] Across the country, unions extended their efforts to find new jobs for displaced workers. The AFL-CIO participated in lobbying for federal and state-level funding to aid in employee training and job assistance, as they had since the 1960s. There was a concerted effort to provide job training and employment counseling, like Jenkins did with REC. For example, when American Motors Corporation shut down its Kenosha plant, UAW Local 72 joined forces with the Job Development Training Corporation to provide retraining and job assistance services led by union leaders.[43]

The tide seemed to turn for Local 180 during the 1987 contract negotiations. While the local contract eliminated some of the job security protections previously negotiated, the contract representing all the unionized Case plants in the nation granted 100 percent job security for all workers not currently on permanent layoff. After months of secret negotiations and two called strikes, union leaders announced what they hailed as a "historic pact" at Case IH (the name changed after Tenneco purchased the farm tractor division of International Harvester). The new agreement promised forty-hour work weeks for the 1250 current workers at Racine plants, instituted a guaranteed employment level at the current rate, and stipulated that extra work requirements would be met by recalling laid-off workers before mandatory overtime.[44]

On the surface, the new contract seemed promising. However, the negotiations forced a change in seniority rules that proved detrimental to skilled trade workers. In fact, skilled trade workers voted overwhelmingly to reject the contract, but were eventually forced to accept the agreement because they were not the majority of union members eligible to vote. The Racine bargaining team had voted to keep the existing contract language but was overruled by other members in the Case chain bargaining units less concerned about skilled workers' protections. As skilled workers predicted, within a year their numbers had been reduced by twenty-three with threats of more layoffs as Case IH management started implementing a contracting-out program to circumvent the labor agreement.[45] Management still refused to engage in good-faith bargaining and held even greater power over workers in the plants.

Recognizing the loss of better paid jobs in industrial settings, activists in Racine intensified their efforts to organize in low-wage industries and to appeal to workers across sectors to actively participate in class-based community events. This is yet another example of how the Racine labor community experiences differ from a tale of labor's decline in this period. High unemployment and unsuccessful strikes to save plants from closing did not deter new organizing campaigns, even at workplaces with recalcitrant management teams who fought every effort to gain union recognition. The Zayre Department Stores had resisted unionization efforts by the UFCW for years. Finally, in the fall of 1983, workers at the two

Racine stores voted to join UFCW in an NLRB election, but the company appealed the election. After the regional NLRB ruled the election valid, the store appealed to the national NLRB. Although, still awaiting a ruling on the vote, members of the Racine labor community came together in January 1984 to have a unity party recognizing the Zayre workers' efforts and welcoming them into the larger labor community.

Members of several different labor bodies organized the party and workers from over forty different union locals attended the event at the Racine Labor Center. With over 350 people in attendance, activists praised the Zayre workers for their persistence and offered continued support as they started making plans for their first contract negotiations.[46] This party and others like it during the 1980s shows that labor activists continued to value a commitment to wide ranging ideas of what and who constituted a labor community. They needed all the allies they could find, since unions were indeed losing ground on the shop floor. Organizing in the Reagan years grew increasingly difficult due to a shift at the federal level in support of corporate managers as opposed to helping level the playing field in the capital-labor relationship. This supports evidence Lane Windham found in her examination of union organizing nationwide during this period. While workers continued to organize and vote to join unions, corporate managers took advantage of the political climate to use unfair labor practices and challenge NLRB elections to hinder worker solidarity.[47]

Always aware of the changing landscape, in Racine, worker activists sought to mitigate the loss of shopfloor power with a concerted effort in other arenas. Events like the Zayre unity party, the Labor Day rallies, the Labor Songfest, and United Fund events held throughout the decade served to reinforce the sense of community activists sought to maintain. It kept unions in the public mind beyond strike actions and built interunion and cross-sector solidarity. A similar party was organized for workers at the Westview Nursing Home after they voted overwhelmingly to join SEIU Local 150. After years of battles with management, a change in ownership, and a federal investigation into the practices at the nursing home, workers recommitted to SEIU Local 150 with the aid of Ron Thomas, who took a position as international business representative after leaving Massey-Ferguson.[48] In organizing the party, Thomas explained, "No worker and no union can afford to go it alone any longer ... So we want to bring together the Westview workers and the labor community to unify for the challenges we face, as well as to celebrate."[49]

Other events also focused on bringing the labor community together and strengthening the sense of community. UAW Local 180 President Kelly Sparks helped coordinate a Labor Songfest in 1986. Sparks organized the concert to help support workers laid off from Case and American Motors in Kenosha. Headlined by Pete Seeger, over 1,000 area residents attended the event and raised over $7000 for food banks in Racine and Kenosha.[50] Concert goers gathered on the UW-Parkside campus to see Seeger and other performers including Daryl Holter, Bobby McGee, Larry Penn, and Joe Glazer.[51]

Pete Seeger rose to prominence as one of the most successful singer/songwriters who came of age in the postwar period and incorporated traditional folk songs and spirituals into what came to be known as freedom music or protest music. Blacklisted during the McCarthy period, Pete Seeger gained a mass following by grafting leftist political messages onto traditional folk songs. He used his music to encourage social change, support civil rights and labor, and to protest against the Vietnam War.[52] His broad appeal among progressive activists and others led to the large crowd participating in the Labor Songfest.

Following their 1987 contract negotiations, Kelly Sparks and UAW Local 180 members organized a food drive and "solidarity meal" for the striking UFCW Local P-40 members at the Patrick Cudahy meatpacking plant. Workers had been on strike since January because they refused to accept another round of wage cuts after accepting concessions in the 1982 and 1984 negotiations. As Local 180 member Gilbert Delgado explained, "We know how it is to be out on strike . . . We also want to show that Local 180 is again involved in the community, and to get people feeling good about being members of Local 180."[53] Battling layoffs and fighting for better contracts had taken a toll on the largest union in the city, but they still held a commitment to being a leader in the labor community as far as community outreach.

The Cudahy strike, which culminated a series of battles at the company over the decade, highlighted the impact of corporate restructuring, government deregulation, and increased management attacks on labor and working conditions in the United States by the end of the twentieth century. In the meatpacking industry, corporate consolidation and technological advancements allowed management to combine and eliminate higher skilled positions such as meat cutters and butchers. Deregulation at the federal level led to meatpacking becoming one of the most hazardous industries in the country by the 1990s. Management targeted unions to reduce resistance to production speedups and reduced wages and went on a concerted attack against the UFCW in the early 1980s by gutting membership and demanding wage and benefit concessions. Average wages in the industry declined from eleven dollars an hour in the late 1970s to about eight dollars an hour by 1982.[54]

The worsening conditions and economic uncertainty pushed out those workers with the means to find other employment, further weakening unions. Meatpacking plants like Hormel, IDP, and Cudahy started relying on an increasingly nonwhite (mostly Mexican), vulnerable workforce. Workers did fight back, but their decreased power and lack of government support offered little hope for victory. For example, in 1982, 1984, and 1985, workers at a Hormel plant in Austin, Minnesota, went on strike and the governor sent the National Guard to protect strikebreakers against the union. Workers in Austin lost their strike, and many lost their homes, prompting them to relocate.[55]

Corporate efforts weakened but did not end worker militancy and the fight by UFCW and their labor movement allies. In 1984 in Cudahy, Wisconsin (just outside Milwaukee) Local P-40 members refused wage and benefit cuts amounting to four and a half dollars an hour. The company threatened to close and move the plant that had existed in the city since the early twentieth century. However, workers blocked the sale of the company and forced continued negotiations. By the end of the year, workers accepted wage cuts of nearly two dollars an hour and reduced benefits but saved the plant. Cudahy management continued its efforts to bust the union, but Local P-40 and the surrounding labor communities kept fighting. The ongoing labor dispute would cause strikes for the next three years to maintain some sort of economic and workplace protections for the meatpackers.[56] Even in a pronounced weakened state and representing a high number of immigrant workers, UFCW P-40 continued to fight. They did this with the help of their neighbors, the Racine labor community. As the solidarity meal Local 180 prepared highlights, Racine worker activists kept a broad view of the labor community. They supported workers in the greater Milwaukee area, even while dealing with job loss, corporate restructuring, and concession bargaining in Racine.

Labor activists used local history to reinforce a sense of solidarity during the late 1980s as they had since after World War II. The Wisconsin Labor History Society's annual meeting was held in Racine on 10 May 1986. The theme for the year was to focus on the history of industrial unions in the state. Speakers included Charles Heymanns, who was president of the union at Kohler Industries in 1934 and helped lead their fight for union recognition; Victor Cooks, one of the founding members of what would become Local 180; and William Jenkins in his leadership role at Belle City Malleable (Racine Steel Castings) and as the first Black president of the city's labor council. The speakers talked about the history of organizing early AFL and CIO unions and the importance of educating and politicizing rank-and-file workers. Cooks and Jenkins both spoke to the need

148   CHAPTER 6

to continue that trend, urged union leaders to teach workers about the history of unions, and to do more than just have them sign union cards in order to recreate the militancy of the postwar years. Their lessons seemed even more important as only 100 people turned out to the Racine Labor Center to attend the conference.[57] Despite the low attendance, the legacy of Jenkins and the others were represented by Kelly Sparks, Ron Thomas, Paul Whiteside Jr., and many other union activists in the 1980s.

Organizing in the New Political Climate

At the same time, a new sense of militancy fueled activities at the end of the decade. The fight in the city to keep Harris Metals in town after a threatened move to Tennessee, the rallying around the workers at the Westview Nursing Home, the activities by SEIU Local 150 members at St. Luke's Hospital, and other campaigns fueled this sense of labor's resurgence. Younger union activists with a "rebellious attitude" also held the reins at several locals and pushed for greater resistance from the whole labor community as seen in the actions and language of Ron Thomas, Mike Webster, and Albert Herron, who motivated union members and residents in Racine to come together and stand strong against corporate attacks on their community.

A history of Local 150 workers at St. Luke's Hospital is illustrative. Local activists continued to work toward better wages and working conditions after the 1976 strike. Following three months of negotiation, the contract with St. Luke's for 1982–1985 provided for wage increases, although chief steward Brenda Feick admitted, "We accepted less than what we wanted, and the hospital kept the wage issue open for the third year." At this time, Local 150 represented 242 workers at St. Luke's Hospital.[58]

Labor activists in Local 150, like others in the community, also sought to improve conditions for those outside of their local labor movement. In January 1985, SEIU Local 150 participated in a Milwaukee fundraiser to send food aid to the people of Ethiopia. They joined forces with five community organizations, and Local 150 members contributed over $1,000 to the fund, despite their low wages.[59] In an effort to remain involved in political activities, new president Dan Iverson and other officials voted to join a statewide organization, the Wisconsin Action Coalition (WAC), that collectively challenged issues at the state and federal level related to tax, utility, and job issues. WAC engaged in voter registration drives in 1984, pushed for the full-employment campaign, and successfully fought against phone and utility rate increases.[60] In his report to the international union, Iverson detailed an ambitious program to improve internal organizing and political action for Local 150 members.[61] In 1985 Racine labor unions established a Labor Roundtable to discuss shared concerns affecting the labor movement. In the second meeting, Local 150 Chief Steward Brenda Feick and Business Representative Steve Cupery reported on the union's standing. They acknowledged a concerted effort to develop a "strong progressive orientation" to improve the image problems associated with the local's handling of the 1976 strike at St. Luke's.[62]

The change in the atmosphere between Local 150's Milwaukee leadership and the Racine labor community can be seen in the increased coverage of contract negotiations by *Racine Labor*. As negotiations began, the bargaining unit stated its desire to improve contract language related to job security, health insurance premiums, pension plans, grievance procedures, and health and safety language. The committee also expected to raise salaries to reflect the decline in real wages due to inflation. Members at St. Luke's received questionnaires so they could voice their concerns as the bargaining committee planned negotiations. Membership had fallen from 250 in 1976 to 186 by April 1985, mostly because of layoffs at the hospital. The bargaining committee expressed the desire to capitalize on St. Luke's economic situation, which was better than other hospitals in the area.[63]

The activities of St. Luke's workers during the 1985 negotiations demonstrated a continued effort to address economic, political, and workplace democracy issues despite the setbacks of failed strikes, economic recession, and union leadership conflict. In an attempt to sway the public, Local 150 pointed to a study by the Greater Milwaukee Area Hospital Council published in the local newspaper, which illustrated that pay rates at St. Luke's ranked near the bottom of the twenty-four hospitals polled. The report indicated that nurse's aides' minimum pay ranked twenty-third and housekeepers ranked twenty-second. Members of Local 150 also launched a campaign urging more patients to patronize St. Luke's Hospital. In an appeal to the labor community, Local 150 Business Representative Steve Cupery acknowledged that as the only union hospital in the two cities of Racine and Kenosha, St. Luke's should be the destination of choice for members of the labor community whenever possible. This would increase the client base, which would benefit both the hospital and the union members. Union officials met with leaders of other locals in order to gain their support.[64] Unlike the boycott of St. Luke's during the 1976 strike, this linking of union and hospital fortunes had the potential of creating a positive image in the Racine community and bringing St. Luke's management closer to an accord. Scholars point to the ways in which Hospital Workers' 1199 captured public support for their workers' cause and mark it as one of the key factors of 1199's success.[65] Positive press also would benefit Local 150's reputation and apply needed pressure to hospital negotiators during the bargaining period.

Members voted on the negotiated labor agreement on 13 May 1985. The bargaining committee members reported that they were able to convince St. Luke's negotiating team to remove proposed wage concessions and to accept instead wage increases of 1.6 percent for the first two years of the contract. Members approved the contract by a vote of 104 to 9. Cupery believed success came from the positive pressure the union was able to generate against St. Luke's board members.[66] As Cupery celebrated the successful contract negotiations, he also advertised Local 150's plans for the future. The bargaining team and leadership members of St. Luke's unit of Local 150 planned a three-part action plan. Elements included preparing for the next wage negotiations, due in two years, by keeping pressure on St. Luke's Hospital management and continuing to advertise that service workers at the hospital were the lowest paid in the area. They implemented "a major publicity program to encourage union members to patronize St. Luke's," and encouraged alliances with community organizations, such as senior citizen groups, to get more labor-friendly people on the hospital's board of directors.[67]

Workers at St. Luke's remained engaged and motivated to continue their struggle for better wages and workplace influence. Leadership changes at the state level, including the introduction of Dan Iverson as president, seemed to settle the disputes between Racine's members and Local 150 leadership. Workers participated in more collaborative activities with other social justice organizations and within the Racine labor community. Therefore, the sudden dismissal, just one month after the new contract went into effect, of the fifteen nursing assistants employed at St. Luke's came as a shock, not only to those employees, but to the entire Racine labor community. As Cupery argued, the newly-signed labor agreement contained language protecting members from job loss. Hospital management argued that because the whole job line had been eliminated, the workers did not qualify for job placement in other lines, as stipulated under the contract. Although Local 150 representatives filed a grievance on behalf of the workers, the fate of the nursing assistants was tied up for years as St. Luke's refused to abide by the arbitrator's rules.[68] This again shows the changed political landscape and increased power of management when labor laws and government enforcement did not support workers' rights.

St. Luke's decision to fire the nursing aides might have had several causes. By the mid-1980s, businesses across the country responded to the shifting political and legal landscape and fought back against gains made by labor unions in earlier periods. Professionalization within the health care industry also may have played a role in St. Luke's decision. As anthropologist Karen Brodkin Sacks discovered in her study of the Duke Medical Center, health care institutions started to rely on professional certification instead of on-the-job training for nurse's aides, lab technicians, and some clerical positions. Sacks also details the ways in which Duke Medical Center management started to relegate more duties to registered nurses, while reducing the number of licensed practical nurses, nurses' aides, and other service workers.[69]

Ron Thomas, though working closely with the Westview Nursing Home workers, also kept involved with the battle to find jobs for the laid-off nursing assistants at St. Luke's. Arbitrators ruled that St. Luke's had to rehire the most senior nursing assistant with twenty-seven years' experience, Ruth Holston, and pay back pay dated to the 1985 firing. The arbitration ruling also stated that all the nursing assistants had recall rights at the hospital. Yet, Thomas and SEIU Local 150 argued that the hospital management, led by a famous antiunion law firm, was purposefully delaying implementation of the ruling. Although the hospital rehired Holston, they never paid the back pay and laid her off again after a month on her new job. Layoffs at the hospital reduced union membership to 165 by January 1987. Local 150 reached out to federal arbitrators to again deal with the recall rights of the nursing assistants and also to help with contract negotiations. The hospital called for a wage freeze and the union called for wage increases for members. The hospital also wanted to eliminate the arbitration and grievance procedures built into the contract. In an effort to keep members informed and involved, Ron Thomas arranged training sessions for members and informational meetings on the current negotiations at the Racine Labor Center. Thomas's experiences as president of the UAW local at Massey-Ferguson, especially during the fight to save the jobs in Racine, opened the door to introduce the type of rank-and-file participation that was more common in Racine's UAW locals than SEIU Local 150 had experienced as a statewide union. The union also voted to start a petition drive among all the workers at St. Luke's to show support for their wage demands and convinced the hospital to agree to monthly "management-labor" meetings to build a better working relationship.[70]

SEIU Local 150 won its third arbitration agreement for the nursing assistants in July 1987. Three years after the original firings, the federal arbitrator again maintained that St. Luke's should have provided the nursing assistants with recall rights and granted them back pay and benefits. As Local 150 President Dan Iverson asserted, "This decision shows that it really pays to have a union behind you." The years without jobs of course took a heavy toll on the nursing assistants as they all suffered varying degrees of financial hardship. It also points to the growing trend of low-wage women workers becoming trapped in a cycle of underpaid jobs and welfare when faced with life's emergencies, a vicious cycle that would continue into the next century.[71] The situation also reiterated the resistance of the hospital to abide by the rules of the NLRB, federal arbitrators, and the agreements they signed with unions. A federal judge upheld the arbitrator's ruling and held St. Luke's accountable for back pay plus 9 percent interest for the fired nursing assistants, charging the hospital with about $80,000 in fees to the workers. After the ruling, Ron Thomas and union leaders pushed to get the wage agreement back on the bargaining table. Finally, in May 1988, Local 150 members ratified a new three-year agreement with the hospital that included the long-sought-for wage increases. In his usual willingness to speak to the press, Thomas praised the bargaining committee and the rank-and-file members for their persistence against St. Luke's hard line, "Without a doubt, they held together under extremely adverse circumstances. Despite all the stress they held firm," he told *Racine Labor* reporters.[72]

The long-fought battle with St. Luke's did not limit the organizing efforts by Local 150 in Racine. Unlike the situation in the 1970s when Racine activists accused the Milwaukee-based local of signing sweetheart deals with management and getting workers to sign union cards and then not offering them real representation, by the 1980s, with new union leadership and local activists who were committed to educating and engaging workers, changes in the organizing efforts of Local 150 helped create the momentum of the last years of the decade. On the national level, SEIU boosted its organizing efforts by purposefully organizing the unorganized, emphasizing the union's commitment to social justice issues in the political arena. SEIU expanded to five divisions including healthcare, public sector, clerical, building services, and industrial and allied services workers.[73]

As Local 150 leaders worked to get wage increases and better working conditions at St. Luke's, they also worked closely with workers at the Westview Health Care Center. Workers worried about job loss when the nursing home was sold and then failed a federal inspection to receive Medicare benefits. Workers saw organizing a union as the best way to deal with the changes that occurred when a new owner, Ted Dremel, a local realtor, took over the home's administration. During the August 1987 organizing drive, over 75 percent of the 180 service and maintenance workers signed union cards seeking representation. Of immediate concern to the workers was what they described as a crisis in staffing. The owners tried to reduce expenses by having fewer aides care for a growing number of patients. Workers also wanted to open negotiations on wages and benefits as the owners had eliminated a profit-sharing plan at the nursing home and cut employees' hours. Workers arranged a march to Dremel's real estate office to encourage him to voluntarily recognize the union and start bargaining instead of waiting for a NLRB election. Dremel did agree to meet with workers and claimed he was not aware of staffing issues and that he would consider voluntary union recognition. Keeping the pressure high, workers also submitted a list of complaints by workers, residents' family members, and residents to the state office that oversaw nursing homes.[74]

The public pressure paid off and Dremel agreed to a quick vote for union representation. On 5 September 1987, workers voted 128–4 to be represented by SEIU Local 150. As employee Coronett Sykes said about the vote, "I'm overwhelmed. It was a long time coming. We've needed this for years." President Dan Iverson agreed and pointed out that the vote should serve as notice to the nursing home industry in Wisconsin that changes are needed for patient care.[75] As we have seen, the union victory at Westview was celebrated in the Racine area with a unity party at the Labor Center. It also had larger implications in Wisconsin because activists had been lobbying for a nursing home reform bill that was recently vetoed by Governor Tommy Thompson. Union leaders hoped to bring the same concerns to the bargaining table and keep up their efforts to introduce changes in nursing home care and administration. State AFL-CIO Secretary-Treasurer David Newby celebrated the union recognition vote and issued a statement placing the vote in the context of the momentum of the larger Wisconsin labor movement. Newby also asserted that the victory was even more important because the workers at Westview represented the lowest paid and most exploited members of the labor community.[76]

While the labor community was rallying around the low-wage service workers at St. Luke's and Westview in 1987, workers in the industrial sector were also fighting to keep their jobs and to resist corporate restructuring efforts. Led by President Albert Herron, members of Boilermakers Local 1703 decided to pursue an all-out effort to prevent Harris Metals from shifting jobs to a nonunion plant in Tennessee. The projected move would cost about sixty jobs for workers in Racine, representing nearly half of the membership of the local. Workers at the Harris Metals foundry produced specialty alloy-steel castings. The company was part of an international conglomerate that owned twenty-four plants in three countries. Harris Metals threatened to move after workers rejected another round of wage concessions. Instead, workers voted to take a two-pronged approach that included negotiating for a severance package and applying for local aid for the expected layoffs. Pointing to the support that Congressman Les Aspin put into keeping Harris Metals in the city, Herron said that the union's

154   CHAPTER 6

approach would be to remind management and the broader Racine community of the efforts both workers and politicians had used to keep Harris Metals in Racine and operating at a profit.[77]

Despite rain, over two hundred people showed up at a Jobs with Justice rally held in conjunction with Labor Day festivities and to build opposition to the Harris Metals move and other instances of corporate abuse in the Racine area on 6 September 1987. The Jobs with Justice Campaign started earlier that year with a meeting in Miami, Florida. Their platform called for workers to pledge to at least five acts of solidarity with other workers, stand up for the rights of working people, support the rights of all workers to bargain collectively, organize the unorganized, and otherwise mobilize around efforts for good jobs for all workers. The movement, initiated by members of several progressive unions, also urged coalition building and political action.[78] Albert Herron was one of the key speakers at the rally and he urged the crowd to remember the high stakes for plant closings, demanding, "We can't let management have its way!" Other speakers also encouraged workers to "stand firm" in the fight for economic justice and pursue political action.[79]

The focus on politics played out over the weekend with many Democratic candidates speaking to Labor Day attendees about their roles in working to prevent plant closings and other issues impacting the city and county. Corinne Reid-Owens, Racine NAACP President, issued a statement reconfirming the organization's support for the Racine labor community. In part, the statement spoke to the history of the civil rights organization's support of the labor movement: "we have marched shoulder to shoulder in the struggle for justice and must continue." The speakers also included the new Westview union members and Patrick Cudahy strikers. The mood of the event was evident in the theme of "Spirit of Resurgence." Workers and union leaders felt a sense of revitalization and took the time to celebrate victories even while real fights were still unfolding in the city and clear victories were hoped for but not yet achieved. As the award committee noted, part of the deliberation for the Labor Person of the Year award that went to CWA Local 4611 President Mike Webster included his reputation as being a progressive and militant young union leader. He displayed just the kind of enthusiasm the committee and rank-and-file activists had been calling for over the past few years.[80]

Public pressure motivated Senator Joseph Strohl to intervene and send a letter to the Chicago-based Harris Metals asking them to reconsider the move to Tennessee. Using the slogan that "Harris is taking the money and running," Herron and other union activists convinced politicians and the larger Racine community that wage concessions and the appeal by

Congressman Aspin to bring contract work from Texas Instruments to Harris Metals constituted a commitment by workers and government officials to save the Racine production operations. It was time, they argued, for the company to follow through on those efforts. At a rally on 25 September held at the plant gates, US Senate candidate Ed Garvey, Sister Brenda Walsh, CWA Local 4611 President Mike Webster, and SEIU Local 150 Business Representative Ron Thomas all showed up to speak in support of the Harris Metals workers. During efforts to keep the company from transferring jobs out of state, union bargaining team members continued to negotiate for concessions for the affected workers. However, when the company moved from no packages to $200 severance pay offers in bargaining sessions, it infuriated union leaders and workers.[81]

Even as Harris Metals officials started moving equipment out of the plant and laying off workers, bargaining team members refused to send the severance package offers to Local 1703 members. President Herron explained, "We feel like we're owed a hell of a lot more than $200 for being kicked out the door . . . I think their offer is disgusting." Workers recognized the continuation of a trend that started in the postwar years: large corporations buying locally owned manufacturing firms, bringing in outside managers with expertise in finance and no experience in production, and then squeezing everything out of the plant and workers before closing. Herron urged his members and the community to fight against plant closings and hold corporations accountable for their actions in Racine. Even after everyone knew that Harris Metals was closing the specialty line he argued, "We have got to keep fighting to save jobs for our community." The company revised their offer twice and their "final" offer to Local 1703 included $50 for each year of service or $200, whichever was greater. However, with the increased monetary offer the company stripped laid-off employees of their seniority rights and included a clause that said members would be required to "refrain from future activities which disparage Harris Metals and its parent company, Lindberg Corporation." Members voted to reject the offer by a margin of four-to-one.[82]

In explaining why members voted against the final offer, Albert Herron explained it was about dignity. Workers felt that the company betrayed both their loyalty to the company and willingness to take pay cuts in the last round of contract negotiations by making the decision to move production to plants outside of Racine. Workers recognized that the proposed severance package would not even cover their monthly expenses and that the loss of seniority would also affect their ability to take job openings in the foundry divisions at their current pay levels. The "disparage" clause was also a personal affront. Herron explained, "The company was telling

156 CHAPTER 6

us to give up our political freedom for some money . . . These people won't let the company take their dignity away." He put the vote in terms of worker solidarity, "Boilermakers Lodge 1703 may have lost some jobs, but we still have our solidarity, and we're letting people know we don't appreciate losing the jobs."[83]

The union's militant resistance paid off with a new "final offer" from the company. Harris Metals management increased the severance package to $75 per year of service, returned seniority rights, and removed the disparage clause from the agreement. Although still unhappy with the severance rate, workers approved the adjustments in November, nearly two months after the final layoffs of the sixty-five workers. Union leaders also finalized aid for the laid-off workers through the Dislocated Worker Program, funded through the Job Training and Partnership Act. Workers could receive training through Gateway Technical College, job search assistance, and on-the-job training through participating employers.[84]

The momentum from the Labor Day celebrations in 1987 and the Harris Metals workers' militancy fed into the last years of the decade. Workers continued to rally around progressive politicians willing to support working-class issues, planned new and aggressive tactics to protect the economic security of the city and state, and continued to fight against moving jobs out of the area. The fight to save Harris Metals underlines the importance of strong state support for working-class economic justice. Even with widespread support from individual politicians, with weak labor laws and lax enforcement, workers were left with unions as their only defense against corporate mobility. This severely limited labor's power in this period.

Labor activists across the state organized a "New Directions for Labor" conference for May 1988 held in Madison, Wisconsin. The conference featured labor organizers and leaders, community activists, and scholars, all committed to finding new strategies to deal with the changing economic and political realities. A Wisconsin Labor Management Conference brought SEIU President John Sweeney to Milwaukee to help build better labor-management relationships in the state.[85] The local labor community also celebrated successes as several UAW locals won wage increases in contract negotiations, city workers won against outsourcing services, and state workers gathered their resources to challenge Governor Thompson's attack on retirement plans. The 1988 presidential campaigns created an opportunity to repudiate the conservative political agenda.

Labor activists in Racine highlighted the central role of working-class issues in the Democratic primaries and local elections. Although the nomination eventually went to Governor Michael Dukakis, Jesse Jackson's campaign focused on government intervention in the economy, closing the gaps in the social safety net, and putting an end to discrimination that labor liberals had continued to demand throughout the second half of the twentieth century. Dukakis ran against Vice President George H. W. Bush on a campaign of efficiency and competence in the postwar liberal tradition of practical solutions to public problems. The labor community celebrated the success of organizing around politicians working to support their causes. Despite the defeat of Michael Dukakis, workers felt encouraged by the victories against strong opponents at the city, county, and state level in the November 1988 elections. And workers ended the decade militantly resisting the shifting production of crayon boxes to China by Western Printing. Workers arranged a boycott of China-produced crayons, rallied and marched against the company offices, and arranged a communitywide unity rally.[86]

The Racine labor community had built a strong foundation over the years while also remaining flexible in response to internal and external demands. The sense of community, their commitment to a strategic political use of history, and their willingness to face changes with solidarity and militancy paid off to a degree even during the hard economic times of the 1980s. The decade brought a steep decline of access to unionized jobs, rising unemployment across sectors, and concentrated corporate power. Yet, workers continued to join unions, to actively work together to solve both workplace and social problems, and to resist corporate and political strategies to turn back the gains of the labor community. Their willingness to organize new sectors and shift tactics offered them not only hope but also concrete gains in workplace democracy and economic security. The activities and language of labor activists in the 1980s and the rank-and-file support for their efforts demonstrates the need to look for determination and resilience from the historical actors of the period of deindustrialization. Workers in Racine did not know what the future held, but they expected to face it together, as a working-class community. Racine continues to be a union town, a community of activists working together to make their lives and community better in hard social and economic times.

CONCLUSION

How We Get Free

Racine's labor community has not sustained the economic and political strength that inspired activists' hope for change at the end of the 1980s. Despite a slight economic recovery in the 1990s and attempts at a downtown harbor revitalization project to generate tourism revenue, Racine's level of income disparity continues to rise as in other cities across the nation. Hospital workers at St. Luke's Hospital lost a decertification drive in the 1990s, and the service workers are not organized at the newly merged St. Mary's Hospital. However, UAW Local 180, still the largest union in town, continues to fight for justice at work and in the community.

The Racine labor community lost. So did the broader labor movement. But, as the Racine case demonstrates, working-class politics adapted to the transformations in the postwar period—the empowerment of women and nonwhite men, the shift from manufacturing to service work, the decline of New Deal liberalism, as well as the rise of neoliberalism and conservative political power. They did so without losing sight of the economic inequality and exploitation that undergirded racial capitalism in the United States. They seized the economic and political opportunity of the postwar period to consolidate the power that they could access. Racine's activists pursued their shifting working-class agenda to transform the Democratic Party into the liberal powerhouse they recognized was needed to thwart the power of corporate leaders. As the economic and political landscape changed, labor activists in Racine found new ways to organize the growing low-wage service industry workforce. Their broad-based class solidarity inspired a sense of collective class identity for these often-marginalized workers. The community banded together to fight against plant closings and to offset

160 Conclusion

some of the economic, social, and political costs of these departures while also organizing and celebrating new union members in other sectors.

The story told in *A Blueprint for Worker Solidarity* shows that collective worker action can impact the economic and social lives of US workers. A robust, engaged labor movement is vital for the improvement of working people's lives. Workers' ability to freely organize facilitates access to good jobs for all. When white workers joined in broad-based social justice unionism, they helped disrupt the harms of racial capitalism.[1] Throughout the twentieth century in Racine, workers across sectors and skill levels enjoyed at least some form of power on the shop floor, successfully bargained for better wages and working conditions, and in a more limited fashion, held back the tide of management backlash. Workers rallied around social justice issues, elected local, state, and national politicians who represented their interests, and shaped the city into their vision of a militant union town.

Yet, workers and the unions that represent them cannot operate on a level playing field without the legal protection offered by an active federal government and robust labor law. When the economic crisis of the Great Depression and worker unrest forced federal involvement in the economy leading up to World War II, the labor movement amassed the members and resolve necessary to improve the working conditions and economic citizenship for all workers. During the more favorable years of postwar prosperity, labor activists pushed liberal policymakers to guarantee protections for workers' collective action. The labor-liberal coalition, always an unequal relationship, suffered as postwar liberals shifted focus away from management of the domestic economy to Cold War foreign policy. The failure to pass effective labor law reform or repeal Taft-Hartley allowed conservative actors to whittle away at the legal power workers had to operate from a position of united strength. However, labor activists have not stopped calling for government action to restore the social safety net, provide full employment, and protect workers' right to organize. Labor activists remain committed to the broad notions of economic security and full citizenship rights that liberals espoused in the New Deal era.

Workers' enduring notions of class solidarity and continued efforts to organize new workers complicate the declension narrative of post-1960s US society. The Racine case shows how a political use of labor history, broad-based class politics, and an expansive understanding of who belonged in the labor community inspired more and more workers to join unions, exercise their civic responsibilities, and unite to resist conservative attacks and corporate intransigence. As engaged labor activists continue to respond to and adapt class politics, new avenues of organizing and politicizing

Conclusion   161

workers emerge. Racial politics in Racine did not undermine notions of class solidarity. Postwar racial politics impacted and reshaped class politics in this urban setting and the community adapted to new circumstances. New demographics will also change the avenues toward producing class solidarity. More and more immigrant workers, women, and contingent workers are joining the workforce due to migration, shifts in employment opportunities, and the slow-moving economy. As seen in Racine, new workers bring new ideas and influences into the labor movement.

Just as activists saw the need to organize the unskilled industrial workers in the 1930s, union members have been responding to changing workforce populations over time. In 1995, reform activists in the AFL-CIO contested for and won the presidency. The "New Voice" ticket led by John Sweeney, president of SEIU, took over a campaign to rejuvenate the labor movement by becoming more active in public debate and organizing new workers.[2] In 2005, another reform movement within labor chose to separate from the AFL-CIO and formed a new federation, Change to Win (CTW). CTW, composed of SEIU, the merged textile and hotel workers union UNITE HERE, the United Food and Commercial Workers, the Teamsters, and a few other smaller unions, represents a large and growing number of female, low-wage service, domestic, and home care workers.[3] These changes and the increasing number of rank-and-file mobilizations in this period of economic instability have inspired new organizing and new ways of representing workers' interests in the larger society. Home health care, domestic, fast-food, and precarious higher education workers, have been mobilizing to gain more economic security and workplace democracy in the Fight For $15 movement. The uprising for Black Lives Matter since the murder of Trayvon Martin in 2012, which intensified during the summer of 2020 after the murder of George Floyd, also sparked new worker solidarity efforts.[4] This is exemplified and embodied in the workplace struggles taking place in 2021 and 2022 in Amazon warehouses and Starbucks coffee shops across the United States. More and more workers are coming together and leveraging their collective power to win racial and economic justice for all. Tamara Lee and Maite Tapia are leaders in a growing scholarship on these intersectional organizing campaigns. This critical framing of worker mobilizations can support workers' efforts.[5]

The Racine case also highlights the need to better frame the narratives of the ways labor activists created and built coalitions for economic and social justice movements. In Racine, workers participated in and responded to the civil rights and women's movements. As globalization continues, workers will need to strengthen solidarities across regions, ethnicities, and systems of work. And as Erica Smiley and Sarita Gupta argue, this is also about the choices we make, as activists, social justice movements, and power brokers. We must learn to adapt to changing political environments as we continue to harness our collective power. Workers understand what it looks like to win and know the value of overcoming internal challenges.[6] Reframing the narrative of labor power in this period opens the door to further research on the role of worker centers in the labor movement as well as collaborations between labor and immigrant rights activists. The UAW has been working with building connections across nations to unionize auto factories in the US South. Workers in Brazil, Japan, and France have banded together with workers in Tennessee and Mississippi to provide better wages and working conditions for workers in the global automobile economy.[7] These studies will continue to uncover the important legacies of class solidarity and movements for economic and social justice in the late twentieth century.

Ultimately, the Racine labor community of the postwar period offers avenues for scholars and activists to take "more seriously the possibilities embedded in postwar urban turmoil," because "we find that determination—not decline or decay—best characterizes our nation's cities."[8] Labor activists in Racine and across the nation sought to change the lives of all working people. Yet, workers and their organizations cannot do it alone. Active government involvement and an engaged citizenry that recognizes the value of collective action for change are needed to protect economic, social, and political livelihoods in US society. The continued salience of working-class identity and politics in Racine, even its current state of postindustrial decline, offers a blueprint for activists seeking to make the world a better place.

Notes

Introduction

1. Patrick Caldwell, "The County that Swings Wisconsin," *The American Prospect*, October 25, 2012, online edition, accessed 25 October 2012, http://prospect.org/article/county-swings-wisconsin.

2. Caldwell, "The County that Swings Wisconsin."

3. Racine County, "Election Results," accessed March 18, 2013, racineco.com/crepository/pastelection/s20121106.pdf.

4. Nelson Lichtenstein, *State of the Union: A Century of American Labor* (Princeton University Press, 2002); Jefferson Cowie, *Stayin' Alive: The 1970s and the Last Days of the Working Class* (The New Press, 2010); Judith Stein, *Pivotal Decade: How the United States Traded Factories for Finance in the Seventies* (New Haven: Yale University Press, 2010).

5. Jane L. Collins and Victoria Mayer, *Both Hands Tied: Welfare Reform and the Race to the Bottom in the Low-Wage Labor Market* (University of Chicago Press, 2010).

6. "Summary of Provisions of 2011 Act 10," Wisconsin Legislature, accessed June 2, 2014, http://legis.wisconsin.gov/lfb/publications/budget/2011-13-Budget/documents/act32/act%2010.pdf.

7. William Jenkins, interview by George H. Roeder, January 3 and 29, 1974, transcript, Wisconsin Historical Society.

8. Tom Valeo interview by author, January 31, 2014, in author's possession, Madison, WI.

9. Steven High, *Industrial Sunset: The Making of North America's Rust Belt, 1969–1984* (Toronto: University of Toronto Press, 2003), 5–6.

10. Nelson Peter Ross, "Two Civilizations: Indians and Early White Settlement," 33; Chelvadurai Manogaran, "Geography and Agriculture," 137–138; Richard H. Keehn, "Industry and Business," in *Racine: Growth and Change in*

a Wisconsin County, ed. Nicholas C. Burckel (Racine: Racine County Board of Supervisors, 1977), 280.

11. John Buenker, *Invention City: The Sesquicentennial History of Racine, Wisconsin* (Racine: Racine Heritage Museum, 1998), 120–121.

12. Lizabeth Cohen, *Making a New Deal: Industrial Workers in Chicago, 1919-1939* (Cambridge: Cambridge University Press, 1990), 2, 355–360.

13. Harvey Kitzman, interview by Jack W. Skeels, 4 March 1963, Walter P. Reuther Library (hereafter WPR), Wayne State University, Detroit, MI.

14. "Firefighters at Peak Strength; Department Makes Steady Gains," *Racine Labor*, 6 Jan 50, 1.

15. Michael Sherry, *In the Shadow of War: The United States Since the 1930s* (New Haven: Yale University Press, 1997).

16. Lichtenstein, *State of the Union*, 54–59.

17. Robert Korstad and Nelson Lichtenstein, "Opportunities Found and Lost: Labor, Radicals, and the Early Civil Rights Movement," *JAH* 75, no. 3 (Dec 1988): 786–811; Blair LM Kelley, *Black Folk: The Roots of the Black Working Class* (New York: Liveright Publishing Corporation, 2023).

18. Dorothy Sue Cobble, *The Other Women's Movement: Workplace Justice and Social Rights in Modern America* (Princeton University Press, 2004), 6, 100.

19. Crystal Marie Moten, *Continually Working: Black Women, Community Intellectualism, and Economic Justice in Postwar Milwaukee* (Vanderbilt University Press, 2023).

20. Paul Whiteside, interview by James A. Cavanaugh, Kenosha, WI, 13 August 1981, tape 3 side 2, Wisconsin Labor Oral History Project, 1981–1982, Wisconsin State Historical Society, Madison, WI.

21. Nancy MacLean, *Freedom is Not Enough: The Opening of the American Workplace* (Cambridge: Harvard University Press, 2006).

22. Jacquelyn Dowd Hall, "The Long Civil Rights Movement and the Political Uses of the Past," *JAH* 91, no. 4 (Mar 2005): 1233–63.

23. Joseph M. Kelly, "Growth of Organized Labor," in *Racine: Growth and Change in a Wisconsin County*, ed. Nicholas C. Burckel (Racine: Racine County Board of Supervisors, 1977), 345–353.

24. Jefferson Cowie, "Vigorously Left, Right, and Center": The Crosscurrents of Working-Class America in the 1970s," in *America in the Seventies*, eds. Beth Bailey and David Farber (Lawrence: University Press of Kansas, 2004), 76, 80–81.

25. Lane Windham, *Knocking on Labor's Door: Union Organizing in the 1970s and the Roots of a New Economic Divide* (Chapel Hill: University of North Carolina Press, 2017); See also Judith Stein, *Pivotal Decade* (New Haven: Yale University Press, 2010).

26. Ross, "Two Civilizations: Indians and Early White Settlement," 33; Manogaran, "Geography and Agriculture," 137–138; Richard H. Keehn, "Industry and Business," in *Racine: Growth and Change in a Wisconsin County*, ed. Nicholas C. Burckel (Racine: Racine County Board of Supervisors, 1977), 280;

Barry Bluestone and Bennett Harrison, *The Deindustrialization of America: Plant Closings, Community Abandonment, and the Dismantling of Basic Industry* (NY: Basic Books, 1982).

27. Collins and Mayer, *Both Hands Tied*, 31–39.

28. Jon Shelton, *Teacher Strike! Public Education and the Making of a New American Political Order* (Urbana: University of Illinois Press, 2017).

29. Joseph A. McCartin, "'A Wagner Act for Public Employees': Labor's Deferred Dream and the Rise of Conservatism, 1970–1976," *Journal of American History* 95, no. 1 (June 2008): 123–148.

30. Buenker, *Invention City*, 120–121.

31. Guian A. Mckee, *The Problem of Jobs: Liberalism, Race, and Deindustrialization in Philadelphia* (University of Chicago Press, 2008), 5, 6.

32. Cohen, *Making a New Deal*, 228.

33. Alan Brinkley, *The End of Reform: New Deal Liberalism in Recession and War* (New York: Vintage Books, 1995), 143; Lichtenstein, *State of the Union*, 27; Elizabeth Borgwardt, *A New Deal for the World: America's Vision for Human Rights* (Cambridge: Harvard University Press, 2005).

34. See Cohen, *Making a New Deal* for Chicago and Guian A. Mckee, *The Problem of Jobs: Liberalism, Race, and Deindustrialization in Philadelphia* for Philadelphia.

35. Andrew Battista, *The Revival of Labor Liberalism* (Urbana: University of Illinois Press, 2008), 9; Thomas J. Sugrue, *The Origins of the Urban Crisis: Race and Inequality in Postwar Detroit*, 2nd ed. (Princeton University Press, 2005), 6.

36. Cohen, *Making a New Deal*; Similar to Battista, I will use the terms labor liberalism and labor liberal to encapsulate this agenda throughout the book.

37. Bluestone and Harrison, *The Deindustrialization of America*.

38. Robert O. Self, "California's Industrial Garden: Oakland and the East Bay in the Age of Deindustrialization," *Beyond the Ruins: The Meanings of Deindustrialization*, eds. Jefferson Cowie and Joseph Heathcott (Ithaca: ILR Press, 2003), 159–180.

39. Richard Newman, "From Love's Canal to Love Canal: Reckoning with the Environmental Legacy of an Industrial Dream," *Beyond the Ruins*, 112–138.

40. Steve May and Laura Morrison, "Making Sense of Restructuring: Narratives of Accommodation among Downsized Workers," *Beyond the Ruins*, 259–283; Joy L. Hart and Tracy E. K'Meyer, "Worker Memory and Narrative: Personal Stories of Deindustrialization in Louisville, Kentucky," *Beyond the Ruins*, 284–304; Dale A. Hathaway, *Can Workers Have a Voice?: The Politics of Deindustrialization in Pittsburgh* (University Park, PA: The Pennsylvania State University Press, 1993).

41. Jefferson Cowie, *Capital Moves: RCA's Seventy-Year Quest for Cheap Labor* (Ithaca: Cornell University Press, 1999), 3, 4.

42. "About Call me Latine," accessed 28 May 2022, *About Call me Latine—Call me Latine*.

Notes to Chapter 1

Chapter 1. Building Racine's Labor Community

1. William Jenkins, interview by George H. Roeder, January 3 and 29, 1974, transcript, Wisconsin Historical Society.

2. Jenkins, interview.

3. Robert Bussel, *Fighting for Total Person Unionism: Harold Gibbons, Ernest Calloway, and Working-Class Citizenship* (Urbana: University of Illinois Press, 2015) quote from page 5.

4. Joseph M. Kelly, "Growth of Organized Labor," in *Racine: Growth and Change in a Wisconsin County*, 346.

5. Kelly, "Growth of Organized Labor," 346–347.

6. Kelly, "Growth of Organized Labor," 347.

7. "Squibs," *Racine Labor*, April 22, 1960, 1.

8. Kelly, "Growth of Organized Labor," 356.

9. Paul Whiteside, interview by James Cavanaugh, August 13, 1981, Wisconsin Historical Society; Jenkins, interview: Hugh Reichard, "Racine Again," *Ammunition* vol. 4, no. 3 (March 1946): 18–19.

10. RTLC records, WHS, Box 1, folder 5.

11. Hugh Reichard, "Racine Again," *Ammunition* vol. 4, no. 3 (March 1946): 18–19.

12. RTLC records, Box 1, Folder 6.

13. Whiteside, interview.

14. Richard W. Olson, "An Isolated Survivor: *Racine Labor*," in *The New Labor Press: Journalism for a Changing Union Movement*, eds. Sam Pizzigati and Fred J. Solowey (New York: ILR Press, 1992), 174–183.

15. UAW Local 180, WPR, Box 6, Folder 15.

16. UAW Local 180, WPR, Box 2, Folder 4.

17. Richard C. Haney, "The Rise of Wisconsin's New Democrats: A Political Realignment in the Mid-Twentieth Century," *The Wisconsin Magazine of History* 58, no. 2 (Winter 1974–1975): 90–106.

18. Haney, "The Rise of Wisconsin's New Democrats"; "Racine DOC to Meet Jan. 27, Will Pick Officers For Year," *Racine Labor*, Jan. 13, 1950, 1.

19. Michael Holmes, "Politics and Government, 1920–1976" in *Racine: Growth and Change in a Wisconsin County*, 252–253; RTLC Box 1; Folder 6.

20. Michael Holmes, "Politics and Government, 1920–1976," in *Racine: Growth and Change in a Wisconsin County*, 252–253.

21. "Many Union Men Active in Civic, Political Posts Here," *Racine Labor*, September 1, 1950, Section 3, 1, 15.

22. Heritage Research Center, "WWII Industrial Facilities: Authorized Federally Funded Facilities," accessed September 16, 2012, http://www.heritage research.com/ourlibrary/databases/wwii/industries/wisconsin.htm.

23. U.S. Bureau of the Census, *Wisconsin: Population of Counties by Decennial Census: 1900–1990*, ed. Richard L. Forstall (Washington, DC: Government Printing Office, 1995).

Notes to Chapter 1   167

24. Colin Gordon, *New Deals: Business, Labor, and Politics in America, 1920–1935* (Cambridge: Cambridge University Press, 1994), 164–165, 215–220; Kim Phillips-Fein, *Invisible Hands: The Making of the Conservative Movement from the New Deal to Reagan* (New York: W.W. Norton, 2009), 8, 9.

25. Lichtenstein, *State of the Union*, 105.

26. Kim Phillips-Fein, *Invisible Hands*, 14.

27. Brinkley, *The End of Reform*, 41.

28. Lichtenstein, 98, 127. Lichtenstein describes how in the 1980s as labor lost significant ground to corporate capitalists the myth of a labor-management accord became popular among activists, historians, and policymakers who sought to critique the federal government's retreat from protecting collective bargaining. He quotes John Sweeney, AFL-CIO president calling for a return to the "unwritten social contract" on page 98.

29. Lichtenstein, *State of the Union*, 115; Cohen, *Making a New Deal*, 366–367. Black postal workers stand as at least one exception to blanket expulsions after Taft Hartley. See Blair LM Kelley, *Black Folk: The Roots of the Black Working Class* (New York: Liveright Publishing Corporation, 2023).

30. Nelson Lichtenstein, *Labor's War at Home: The CIO in World War II* (Cambridge: Cambridge University Press, 1982), 238–239.

31. Lichtenstein, *State of the Union*, 117.

32. Lichtenstein, *State of the Union*, 176.

33. Phillips-Fein, *Invisible Hands*, 125–126; Nelson Lichtenstein, *The Most Dangerous Man in Detroit: Walter Reuther and the Fate of American Labor* (New York: Basic Books, 1995), 347–350.

34. J. I. Case Company, *CASE: A Case History* (Racine: Case Company, n.d.).

35. "An Evening Dedicated to Harvey Kitzman," Kitzman Papers, WHS; Kelly, "Growth of Organized Labor," 356–362.

36. "Ex-Case Chief Clausen, 87, Dies; Known as a Rugged Individualist," *Racine Journal Times*, August 15, 1965, 1, 3A.

37. "Clausen's Death Marks By-Gone Era," *Racine Labor*, August 20, 1965, 9.

38. See chapter 3.

39. Robert O. Self, *American Babylon: Race and the Struggle for Postwar Oakland* (Princeton University Press, 2003), 35–36.

40. Cohen, 292, 297.

41. Harvey Kitzman, interview, WPR.

42. "History of Region 10," Harvey Kitzman Papers, WHS; Biography, Harvey Kitzman Papers, WHS.

43. Kelly, "Growth of Organized Labor," 370–371.

44. Kelly, "Growth of Organized Labor," 370–371.

45. Kitzman, interview, WPR, 17 and 18.

46. UAW Local 180, WPR, Box 2, Folder 10.

47. UAW Local 180, WPR, Box 5, Folder 6.

48. The UAW Local 180 collection, WPR, Box 5, Folder 6, letters Jan. 17, 1945, Jan. 22, 1945, Feb. 6, 1946, Feb. 14, 1946.

168 Notes to Chapter 1

49. Michael Holmes, "Politics and Government, 1920–1976," in *Racine: Growth and Change in a Wisconsin County*, 254.

50. The UAW Local 180 collection, WPR, Box 5, Folder 6.

51. "Hurls Advice at J.I. Case," *Racine Labor*, June 3, 1946, 1.

52. Kelly, "Growth of Organized Labor," 375; Kitzman, interview.

53. The UAW Local 180 collection, WPR, Box 1, folder 26; Kitzman, interview.

54. The UAW Local 180 collection, WPR.

55. John W. Cole, "Number of Blacks in State Rises 72%," *Milwaukee Journal*, March 3, 1971, 1; Joe William Trotter, Jr., *Black Milwaukee: The Making of An Industrial Proletariat, 1915–45*, 2nd ed. (Urbana: University of Illinois Press, 2007), 149–150; Tex Reynolds, "Between the Lines," *Racine Journal-Times*, Feb. 13, 1959, 1–2.

56. Jenkins, interview, WPR, transcript p. 16.

57. Jenkins, interview; Julia Pferdehirt, *Blue Jenkins: Working for Workers* (Madison: Wisconsin Historical Society Press, 2011), 6–15.

58. Jenkins, interview; Pferdehirt, *Blue Jenkins*, 79.

59. Jenkins, interview; Kelly, "Growth of Organized Labor," 378–379; Pferdehirt, *Blue Jenkins*, 96.

60. August Meier and Elliott Rudwick, *Black Detroit and the Rise of the UAW* (New York: Oxford University Press, 1979), 108–175.

61. Trotter, *Black Milwaukee*, 13.

62. Trotter, *Black Milwaukee*, 42, 46, 47, 61, 148–150, and 162–166.

63. Andrew Kersten, *Race, Jobs, and the War: The FEPC in the Midwest, 1941–46* (Urbana: University of Illinois Press, 2000), 14–17; William P. Jones, "The Unknown Origins of the March on Washington: Civil Rights Politics and the Black Working Class," in *Labor: Studies in Working-Class History of the Americas* 7, no. 3 (2010): 33–52; and Anthony Chen, *The Fifth Freedom: Jobs, Politics, and Civil Rights in the United States, 1941–1972* (Princeton University Press, 2009), 36–37.

64. Meier and Rudwick, *Black Detroit*, 213–215.

65. Meier and Rudwick, *Black Detroit*, 215.

66. Trotter, *Black Milwaukee*, 166.

67. Jenkins, interview.

68. Robert Korstad and Nelson Lichtenstein, "Opportunities Found and Lost: Labor, Radicals, and the Early Civil Rights Movement," *JAH* 75 (Dec 1985): 786–811.

69. Meier and Rudwick, *Black Detroit*, ix.

70. Jenkins, interview.

71. Cindy Hahamovitch, *No Man's Land: Jamaican Guestworkers in America and the Global History of Deportable Labor* (Princeton University Press, 2011), 2, 3, 83.

72. Jenkins, interview.

73. Jenkins, interview.

74. Jenkins, interview; Pferdehirt, *Blue Jenkins*, 72–80.

Notes to Chapter 1 169

75. Jenkins, interview.

76. UAW Local 180, WPR, Box 2, Folder 4.

77. Jenkins, interview; Tex Reynolds, "Negroes," *Racine Journal Times*, Feb. 13, 1959.

78. "Race Relations and Equal Opportunity in Racine County," Community Forum on Race Relations in Racine County, Wisconsin, accessed Sept. 25, 2012, http://www.usccr.gov/pubs/sac/wi0301/ch3.htm.

79. Meier and Rudwick, *Black Detroit*, 78–79.

80. Roger Horowitz, *'Negro and White, Unite and Fight!' A Social History of Industrial Unionism in Meatpacking, 1930–90* (Urbana: University of Illinois Press, 1997), 224–225; Cobble, *The Other Women's Movement*, 81–82.

81. Jenkins, interview; "Entire Union Group Affiliates with NAACP," *Racine Labor*, Feb. 13, 1959, 1.

82. Alyssa Mauk, "Remembering Racine's Leaders: Corinne Reid Owens was 'Racine's Rosa Parks,'" *Journal Times*, November 28, 2019; Crystal Marie Moten, *Continually Working: Black Women, Community Intellectualism, and Economic Justice in Postwar Milwaukee* (Nashville: Vanderbilt University Press, 2023), 36–37.

83. "Low-Rent Home Plan Squeaks Past Council," *Racine Labor*, Jan. 13, 1950, 1; "Race Relations and Equal Opportunity in Racine County," Community Forum on Race Relations in Racine County, Wisconsin, accessed Sept. 25, 2012, http://www.usccr.gov/pubs/sac/wi0301/ch3.htm.

84. RTLC records, box 1, folder 6, WHS.

85. "Housing Project Misrepresented," *Racine Labor*, Jan. 20, 1950, 1; "Defer Housing Plan," *Racine Labor*, Jan. 20, 1950, 1, 2; Loren Norman, "Squibs," *Racine Labor*, Feb. 24, 1950, 4; "Race Relations and Equal Opportunity in Racine County"; "Group Discusses Possibilities For Solving Negro Housing," *Racine Journal Times*, May 25, 1956, 4.

86. Eric Fure-Slocum provides a detailed history of how this battle played out in Milwaukee in *Contesting the Postwar City: Working-Class and Growth Politics in 1940s Milwaukee* (Cambridge University Press, 2013), 71, 74, 76–77.

87. Cobble, *The Other Women's Movement*, 56–58.

88. Cobble, *The Other Women's Movement*, 19.

89. For example, see "Sister Sue Says," *Ammunition*, vol. 2, no. 1 (Jan. 1944), 23; and vol. 3, no. 3 (March 1945), 11.

90. *Growth and Change*, 384–385; RTLC Records, WHS, Box 1, Folder 3; Cobble, *The Other Women's Movement*, 27.

91. "Trade Union League Ends 15 Years of Service to Racine," *Racine Labor*, January 5, 1951, 5.

92. "Women Play Vital Role in Many Racine Locals," *Racine Labor*, October 1, 1954, 7.

93. "Webster Girls Win Championship," *Racine Labor*, September 10, 1954, 1.

94. Dorothy Haener interview, Documenting the Midwestern Origins of the 20th-Century Women's Movement, 1987–1992, WHS; Clara Day interview,

170 Notes to Chapters 1 and 2

Documenting the Midwestern Origins of the 20th-Century Women's Movement, 1987–1992, WHS.

95. Executive board minutes, April 5, 1940, UAW Local 180 Collection, WPR, Box 1, Folder 30.

96. UAW Local 180, WPR, Nov. 20, 1944, Box 5, Folder 5.

97. "Five Women Win Contested Jobless Pay Claim Against J. I. Case Co.," *Racine Labor*, Jan. 12, 1945, 5.

98. "Negotiation Minutes," The UAW Local 180 Collection, WPR, Box 1, Folder 24, April 18, 1950.

99. "Women Employees Have Rights Too, Case Hearing Set," *Racine Labor*, May 5, 1950, 1; "Hearing on Case Women Employees to Resume June 2," *Racine Labor*, May 26, 1950, 3.

100. "UAW Plans Women's Confab," *Racine Labor*, Feb. 3, 1950, 1.

101. "Newest Dance Star," *Racine Labor*, April 14, 1950, 10.

102. See Chapter Four.

103. For example see worker correspondence in SEIU Executive Office—David Sullivan Files, WPR, Box 19, Folders 38, 39; The UAW Local 180 Collection, WPR, Box 1, Folders 3, 9; Box 6, Folder 4; Letters to the Editor, *Racine Labor*, March 20, 1953, 5.

Chapter 2. Labor Politics and Solidarity in the 1950s

1. Joseph E. Slater, "Wisconsin Public Sector Labor Laws," in *Public Workers: Government Employee Unions, the Law, and the State, 1900–1962* (Ithaca: ILR Press, 2004), 158–192.

2. For narratives addressing the postwar boom as leading to greater security for workers see Robert J. Gordon, *The Rise and Fall of American Growth: The U.S. Standard of Living since the Civil War* (Princeton University Press, 2016); Marc Levinson, *An Extraordinary Time: The End of the Postwar Boom and the Return of the Ordinary Economy* (New York: Basic Books, 2016); and Jefferson Cowie, *The Great Exception: The New Deal and the Limits of American Politics* (Princeton: Princeton University Press, 2016). Works that complicate this narrative include Daniel J. Clark, *Disruption in Detroit: Autoworkers and the Elusive Postwar Boom* (Urbana: University of Illinois Press, 2018); Nelson Lichtenstein, *State of the Union: A Century of American Labor* (Princeton: Princeton University Press, 2002), especially chapter 3; Tami Friedman, ""Acute Depression . . . in . . . the Age of Plenty": Capital Migration, Economic Dislocation, and the Missing "Social Contract" of the 1950s," *Labor: Studies in Working-Class History of the Americas* 8, no. 4 (January 2011): 89–113.

3. Howell John Harris, *The Right to Manage: Industrial Relations Policies of American Business in the 1940s* (Madison, WI: University of Wisconsin Press, 1982).

4. Harvey Kitzman Papers.

Notes to Chapter 2   171

5. University of Wisconsin–Parkside, "Proposal for a Records Survey of Manufacturing Firms in the Cities of Racine and Kenosha, Wisconsin, As Part of an Archives of Industrial Society Project" (Kenosha, WI, 1978). Business Survey Records, Wisconsin Historical Society, UW-Parkside Area Center, Box 1, Folder 11.

6. "Webster Local Wins Election on Union Shop," *Racine Labor*, Feb. 17, 1950, 1; "Union Shop Won in New Webster Pact," *Racine Labor*, March 31, 1950, 16.

7. "Belle City Local Wins Pensions, 10c Increase," *Racine Labor*, August 18, 1950, 1; "Victory at Walker's," *Racine Labor*, August 11, 1950, 1; "Raise for Belle City Employes," *Racine Labor*, October 24, 1952, 2.

8. "A. B. Modine: A Remembrance," accessed August 11, 2013, www.modine.com\web\about-modine\history.

9. "Local 244 Strike in Second Week," *Racine Labor*, October 3, 1952, 1, 2.

10. "Conciliator Sets Date for Meeting in Modine Strike," *Racine Labor*, October 10, 1952, 1; "Talk Over Strike at Modine Co.," *Racine Labor*, October 17, 1952, 3; "Modine Union, Backed by all Labor, Fights On," *Racine Labor*, December 5, 1952, 1; "Why Modine is Striking," *Racine Labor*, December 5, 1952, 4; "What's Happening in the Modine Strike," *Racine Labor*, January 30, 1953, 1, 4.

11. See Chapter One.

12. "UAW Backs Modine Strikers to Hilt, Declares Kitzman," *Racine Labor*, April 3, 1953, 2.

13. "Be Fair Says Modine Worker," *Racine Labor*, February 20, 1953, 1; "Membership Gives Vote of Confidence to Modine Local Bargaining Committee," *Racine Labor*, March 6, 1953, 1; "Modine Wife View," *Racine Labor*, March 20, 1953, 5.

14. "Locals Leap to Help Modine Strikers," *Racine Labor*, November 14, 1952, 1; "Case Local Votes to Aid Modine Strike," *Racine Labor*, November 14, 1952, 1; "Modine Strike Drags On," *Racine Labor*, November 21, 1952, 2; Modine Union, Backed by all Labor, Fights On," *Racine Labor*, December 5, 1952, 1, 3; "Modine Strikers Get Strong Support," *Racine Labor*, December 12, 1952, 1.

15. "Mediators Active but Modine Strike Goes On," *Racine Labor*, January 23, 1953, 1; "Modine Strike," 2; "Modine Co. Mistakes," *Racine Labor*, March 20, 1953, 4.

16. "U.S. Moves in Modine Strike, Meeting Monday," *Racine Labor*, March 20, 1953, 1; "Seventh-Month Old Modine Strike Ends," *Racine Labor*, April 24, 1953, 1, 7; "Radiations: What's Doing at Modine's," *Racine Labor*, June 5, 1953, 5; "Modine Strike, 212 Days Old, Comes to End," *Racine Journal-Times*, April 20, 1953, 1.

17. Robert W. Ozanne, *The Labor Movement in Wisconsin: A History* (Madison: State Historical Society of Wisconsin, 1984), 72–74, quote from page 74; Joseph E. Slater, *Public Workers: Government Employee Unions, the Law, and the State, 1900–1962* (Ithaca: ILR Press, 2004), 164–165.

Notes to Chapter 2

18. "Water Department Employees Local 63, Was Chartered in 1937," *Racine Labor*, September 3, 1965, 33.

19. Kelly, "Growth of Organized Labor," 386–389.

20. "Municipal Employees On Strike," *Racine Labor*, Jan. 4, 1952, 1; "Dispute Situation: City Council Offers Strikers 5 Proposals," *Racine Labor*, Jan. 11, 1952, 1; "Journal-Times Goes Berserk," *Racine Labor*, January 11, 1952, 4; "City Workers Win Point, End Strike," *Racine Labor*, January 18, 1952, 3; "Good Deal for City Workers," *Racine Labor*, January 18, 1952, 4; Tex Reynolds, "Between the Lines," *Racine Journal-Times*, January 3, 1952, 1; "City Employes Strike Over Wage Demands," *Racine Journal-Times*, January 3, 1952, 1, 3A; "City Workers' Strike Unjustified," *Racine Journal-Times*, January 3, 1952, 10A.

21. Lichtenstein, *State of the Union*, 46, 115–116; "Growth of Organized Labor," 364–366; Kitzman, interview; Ozanne, *The Labor Movement in Wisconsin*, 86–94.

22. Lisa Phillips, *A Renegade Union: Interracial Organizing and Labor Radicalism* (Urbana: University of Illinois Press, 2013), 101, 105, 107, 115; Ozanne, 91; Steve Rosswurm, "An Overview and Preliminary Assessment of the CIO's Expelled Unions," in *The CIO's Left-Led Unions*, ed. Steve Rosswurm (New Brunswick: Rutgers University Press, 1992), 1–2; and Toni Gilpin, *The Long Deep Grudge: A Story of Big Capital, Radical Labor, and Class War in the American Heartland* (Chicago: Haymarket Books, 2020).

23. "City Employees Sever Tie to Public Workers Union," *Racine Labor*, March 21, 1952, 1; "Keep Racine Clean," *Racine Labor*, March 21, 1952, 1.

24. Kitzman interview; See also, Joseph E. Kelly, "Growth of Organized Labor," 364, 365.

25. "County Wage Tiff Sizzles," *Racine Labor*, February 15, 1952, 1; "County Workers Win," *Racine Labor*, February 22, 1952, 1, 5; "Approve County Pay Pact," *Racine Labor*, February 29, 1952, 1.

26. "Trades Council Backs Request of Firemen," *Racine Labor*, November 7, 1950, 1; "Firefighters 'Burned Up' About Wages," *Racine Labor*, October 16, 1953, 1.

27. "Group Aims to Publicize Joe's Record," *Racine Labor*, June 6, 1952, 1; "State Leaders Endorse Booklet Exposing McCarthy," *Racine Labor*, July 4, 1952, 2; The Wisconsin Citizens' Committee on McCarthy's Record, "The McCarthy Record," 1952.

28. "Racine Votes for Ike but Not McCarthy," *Racine Labor*, November 7, 1952, 7.

29. UAW Local 180, WPR, April 19, 1955; Slater, *Public Workers: Government Employee Unions, the Law, and the State, 1900–1962*, 180.

30. See Chapter 1 for history of Taft-Hartley; Lichtenstein, *State of the Union*, 164–166; UAW Local 180, WPR, June 21, 1955, Box 3, Folder 9.

31. Matthew M. Reiter, "The Last Family Men: Independent Firms, Anti-Unionism, and Right Wing Politics in Twentieth-Century Wisconsin" (PhD diss., University of Wisconsin-Madison, 2019), 40; Tula Connell, *Conservative*

Counterrevolution: Challenging Liberalism in 1950s Milwaukee (Urbana: University of Illinois Press, 2016); Phillips-Fein, *Invisible Hands*, 125–129.

32. UAW Local 180, WPR, Box 3, Folder 9, 6 Sept 55–20 Sept 55.

33. Ozanne, *The Labor Movement in Wisconsin*, 147; "Labor Proves Legality of Catlin Law," *Racine Labor*, January 11, 1956, 2.

34. "Candidates Popping Up For City Jobs," *Racine Labor*, January 8, 1954, 1.

35. "City to Have New Mayor, 9 New Aldermen," *Racine Labor*, April 13, 1955, 2.

36. "Landslide Buries GOP," *Racine Labor*, November 7, 1958, 1.

37. Slater, *Public Workers*, 158–184.

38. Wisconsin Legislative Documents, "Municipal Employee Relations Act," http://docs.legis.wi.gov/statutes/statutes/111/IV, accessed Sept. 21, 2012.

39. Robert H. Hayes and William J. Abernathy, "Managing Our Way to Economic Decline," *Harvard Business Review* 58, no. 4 (1980): 67–77.

40. Bluestone and Harrison, *The Deindustrialization of America*, 1982.

41. "Nash Layoff Hits 1300 at Kenosha," *Racine Labor*, February 26, 1954, 1; "Hudson and Nash Merger is Now Final," *Milwaukee Sentinel*, April 23, 1954, 6, part 2; University of Wisconsin–Parkside, "Proposal for a Records Survey of Manufacturing Firms in the Cities of Racine and Kenosha, Wisconsin, As Part of an Archives of Industrial Society Project" (Kenosha, WI, 1978). Business Survey Records, Wisconsin Historical Society, UW-Parkside Area Center, Box 1, Folder 11.

42. Clark examines a similar cyclical pattern in the auto industry in Detroit during this same time. As he argues, a national rise in living standards and wage increases within the auto industry did not lead to greater job security for autoworkers in the 1950s because many workers were unemployed so often throughout the year. See *Disruption in Detroit*.

43. "Plan Meeting on Closing of Tannery," *Racine Labor*, January 11, 1956, 1.

44. "Local 244 Hard Hit by Layoffs," *Racine Labor*, August 29, 1956, 8; "New Pact, Layoffs Concern Local 180," *Racine Labor*, August 29, 1956, 3, part 2; "Despite Layoffs, Work Here Holding Up Well," *Racine Labor*, October 3, 1956, 1.

45. Melvyn Dubofsky, "Technological Change and American Worker Movements, 1870–1970," in *Technology, the Economy, and Society: The American Experience*, eds. Joel Colton and Stuart Bruchey (New York: Columbia University Press, 1987), 162–185.

46. "Legislative Program," *Ammunition* 11, no. 4 (April 1953): 38–39.

47. "Warns about Shock of Automation," *Racine Labor*, March 30, 1955, 1.

48. "A Kenosha Engineer Looks at Automation," *Racine Labor*, January 18, 1956, 4.

49. "Population Growth Automation Give U.S. Problem, State AFL-CIO," *Racine Labor*, September 4, 1959, 8.

174 Notes to Chapter 2

50. The UAW Local 180 Collection, WPR, Box 3, Folder 10, April 17, 1956, regular membership meeting minutes.

51. "Big CIO Dance is Set to Go," *Racine Labor*, November 21, 1952, 3; "Webster Electric Fields two Baseball Teams," *Racine Labor*, August 14, 1953, 2; "Recreation Council Set Up by UAW Here," *Racine Labor*, November 13, 1953, 1; "All Out for Big Rally," *Racine Labor*, February 5, 1954, 1; "A Hearty Welcome to our New Readers," *Racine Labor*, February 12, 1954, 1; As Finn Enke demonstrates in their study of the feminist movement, understanding the ways in which group identity unfolds "on the ground," through spatial analysis reveals how spatial practices help consolidate group identity, *Finding the Movement: Sexuality, Contested Space, and Feminist Activism* (Durham: Duke University Press, 2007), 8–9.

52. UAW-CIO Local 833. "All My Life My Daddy's Been on Strike to Make My Future Better: The Kohler Worker's Story." ([Indianapolis, Ind.]: UAW-CIO International Union: UAW-CIO Local 833, 1955); online facsimile at http://www.wisconsinhistory.org/turningpoints/search.asp?id=1525; Visited on: 9/23/2012, 7.

53. "All My Life," 1.

54. "All My Life," 10.

55. *Kohler of Kohler News*, April 1955, Kohler, Wisconsin, 1, 37.

56. Lichtenstein, *The Most Dangerous Man in Detroit*, 347.

57. UAW Local 180 Collection, WPR, eboard and regular membership meeting minutes 1954–1955.

58. "Sexton Praises Local 180," *Racine Labor*, March 28, 1952, 1; "Case Company Helps Fight Jobless Compensation," *Racine Labor*, April 18, 1952, 1; "Proposal is Rejected by Case Local," *Racine Labor*, January 30, 1953, 3; "Case Local Rejects Company Offer," *Racine Labor*, May 15, 1953, 1; "UAW Now Represents all Case Co. Workers," *Racine Labor*, August 7, 1953, 1; "Strike Authorization Voted by Case Local," *Racine Labor*, October 23, 1953, 1; "Case Stewards Go to School," *Racine Labor*, December 18, 1953, 2; "Case Local 180 Membership Backs Bargaining Committee," *Racine Labor*, January 8, 1954, 1, 6; "Officers Meet to Help Local 180," *Racine Labor*, January 15, 1954, 1; "Mass Meeting Called by CIO to Back Case Local," *Racine Labor*, January 5, 1954, 1; "Case Local to Hold Strike Vote May 8," *Racine Labor*, April 23, 1954, 1; "Case Strike," *Racine Labor*, May 7, 1954, 1, 8; "Case Local Rejects Proposal," *Racine Labor*, May 21, 1954, 3; "Case Local Strike Vote Fails to Win Two-Thirds Majority," *Racine Labor*, December 15, 1954, 3; "Case Local Rejects New Company Offer," *Racine Labor*, August 31, 1955, 5; "Case Local Defers Action on Strike Vote," *Racine Labor*, January 11, 1956, 3; "New Pact, Layoffs Concern Local 180," *Racine Labor*, August 29, 1956, 3, part 2.

59. UAW Local 180, WPR, Box 3, Folder 8.

60. UAW Local 180, WPR, Box 6, Folder 12, May 1956.

61. Lichtenstein, *The Most Dangerous Man*, 347; Kim Phillips-Fein, *Invisible Hands*; and Lichtenstein, *State of the Union*, 138–139.

Notes to Chapters 2 and 3

62. Phillips-Fein, 127–128; Elizabeth Tandy Shermer, "Origins of the Conservative Ascendancy: Barry Goldwater's Early Senate Career and the Delegitimization of Organized Labor," *JAH* 95 (Dec 2008): 678–709.

63. Elizabeth Tandy Shermer, "Origins of the Conservative Ascendancy: Barry Goldwater's Early Senate Career and the Delegitimization of Organized Labor," in *JAH* 95 (Dec 2008): 678–709; Phillips-Fein, *Invisible Hands*, 125–126; Lichtenstein, *The Most Dangerous Man*, 347–350.

64. Walter Uphoff, *Kohler on Strike: Thirty Years of Conflict* (Boston: Beacon Press, 1966), 300–314.

65. "CIO Locals to Discuss Unity," *Racine Labor*, January 4, 1956, 3; "Start Merger Talks Now, Urges Heymanns," *Racine Labor*, January 18, 1956, 1; "View on Local Merger: The Sooner the Better," *Racine Labor*, February 22, 1956, 1.

66. "Merger Constitution Refereed Back by AFL," *Racine Labor*, October 18, 1957, 1; "Will Continue Working for Unity in 58 Haberrman Says," *Racine Labor*, December 27, 1957, 10; "More Delay Seen in State Labor Merger," *Racine Labor*, February 7, 1958, 1, 5; "No April 16 Meeting of AFL Council," *Racine Labor*, April 11, 1958, 1; "Proxmire, Nelson Endorsed by Labor, " *Racine Labor*, August 1, 1958, 1, 3; "Merger Meeting Wednesday," *Racine Labor*, October 24, 1958, 1; "Merger of Racine Labor Councils Near at Hand," *Racine Labor*, October 9, 1959, 1; "Merger of Two Councils Here Moves Slowly Ahead," *Racine Labor*, December 24, 1959, 1, 9.

Chapter 3. UAW Local 180 and the Attack on New Deal Liberalism

1. Tom Valeo, interview; "UAW's Anthony Valeo Labor Person of the Year," *Racine Labor*, September 5, 1980, 1, 10.

2. Tom Valeo, interview.

3. The Local 180 collection, WPR, Box 6, Folder 15, letter, Jan. 14, 1960.

4. "Set Strike Vote at Case: Local 180 To Ballot Saturday," *Racine Labor*, Feb. 19, 1960, 1, 2; "Strike By Local 180 Approved," *Racine Labor*, Feb. 26, 1960, 1.

5. "Set Strike Vote at Case: Local 180 To Ballot Saturday," *Racine Labor*, Feb. 19, 1960, 1, 2.

6. UAW Local 180, WHS (accessed copies, originals at WPR), March 3, 1960, letter from Case to workers; The Local 180 Collection, WPR, Box 6, Folder 15, letters, March 23, 1960, April 6, 1960; UAW Local 180, Box 1, Folder 1; "'180' Sets Strike Meeting Saturday," *Racine Labor*, July 15, 1960, 1.

7. UAW Local 180, WHS, Box 1, Folder 1, letter, March 15, 1960.

8. UAW Local 180, WPR, Box 7, Folder 1.

9. "Mass Meeting Planned," *Racine Labor*, August 5, 1960, 1; "Full Facts to be Told on Case Strike at Big Rally," *Racine Labor*, August 12, 1960, 1, 5; "Case Mass Meeting," *Racine Labor*, August 26, 1960, 1, 3.

10. UAW Local 180, WPR, March 25, 1960, Box 6, Folder 15.

11. UAW Local 180, WPR, April 5, 1940, Box 1, Folder 30; Box 1, Folder 3

176 Notes to Chapter 3

negotiation minutes, May 11, 1937; Box 5, Folder 5, letter from Wisconsin Industrial Commission, November 20, 1944.

12. Kitzman, interview.

13. UAW Local 180, WHS, June 10, 1960, letter to strikers from union.

14. "More Locals Help Local 180 Strikers," *Racine Labor*, May 20, 1960, 3; "Keep Pushing Strike Aid to UAW Local 180," *Racine Labor*, June 24, 1960, 5.

15. "Local 180 Aid To Strikers Is Increased," *Racine Labor*, June 10, 1960, 3.

16. UAW, WPR, Box 7, Folder 1; "Clerks Boost Food Plan to Aid Strikers," *Racine Labor*, May 27, 1960, 1.

17. UAW Local 180, WHS, newsletter; "Comparison of Insurance Programs in Racine," *Racine Labor*, March 4, 1960, 4.

18. "Strike Brings Out Talent In Two Younger Local 180 Members," *Racine Labor*, June 3, 1960, 2.

19. Lyle W. Shannon and Judith L. McKim, "Attitudes Toward Education and the Absorption of Immigrant Mexican-Americans and Negroes in Racine," *Education and Urban Society*, vol. 6, no. 3 (May 1974): 333–354; Dionicio Nodin Valdes, *Barrios Nortenos: St. Paul and Midwestern Mexican Communities in the Twentieth Century* (Austin: University of Texas Press, 2000), 28, 137, 147.

20. See for example, *Racine Labor*, June 17, 1960, 1; July 1, 1960, 1.

21. "Case Out For Trouble," *Racine Labor*, March 25, 1960, 4.

22. "Tony DeLaat to be Laid Up for Months," *Racine Labor*, April 1, 1960, 2.

23. "Pickets Hit by Scab Cars," *Racine Labor*, June 17, 1960, 1; The Local 180 UAW Collection, WPR, Box 7, Folder 1, letter to members dated June 16, 1960.

24. "Strikebreaking Really Doesn't Pay Very Well," *Racine Labor*, July 8, 1960, 1, 4.

25. "Labor Rallies To Support Embattled Case Strikers: Pledges Aid to Local 180," *Racine Labor*, March 11, 1960, 1; Because the county and state CIO and AFL councils had not merged, the Racine County Industrial Union Council still represented the UAW locals in Racine. For more, see Chapter One.

26. "Case Strikers Carry On; Racine Locals Back Them: Steering Committee is Set Up," *Racine Labor*, March 18, 1960, 1; "Map Plans to Aid Strikers," *Racine Labor*, April 8, 1960, 1.

27. "Local 553 Boosts Aid to Strikers," *Racine Labor*, July 29, 1960, 1.

28. "Nelson Solution: Why Not Bargain?" *Racine Labor*, July 29, 1960, 1.

29. G. Calvin Mackenzie and Robert Weisbrot, *The Liberal Hour: Washington and the Politics of Change in the 1960s* (New York: The Penguin Press, 2008), 42–59.

30. Haney, "The Rise of Wisconsin's New Democrats: A Political Realignment in the Mid-Twentieth Century," 90–106.

31. Bill Cherkasky, interview by Anita Hecht, McLean, Virginia, October 20, 2010, Proxmire Oral History Project, Wisconsin Historical Society,

online transcript, http://content.wisconsinhistory.org/cdm/compoundobject/collection/proxmire/id/3592/rec/3, accessed March 18, 2013; See also, Chapter Two.

32. Gaylord Nelson, "Civil Rights in Wisconsin: Proud Achievements, Unfinished Business," in *The Collected Speeches of Governor Gaylord A. Nelson*, 1959–1960, ed. Edwin R. Bayley (Madison), 1960, 9–16.

33. Harold J. Thompson, The Secretary Says: Gov. Gaylord Nelson!" *Racine Labor*, October 14, 1960, 5; "State AFL-CIO Convo Highlights," *Racine Labor*, October 16, 1964, 9; "Nelson Raps Intervention in Strikes," *Racine Labor*, October 14, 1966, 13; Gaylord Nelson, "Capitol Comments," *Racine Labor*, March 10, 1967, 8.

34. UAW Local 180 Collection, WPR, Box 6, Folder 15, letter to members, April 20, 1960.

35. UAW Local 180 Collection, WPR, Box 7, Folder 1, radio update for August 10–11, 1960.

36. "Case Local Members Give Solid Support," *Racine Labor*, July 22, 1960, 1, 2.

37. "Acceptance of Union Key to Ending Strike," *Racine Labor*, August 26, 1960, 3.

38. E-board to members, April 20, 1960, The UAW Local 180 Collection, WPR, Box 6, Folder 15.

39. George Miller, "Union Ends Case Strike: Expect Callback of All Workers in Two Weeks," *Racine Journal-Times*, September 19, 1960, 1.

40. UAW, Local 180 WPR, Box 7, Folder 1.

41. "Time To Build Kitzman Tells Local 180 Institute: Stewards Discuss Contract," *Racine Labor*, November 18, 1960, 1.

42. "The Weighty One Eighty," *Racine Labor*, March 3, 1961, 10.

43. Kitzman, interview.

44. "Check-Off Won by 180: Is New Era Near at Case Co?" *Racine Labor*, January 4, 1963, 1, 2.

45. "Year of '63 A Milestone for Local 180," *Racine Labor*, August 30, 1963, part 2, 3.

46. "First Western Pact for UAW," *Racine Labor*, January 22, 1960, 1; "Union Shop Vote Won by Local 1007," *Racine Labor*, February 26, 1960, 2.

47. "CIO Council Pledges Aid to Lithos," *Racine Labor*, Feb. 26, 1960, 1; "Litho Turn Down Latest Offer," *Racine Labor*, March 25, 1960, 3; "Litho Get Top Wage," *Racine Labor*, April 15, 1960, 1.

48. "Rae Motor Local Victory," *Racine Labor*, June 24, 1960, 1.

49. Age became a protected category in 1959. See https://dwd.wisconsin.gov/er/civilrights/discrimination/complaintprocess.htm.

50. "Hits Walker's Forced Retirement," *Racine Labor*, January 10, 1964, 1; "Walker Early Retirement," *Racine Labor*, January 31, 1964, 1, 5; "Hits Walker Deal," *Racine Labor*, August 7, 1964, 4; "Local 85 Upheld in Forced Retirement," *Racine Labor*, July 3, 1964, 2.

178 Notes to Chapter 3

51. "One More Hearing is Set in Tangled Walker Retirement," *Racine Labor*, July 31, 1964, 1; *Walker Manufacturing Company v. Industrial Commission*, 27 Wis 2d 669, 135 N.W.2d 307 (1965).

52. Bussel, *Fighting for Total Person Unionism*, 2015.

53. Kitzman, interview.

54. NAACP Racine branch, WHS, Box 1, Folder 1, letter from REA, n.d.

55. "Unions Give Santa a Boost," *Racine Labor*, December 23, 1960, 1.

56. William Jenkins, interview.

57. "AFL-CIO Body to Consider Blood Bank," *Racine Labor*, February 21, 1964, 1; "Pick Labor Team to Spur Racine United Fund Drive," *Racine Labor*, August 23, 1963, 1; "Labor Seeks Post on Staff of United Fund," *Racine Labor*, October 2, 1964, 1; "Resolution Urges Labor Staff Representative for United Fund," *Racine Labor*, October 2, 1964, 8; "Will Keep Pushing for Labor Staff," *Racine Labor*, March 12, 1965, 1; "Valeo Heads United Fund Labor Group," *Racine Labor*, June 4, 1965, 17.

58. "Committee Challenges Claim That Taxes Drive Industry From State," *Racine Labor*, February 5, 1960, 4.

59. "Right to Work Laws a Fraud on the People," *Racine Labor*, July 15, 1960, 1, 4.

60. "Labor Gets Strong Support On Two Measures in Assembly," *Racine Labor*, July 16, 1965, 4; Manny S. Brown, "Legislative Report: Labor Bill Falls Short by Narrow 54–44 Vote," *Racine Labor*, August 4, 1967, 6.

61. Kelly, "Growth of Organized Labor," In *Racine: Growth and Change in a Wisconsin County*, 345–347.

62. Loren Norman, "Squibs," *Racine Labor*, April 22, 1960, 1; "Union Hall to Fight Condemnation Action," *Racine Labor*, April 22, 1960, 1; "Hearing on Union Hall," *Racine Labor*, May 6, 1960, 3; "Fight on Union Hall," *Racine Labor*, May 13, 1960, 1.

63. "Union Hall Association Builds New Home," *Racine Labor*, July 19, 1968, 1; "Union Hall Cornerstone Reveals Historical Items," *Racine Labor*, November 22, 1968, 1, 13.

64. Henri Lefebvre, *The Production of Space*, trans. Donald Nicholson-Smith (Malden, MA: Blackwell, 1991), 33, 62–63, 89–90, and 116–118. Lefebvre represents space as an intersection of spatial practice, representations of space and represented spaces depicting perceived, conceived, and lived space; See also M. Gottdiener, "A Marx for Our Time: Henri Lefebvre and *The Production of Space*," *Sociological Theory* 11, no. 1 (Mar 1993): 129–134; David Harvey, *Justice, Nature and the Geography of Difference* (Malden, MA: Blackwell Publishing, 1996), 417.

65. "Who's Who in Labor," *Racine Labor*, February 25, 1966, 5.

66. "Services Friday for Mrs. Kitzman, Plan Memorial," *Racine Labor*, July 10, 1964, 2; Harold J. Thompson, "The Secretary Says," *Racine Labor*, July 17, 1964, 8.

67. "Loretta Retires," *Racine Labor*, December 20, 1968, 1, 8.

Notes to Chapter 3 179

68. "Two Long-Time City Employees Retiring," *Racine Labor*, December 29, 1967, 1.

69. Racine Trades and Labor Council records, WHS, Box 1, Folder 1, meeting minutes.

70. RTLC records, WHS, Box 1, Folder 3.

71. See for example "Local 67 City Employee Notes," *Racine Labor*, April 1, 1960, 20.

72. Slater, *Public Workers*, 162, 164.

73. See Chapter One.

74. AFL-CIO resolutions, 1964, 1966, Kitzman Papers, WHS; CIO bulletin No. 1, Kitzman Papers, WHS.

75. Letter from Arthur Jung to Fairchild, April 2, 1963, SEIU Executive Office—David Sullivan Files, WPR, Box 51, Folder 5.

76. Tom Beadling, Pat Cooper, Grace Palladino and Peter Pieragostini, *A Need for Valor: The Roots of the Service Employees International Union, 1902–1992* (Washington, DC: SEIU, 1992), 11, 14, 31–34.

77. "AFL-CIO Backs School Employees," *Racine Labor*, July 17, 1964, 1, 2.

78. SEIU Executive Office—David Sullivan Files, WPR, Box 19, Folder 35; Box 19, Folder 38, letter from June Weatherspoon; Box 19, Folder 38, letters from Bernice Joswick, Robert Jahnke, and Valencia Smith; Box 19, Folder 38, letter from Moats to Sullivan, March 19, 1963; Box 20, Folder 2 letter about merger Local 146 into 150, 8 June 1965.

79. William P. Jones, *The March on Washington: Jobs, Freedom, and the Forgotten History of Civil Rights* (New York: W.W. Norton & Company, 2013), 225–227.

80. Quoted in Cobble, *The Other Women's Movement*, 178.

81. Text box, *Racine Labor*, January 6, 1967, 3; Cobble, *The Other Women's Movement*, 110–111, 177–178.

82. SEIU Executive Office—David Sullivan Files, WPR, Box 20, Folder 4, letter from AFL-CIO, July 25, 1966.

83. Leon Fink and Brian Greenberg, "Organizing Montefiore: Labor Militancy Meets a Progressive Health Care Empire," in *Health Care in America: Essays in Social History*, ed. Susan Reverby and David Rosner (Philadelphia, PA: Temple University Press, 1979), 226–228; Lichtenstein, *State of the Union*, 36.

84. SEIU Executive Office—David Sullivan Files, WPR, Box 20, Folder 5; "Ok Labor Contract at St. Luke's Hospital," source unknown.

85. SEIU Executive Office—David Sullivan Files, WPR, Box 20, Folder 6, letter to Sullivan, March 15, 1968.

86. "Plans For Technical Institute Outline To Union Group Here," *Racine Labor*, March 18, 1960, 3.

87. "Vocational School Launches Program to Train Technicians," *Racine Labor*, September 2, 1960, 13.

88. "New Course Will Help You Improve Skills," *Racine Labor*, January 13, 1961, 1.

180 Notes to Chapter 3

89. "Economics Simple as Barbish Explains It," *Racine Labor*, February 19, 1960, 2.

90. Beadling, et al., *Need for Valor*, 34–45; Ruth Milkman, *L.A. Story: Immigrant Workers and the Future of the U.S. Labor Movement* (New York: Russell Sage Foundation, 2006), 10, 62–69.

91. SEIU Executive Office Files—David Sullivan Records, WPR, Box 20, Folder 2, letter to Beatty from Sullivan, dated April 30, 1965; Beadling, et al., *Need for Valor*, 49.

92. See Chapter Five.

93. "When Production is High but Jobs Decline, Look Out," *Racine Labor*, March 4, 1960, 7.

94. "Automation Must Bring Less Hours," *Racine Labor*, July 8, 1960, 6.

95. "UAW Proposes New Plan To Retrain Factory Workers," *Racine Labor*, April 13, 1962, 15.

96. "Hails City's Concern Over Older Folks," *Racine Labor*, March 11, 1960, 11.

97. "Health Insurance for Retired," *Racine Labor*, January 29, 1960, 6.

98. "Benefits of New U.C. Law Pointed Up by Gov. Nelson," *Racine Labor*, September 2, 1960, 7; Clark, *Disruption in Detroit*, 2018.

99. Kitzman papers, WHS, Box 1, Folder 3, AFL-CIO resolutions.

100. "Back Oster Local: Strike Authorization Approved," *Racine Labor*, March 20, 1964, 1; Richard H. Keehn, "Industry and Business," In *Racine: Growth and Change in a Wisconsin County*, ed. Nicholas C. Burckel (Racine: Racine County Board of Supervisors, 1977), 310–313.

101. Keehn, "Industry and Business," 310–311; "Union Faces Problem of Hamilton-Beach Closing," *Racine Labor*, January 26, 1968, 1, 5.

102. "Not Planning to Move, Says Hamilton-Beach," *Racine Labor*, July 4, 1966, 2.

103. "Union Faces Problem of Hamilton-Beach Closing," *Racine Labor*, January 26, 1968, 1, 6.

104. "Union Faces Problem of Hamilton-Beach Closing," *Racine Labor*, January 26, 1968, 1, 6; Irma Johnson, "Hamilton-Beach UAW Local 577: Layoffs Continue," *Racine Labor*, February 2, 1968, 9.

105. "Union Faces Problem of Hamilton-Beach Closing," *Racine Labor*, January 26, 1968, 1, 6.

106. "Nelson Offers Bill to Curb Plant Pirating," *Racine Labor*, April 7, 1967, 8.

107. Irma Johnson, "Hamilton-Beach UAW Local 577: Placement Not Easy," *Racine Labor*, April 12, 1968, 13; Pauline Partach, "Relief Seems Tempting to Job Hunting Widow," *Racine Labor*, January 17, 1969, 1, 10; Irma Johnson, "Hamilton-Beach UAW Local 577: Meeting Crowded," *Racine Labor*, February 16, 1968, 9; Irma Johnson, "Hamilton-Beach UAW Local 577: 35 at Hearing," *Racine Labor*, March 8, 1968, 18; "Hearing Set On Injunction against Hamilton-Beach," *Racine Labor*, March 8, 1968, 2.

Notes to Chapters 3 and 4

108. "Board Votes to Dissolve Hamilton-Beach Credit Union," *Racine Labor*, February 2, 1968, 1, 5; "Hamilton-Beach Makes it Official: 'Goodbye,'" *Racine Labor*, February 9, 1968, 1; Irma Johnson, "Hamilton-Beach UAW Local 577: Meeting Crowded," *Racine Labor*, February 16, 1968, 9; "Vote to Dissolve Credit Union at Hamilton-Beach," *Racine Labor*, February 23, 1968, 1; "Hamilton-Beach Pension statement Terms Told," *Racine Labor*, February 28, 1969, 5; "Note to former Local 577 members," *Racine Labor*, March 7, 1969, 2.

109. Bluestone and Harrison, *Deindustrialization of America*, 1982.

Chapter 4. Race and Shifting Class Boundaries in Racine

1. Lee B. Roberts, "At 89, Corinne Owens is Anything but Retired," *Journal Times*, May 17, 2002; "Corrine Reid-Owens Obituary," *Journal Times*, November 11, 2012; Alyssa Mauk, "Remembering Racine's Leaders: Corinne Reid Owens was 'Racine's Rosa Parks,'" *Journal Times*, November 28, 2019.

2. Lee B. Roberts, "At 89, Corinne Owens is Anything but Retired," *Journal Times*, May 17, 2002; "Corrine Reid-Owens Obituary," *Journal Times*, November 11, 2012; Alyssa Mauk, "Remembering Racine's Leaders: Corinne Reid Owens was 'Racine's Rosa Parks,'" *Journal Times*, November 28, 2019.

3. Crystal Marie Moten, *Continually Working: Black Women, Community Intellectualism, and Economic Justice in Postwar Milwaukee* (Nashville: Vanderbilt University Press, 2023).

4. See Chapter One.

5. Racine NAACP, WHS, General Correspondence 1959, Box 1, Folder 1.

6. Jenkins, interview.

7. Jenkins, interview.

8. Trotter, *Black Milwaukee*, 126–127, 162–163, and 213.

9. Racine NAACP, WHS, letter from national, April 15, 1963; Angela Y. Davis, *Women, Race and Class* (New York: Random House, 1981), 5.

10. Racine NAACP, WHS, letter to Carroll Dickinson, July 24, 1965, Box 1, Folder 2.

11. Heather Ann Thompson, "Why Mass Incarceration Matters: Rethinking Crisis, Decline, and Transformation in Postwar American History," *JAH* 97, no. 3 (Dec 2010): 703–734; Simon E. Balto, "'Occupied Territory': Police Repression and Black Resistance in Postwar Milwaukee," *Journal of African American History* 98, no. 2 (Spring 2013): 229–252.

12. Racine NAACP, General Correspondence, October 1969, WHS.

13. Loren Norman, "Squibs," *Racine Labor*, March 4, 1966, 1, 4 (emphasis in original).

14. Racine NAACP, General Correspondence, October 1969, WHS.

15. "Total Ward Improvement is Goal of LeRoy Wooley," *Racine Labor*, March 22, 1968, 8.

Notes to Chapter 4

16. Racine NAACP, WHS, general correspondence, Box 1, Folder 1, letter to Current, August 24, 1963.

17. "Cite Discrimination in Obry Moss Case," *Racine Labor*, Sept. 27, 1963, 2; "Background of Moss Case," *Racine Labor*, Sept. 27, 1963, 4, 10.

18. "AFL-CIO Council Backs NAACP in Bank Picketing," *Racine Labor*, October 18, 1963, 1.

19. Jenkins interview; Racine NAACP, WHS, General Correspondence, letter from AMC to Thomas, August 1, 1966, and letter from Jenkins to Thomas, August 11, 1966.

20. "Two New Locals Join AFL-CIO Council Here," *Racine Labor*, September 20, 1963.

21. "UAW Parley on Human Relations and Civil Rights," *Racine Labor*, October 14, 1960, 3.

22. "Unions Urged to Take Steps on Civil Rights," *Racine Labor*, November 18, 1960, 12.

23. Cobble, *The Other Women's Movement*, 155–159.

24. "Mayor Attacked on Minority Hiring," *Racine Labor*, March 23, 1962, 1, 2.

25. Bayard Rustin, "The Blacks and the Unions," *Harper's Magazine*, May 1971, 73–81; for a discussion on union's struggles to represent Black workers see William B. Gould, "Black Workers Inside the House of Labor," *Annals of the American Academy of Political and Social Science* 407 (May 1973): 78–90; for a discussion of labor union politics and minority hiring and social justice see Vernon Coleman, "Labor Power and Social Equality: Union Politics in a Changing Economy," *Political Science Quarterly* 103, no. 4 (Winter, 1988–1989): 687–705; for a discussion of the ways liberal politics hindered cross-racial class solidarity during this period see Paul Frymer, *Black and Blue: African Americans, the Labor Movement, and the Decline of the Democratic Party* (Princeton University Press, 2008) and Stein, *Pivotal Decade*, 2010.

26. Rustin, "The Blacks and the Unions," *Harper's Magazine*, May 1971, 73–81.

27. Frymer, *Black and Blue*, 15; Rustin, "The Blacks," 73–81; This was not true across the labor movement. See Battista, *The Revival of Labor Liberalism*, 2008.

28. William P. Jones, *The March on Washington: Jobs, Freedom, and the Forgotten History of Civil Rights* (New York: W.W. Norton & Co., 2013).

29. "Fair Practices Group Reviews Housing, Jobs," *Racine Labor*, March 6, 1970, 7.

30. Kevin Boyle, *The UAW and the Heyday of American Liberalism 1945–1968* (Ithaca: Cornell University Press, 1995), 161–205.

31. Jones, "The Unknown Origins of the March on Washington," 33–52.

32. Cobble, *The Other Women's Movement*, 78–82.

33. Jenkins interview.

34. Boyle, *The UAW*, 126–131; 145–156; 162–167, quote on page 162; Jones, *The March on Washington*, 194–195, quote on 195.

Notes to Chapter 4

35. Minority Hiring Being Probed," *Racine Labor*, March 6, 1964, 1, 2; "Negro Leader Raps Discrimination Here," *Racine Labor*, May 22, 1964, 1, 14.

36. Jones, *The March on Washington*, 132–139. See also, Blair LM Kelley, *Black Folk: The Roots of the Black Working Class* (New York: Liveright Publishing Corporation, 2023), Chapter Four.

37. "Negro Labor Council Officers Are Installed," *Racine Labor*, September 24, 1965, 7; "Fight for Equal Rights, Housing Get Labor Push," *Racine Labor*, November 19, 1965, 1, 2; "AFL-CIO Answers Criticism," *Racine Labor*, November 19, 1965, 1, 2.

38. Kitzman Papers, WHS, Box 1, Folder 3, 1964 Wisconsin state AFL-CIO resolutions.

39. Jenkins, interview.

40. Jenkins, interview.

41. "New Housing Needed to Save City, Mayor Says," *Racine Labor*, April 22, 1966, 8; "YWCA Franklin Project Gaining Area Acceptance," *Racine Labor*, July 15, 1966, 1; "Hill-Kidd Committee Urges 'Compromise' Educational Campaign for Fair Housing," *Racine Labor*, January 27, 1967, 14; "Mayor Stresses Renewal, Race Relations, Housing," *Racine Labor*, April 21, 1967, 1.

42. "Race Tension Exists in Franklin District," *Racine Labor*, Sept. 3, 1965, 25; "YWCA Franklin Project Gaining Area Acceptance," *Racine Labor*, July 15, 1966, 1, 6; "Find Racial Situation Growing Worse in Racine," *Racine Labor*, June 9, 1967, 10.

43. "Cool It, Baby," *Racine Labor*, August 4, 1967, 1; "Good Advice: Keep Cool and Use Common Sense," *Racine Labor*, August 4, 1967, 2; "Locals Urged to Push Open Housing," *Racine Labor*, November 17, 1967, 7; "Racine Spanish Center," *Racine Labor*, December 29, 1967, 17; "Schmitt Challenges Labor to Rally to Aid of Poor," *Racine Labor*, May 10, 1968, 1; "Race Unity Week to be Marked by Picnic, Panel Discussions," *Racine Labor*, June 7, 1968, 1; "Squibs," *Racine Labor*, August 9, 1968, 1; "Negroes Hit Inaction as Riot Cause," *Racine Labor*, August 9, 1968, 2; "Says Racine's Apathy Keeps Minority Down," *Racine Labor*, August 16, 1968.

44. Shannon and McKim, "Attitudes Toward Education and the Absorption of Immigrant Mexican-Americans and Negroes in Racine."

45. Joshua B. Freeman, *American Empire: The Rise of a Global Power, the Democratic Revolution at Home: 1945-2000* (New York: Penguin Books, 2012), 239–241. For a discussion of Milwaukee see Patrick Jones, *The Selma of the North: Civil Rights Insurgency in Milwaukee* (Cambridge: Harvard University Press, 2010).

46. Michael Holmes, "Politics and Government, 1920–1976," In *Racine: Growth and Change in a Wisconsin County*, ed. Nicholas C. Burkel (Racine: Racine County Board of Supervisors, 1977), 256; Norman, "Squibs," *Racine Labor*, May 9, 1969; "Criticize Curfew," *Racine Labor*, May 9, 1969, 8; "Shame of Racine: Indecent Housing," *Racine Labor*, June 6, 1969, 1; "Welfare Clients Present 31 Demands," *Racine Labor*, August 29, 1969, 6; "CISSS That's Coalition

184 Notes to Chapters 4 and 5

for an Improved Social Service System," *Racine Labor*, August 29, 1969, part 2, 5; "Welfare Crisis Told," *Racine Labor*, September 5, 1969, 6; "Groppi Sparks Legal Hassle; He Gets His Publicity, too," *Racine Labor*, October 10, 1969, 1, 2; Jenkins, interview; Dan Day, "From Father Groppi, Priest and Activist to Father Groppi, father and bus driver," *Kingman Daily Miner*, July 3, 1981, 4.

47. "Social Workers Picket," *Racine Labor*, December 27, 1968, 3; "Welfare Workers on Strike," *Racine Labor*, January 3, 1969, 3.

48. "Mayor Stresses Renewal, Race Relations, Housing," *Racine Labor*, August 21, 1967, 1, 8; "Race Unity Week to be Marked by Picnic, Panel Discussions," *Racine Labor*, June 7, 1968, 1; Norman, "Squibs," *Racine Labor*, August 9, 1968, 1, 4; "Negroes Hit Inaction as Riot Cause," *Racine Labor*, August 9, 1968, 2; "Says Racine's Apathy Keeps Minority Down," *Racine Labor*, August 16, 1968, 3.

49. See Chapter Three.

50. "Squibs," *Racine Labor*, January 10, 1969, 1; "Social Workers Strike," image, *Racine Labor*, January 10, 1969, 1; "Social Workers Strike Spills Into Community," *Racine Labor*, January 17, 1969, 1, 7; "Development Hinted in Social Workers Strike," *Racine Labor*, January 24, 1969, 1; "Should Social Workers Strike," *Racine Labor*, January 24, 1969, 1, 4; "Association of Social Workers OKs Strike Goals," *Racine Labor*, January 31, 1969, 3; "New County Team for Strike Talks," *Racine Labor*, February 14, 1969, 2; "Social Workers Dispute Ended," *Racine Labor*, February 21, 1969, 3; "Lauds Social Workers," *Racine Labor*, February 28, 1969, 3.

Chapter 5. Cross-Sector Solidarity Amid a Shifting Landscape

1. "Proposal," Business Records Survey, WHS, Box 1, Folder 11, 6–8; Joseph M. Kelly, "Growth of Organized Labor," in *Racine: Growth and Change in a Wisconsin County*, 345–397; Richard H. Keehn, "Industry and Business," in *Racine: Growth and Change in a Wisconsin County*, 281, 282, 306–307.

2. Bluestone and Harrison, *The Deindustrialization of America*, 1982; Kim Phillips-Fein, *Fear City: New York's Fiscal Crisis and the Rise of Austerity Politics* (New York: Metropolitan Books, 2017); See also Jon Shelton, *Teacher Strike! Public Education and the Making of a New American Political Order* (Urbana: University of Illinois Press), 2017.

3. See Chapter Four.

4. Micahel Holmes, "Politics and Government: 1920–1976," in *Racine: Growth and Change in a Wisconsin County*, 255–257.

5. Freeman, *American Empire*, 123–124, 240; Lisa McGirr, *Suburban Warriors: The Origins of the New American Right* (Princeton: Princeton University Press, 2001).

6. Self, *American Babylon*, 2003; Sugrue, *The Origins of the Urban Crisis*, 2005.

Notes to Chapter 5

7. "Agreement Is Reached Between Firemen, City, Contract Signed Thursday," *Racine Labor*, Jan. 9, 1970, 1, 3.

8. See discussion of Municipal Employee Relations Act (MERA) in Chapter One.

9. "Suit Against Firemen Dismissed, Strike Ends," *Racine Labor*, January 30, 1970, 1, 5.

10. Joseph McCartin has detailed the backlash against public sector unions and strikes during the 1970s. See "A Wagner Act for Public Employees," 123–148; Joseph McCartin, *Collision Course: Ronald Reagan, the Air Traffic Controllers, and the Strike that Changed America* (Oxford: Oxford University Press, 2011), 215–216; Shelton, *Teacher Strike!*

11. "Firefighters Win Round in City Council," *Racine Labor*, July 3, 1970, 2.

12. McCartin, "'A Wagner Act for Public Employees': Labor's Deferred Dream and the Rise of Conservatism, 1970–1976," 123–148; Marjorie Murphy, "Militancy in Many Forms: Teachers Strikes and Urban Insurrection, 1967–74" in *Rebel Rank and File: Labor Militancy and Revolt from Below During the Long 1970s*, eds. Aaron Brenner, Robert Brenner, and Cal Winslow (New York: Verso, 2010), 230; Shelton, *Teacher Strike!*

13. "SEE Sponsors Meeting on Financing Public Schools," *Racine Labor*, February 20, 1970, 6; "SOS Candidates Rebuffed," *Racine Labor*, April 10, 1970, 5; "Vote on $16.2 million in school bonds Tuesday," *Racine Labor*, May 29, 1970, 1, 4.

14. "Teachers Union Offers Proposals for 1970 Salary Negotiations," *Racine Labor*, January 16, 1970, 2; Kelly, "Growth of Organized Labor," 386–389.

15. NAACP, Racine Branch, WHS, general correspondence, Nov 72, Feb 73.

16. Shannon and McKim, "Attitudes Toward Education," 348–355.

17. "Howell School Study 1971–1972," Racine Unified School District No. 1: Superintendent's Files, 1923–1985, WHS, Racine Series 130, Box 21, Folder 9 Howell School, 1972.

18. "Service Employees Strike Unified School District," *Racine Labor*, January 15, 1971, 1, 3.

19. Naomi R Williams, "Sustaining Labor Politics in Hard Times: Race, Labor, and Coalition Building in Racine, Wisconsin," in *Labor: Studies in Working-Class History* 18, no. 2, 41–63.

20. "Local 152 Notice to Citizens," *Racine Labor*, January 15, 1971, 2; "Heavy Bargaining in School Dispute," *Racine Labor*, January 22, 1971, 8; "Schools Normal as Service Strike Ends," *Racine Labor*, 1.

21. "Racine Teachers Strike Schools," *Milwaukee Journal*, September 25, 1972, 1.

22. "Teachers Return in Racine," *Milwaukee Journal*, October 12, 1972; "Teachers Authorize Strike," *Racine Labor*, September 1, 1972, 3; "Alliance for Labor Action Votes Support of Teachers," *Racine Labor*, September 15, 1972, 1; "Teachers' Strike?" *Racine Labor*, September 22, 1972, 1.

23. "Standard Foundry Down the Drain," *Racine Labor*, July 3, 1970, 14.

Notes to Chapter 5

24. R. J. Steiner, "Case Local 180 Report: Future Moves Told," *Racine Labor*, July 3, 1970, 9.

25. Richard H. Keehn, "Industry and Business," in *Racine: Growth and Change in a Wisconsin County*, 319; "23 Local 82 Men Retire from Modine Plant Here under Special Arrangement," *Racine Labor*, November 20, 1970, 6.

26. "Howard Industries Closes Plant on 15-Minute Notice," *Racine Labor*, February 18, 1972, 3; Keehn, "Industry and Business," 312.

27. "Strikes-Negotiations," *Racine Labor*, August 14, 1970, 1; "UAW Local 553 Hits the Bricks," *Racine Labor*, August 21, 1970, 1.

28. "Kozlik Compares Dumore and Case Says Strikers Just Want to Catch Up," *Racine Labor*, September 18, 1970, 1, 2.

29. "Belle City Letters Returned," *Racine Labor*, September 4, 1970, 1, 8.

30. See Chapter Three.

31. Keehn, 295; "Strikers All-Star Game Set, Belle City to Meet Dumore," *Racine Labor*, August 21, 1970, 6; "Service Union Backs Strikers," *Racine Labor*, August 28, 1970, 1; Williams Jenkins, interview; "Average Hourly Earnings," *Racine Labor*, September 18, 1970, 1, 5; for a discussion of economic turmoil during the postwar period see Clark, *Disruption in Detroit*, 2018.

32. "County Board to Probe Slur on Strikers by Food Chief," *Racine Labor*, August 28, 1970, 1; "Resign AFL-CIO Council tells Surplus Foods Director, Unions Ask Director's Dismissal," *Racine Labor*, August 28, 1970, 5.

33. Phillips-Fein, *Fear City*; Shelton, *Teacher Strike!*

34. "Dumore Strikers Say No, 107–5," *Racine Labor*, October 2, 1970, 1; "Resume Belle City Talks," *Racine Labor*, October 16, 1970, 1, 7; "Belle City Talks are Resumed," *Racine Labor*, October 23, 1970, 1, 5; "Dumore Strikers Accept Contract," *Racine Labor*, October 30, 1970, 2; "Local 553 Waits Word," *Racine Labor*, October 30, 1970, 3; "553 Ends 12-Week Strike; Ratifies 3-Year Pact," *Racine Labor*, November 13, 1970, 1, 7.

35. Shannon and McKim, "Attitudes Toward Education and the Absorption of Immigrant Mexican-Americans and Negroes in Racine," *Education and Urban Society* 6, no. 3 (May 1974): 333–354; Community Forum on Race Relations in Racine County, Wisconsin, "Chapter 3: Race Relations and Equal Opportunity in Racine County, Wisconsin," http://www.usccr.gov/pubs/sac/wi0301/ch3.htm; I use the term *Latine* because the census numbers do not separate between Latine heritages. Mexican Americans made up the majority of this background but increases of Puerto Ricans in the 1970s and 1980s requires a broader term.

36. "Petitions Back Minority Groups Seeking More Help Getting Jobs," *Racine Labor*, February 20, 1970, 6.

37. "WSES Defends Minority Placement Activities," *Racine Labor*, February 27, 1970, 15.

38. For a discussion on union's struggles to represent black workers see Gould, "Black Workers Inside the House of Labor," 78–90; for a discussion of labor union politics and minority hiring and social justice see Coleman,

Notes to Chapter 5 187

"Labor Power and Social Equality: Union Politics in a Changing Economy," 687–705; for a discussion of the ways liberal politics hindered cross-racial class solidarity during this period see Frymer, *Black and Blue*, 2008 and Stein, *Pivotal Decade*, 2010.

39. Marc Eisen, "SER Runs the Gamut," *Racine Labor*, September 29, 1972, 3, 12.

40. "Unions Urged to Join in Anti-Poverty Fight," *Racine Labor*, February 20, 1970, 1.

41. Freeman, *American Empire*, 202–203; Boyle, *The UAW and the Heyday of American Liberalism*, 2003; MacLean, *Freedom is Not Enough*, 2006; For a discussion of the ways communities and workers sought to use War on Poverty programs see Annelise Orleck, *Storming Caesar's Palace: How Black Mothers Fought Their Own War on Poverty* (Boston: Beacon Press, 2005) and Annelise Orleck and Lisa Gayle Hazirjian, eds., *The War on Poverty: A New Grassroots History, 1964–1980* (Athens, GA: University of Georgia Press, 2011), see especially Annelise Orleck, "Conclusion: The War on the War on Poverty and American Politics since the 1960s" in this collection for a discussion of the attack on these programs.

42. "UAW Local 1007 Explains Position in Western Publishing Dispute," *Racine Labor*, August 4, 1972, P3; "1007 Ok's New Western Pact," *Racine Labor*, August 11, 1972, 1.

43. "St. Luke's Pact to Expire Tonight," *Journal Times* (Racine), April 30, 1976.

44. Fink and Greenberg, "Organizing Montefiore: Labor Militancy Meets a Progressive Health Care Empire," in *Health Care in America: Essays in Social History*, 226–228; Lichtenstein, *State of the Union*, 36–37.

45. "St. Luke's Workers Seek to Catch Up on Wages," *Racine Labor*, April 12, 1985.

46. "St. Luke's Pact to Expire Tonight," *Journal Times* (Racine), April 30, 1976; "Hospital official disputes figures," *Journal Times* (Racine), May 1, 1976; "Strike Looming at St. Luke's Hospital," *Racine Labor*, May 7, 1976.

47. Windham, *Knocking on Labor's Door*; McCartin, *Collision Course*.

48. David Pfankuchen, "Hospital Offer to Take Effect," *Journal Times* (Racine), May 20, 1976; "Talks Stalled at St. Luke's," *Journal Times* (Racine), May 7, 1976; "Strike Looming at St. Luke's Hospital," *Racine Labor*, May 7, 1976.

49. "Squad Car Hits Picketer," *Racine Labor*, May 28, 1976; "Bargaining Team Sizes Up Strike," *Racine Labor*, June 25, 1976.

50. "Their Pay is Something to Protest About," *Racine Labor*, May 21, 1976.

51. "UAW Support," *Racine Labor*, May 7, 1976; Jenkins, interview.

52. "Their Pay is Something to Protest About," *Racine Labor*, May 21, 1976; Dean Pettit, "Racine Education Association," *Racine Labor*, June 4, 1976; Ivan D. Israel, "UAW LOCAL 180," *Racine Labor*, June 4, 1976; "AFL-CIO Backs Local Strikers," *Racine Labor*, June 4, 1976; "Strike Fund Set Up to Help Picketers at St. Luke's," *Racine Labor*, June 11, 1976; "She'd Get the Soup, I'd Get

the Crackers," *Racine Labor,* June 11, 1976; "Bargaining Team Sizes Up Strike," *Racine Labor,* June 25, 1976.

53. "Strikers Reject Deal," *Racine Labor,* June 25, 1976; "Bargaining Team Sizes Up Strike," *Racine Labor,* June 25, 1976.

54. Fink and Greenberg, *Upheaval in the Quiet Zone: 1199SEIU and the Politics of Health Care Unionism,* 2nd ed. (Urbana: University of Illinois Press, 2009), 166.

55. "Jay Schwartz Mourned," *Racine Labor,* November 24, 1978, 1, 7; "Machinists Lodge 437 Backs Jay Schwartz," *Racine Labor,* April 20, 1962, 1; "Schwartz is New Local 152 Counsel," *Racine Labor,* May 20, 1966, 5; "Dems Chided by Schwartz on Rights Lag," *Racine Labor,* July 26, 1968, 7.

56. "Jay Schwartz Mourned," *Racine Labor,* November 24, 1978, 1, 7; Dick Olson, "The Roaring 70s," *Racine Labor,* November 24, 1978, 4; "Machinists Lodge 437 Backs Jay Schwartz," *Racine Labor,* April 20, 1962, 1; "Schwartz is New Local 152 Counsel," *Racine Labor,* May 20, 1966, 5; "Dems Chided by Schwartz on Rights Lag," *Racine Labor,* July 26, 1968, 7; Memo from Gene Moats to George Hardy, June 16, 1976, SEIU Executive Office Files: George Hardy Collection, Box 18, Folder 36—Local 150, June 1976, WPR Library.

57. "St. Luke's Fires Four," *Racine Labor,* July 2, 1976; "Hospital Strike Collapses," *Racine Labor,* July 9, 1976.

58. "Bargaining Team Sizes Up Strike," *Racine Labor,* June 25, 1976; *St. Luke's Memorial Hospital Inc v. National Labor Relations Board,* 623 F.2d 1173 (7th Cir. 1980), http://openjurist.org (accessed March 8, 2010). "St. Luke's Fires Four," *Racine Labor,* July 2, 1976; "Fired Striker has Five Kids to Feed and No Job," *Racine Labor,* July 30, 1976; "'I Don't Think the Scars Will Ever Heal,'" *Racine Labor,* May 30, 1980.

59. "St. Luke's Fires Four," *Racine Labor,* July 2, 1976.

60. "Drop Charges against St. Luke's Picketer," *Racine Labor,* November 5, 1976; "Bev Smith Cleared but St. Luke's Fights On," *Racine Labor,* December 10, 1976; "Hospital Blocks U.C. Checks," *Racine Labor,* January 21, 1977.

61. "St. Luke's Fired Burdick Illegally," *Racine Labor* July 15, 1977.

62. "Kovac Case Reopened," *Racine Labor,* September 2, 1977.

63. Letter from David Sullivan to Arthur Heitzer, April 30, 1965, SEIU Executive Office—David Sullivan Files, Box 20, Folder 2—Local 150, Mar–Aug 1965, WPR Library.

64. "St. Luke's Illegally Fired Kovac, Burdick Rules NLRB," *Racine Labor,* September 22, 1978; "St. Luke's Predicts Drawn Out Litigation," *Racine Labor,* September 29, 1978.

65. "Who Will Pay for St. Luke's Lawyers?" *Racine Labor,* September 29, 1978.

66. *St. Luke's Memorial Hospital Inc v. National Labor Relations Board,* 623 F.2d 1173 (7th Cir. 1980), http://openjurist.org (accessed March 8, 2010).

67. "I Don't Think the Scars Will Ever Heal," *Racine Labor,* May 30, 1980.

68. "St. Luke's Pays $80,000 in Strike," *Racine Labor,* October 3, 1980.

69. MacLean, *Freedom Is Not Enough*; Windham, *Knocking on Labor's Door*.

70. "REA Wants Written Rules," *Racine Labor*, August 6, 1976; "REA Leadership Urges Efforts at Legal Action," *Racine Labor*, August 27, 1976; "Schwartz Sets Rules of Settlement," *Racine Labor*, September 3, 1976; "School Board Stall Backs Teachers into Corner," *Racine Labor*, January 14, 1977.

71. Patricia Andrews, "No School? It's Pretty Nice," *Racine Journal-Times*, January 25, 1977, 3a.

72. "Local 152 Won't Cross Picket Lines," *Racine Labor*, January 21, 1977, 1; "Teacher Strike Looms," *Racine Labor*, January 21, 1977, 1, 8; "Request Made Not to Cross Picket Lines," *Racine Labor*, January 21, 1977, 1; Dean Pettit, "REA Teachers Union," *Racine Labor*, January 21, 1977, 6; "Alliance, Labor Groups Go Down Line for REA," *Racine Labor*, January 28, 1977, 1, 5; "Local 180 Backs REA Action," *Racine Labor*, January 28, 1977, 2; "Board's Attitude Blocks Settlement Says Dorman," *Racine Labor*, February 25, 1977, 1; Gerald Kongstvedt, "Why a Teacher Refuses to Obey DuRocher's Order," *Racine Labor*, February 25, 1977, 4; Geeta Sharma, "65 Picketing Teachers Arrested," *Racine Journal Times*, February 25, 1977, 1; "Fifty Day Strike Ends," *Racine Labor*, March 18, 1977, 1, 9.

73. "Stanton Skips 24% of Board Meetings," *Racine Labor*, March 4, 1977, 1; "Board Ignores McClennan 8–1 as He Pleads to Rebuild Trust," *Racine Labor*, March 11, 1977, 1, 4; "Jenkins Runs Because of Concern for 'Kids,'" *Racine Labor*, March 18, 1977, 1; "Happel Believes New School Board is Needed," *Racine Labor*, March 25, 1977, 1, 8.

74. "Labor Goes All Out to Change School Board," *Racine Labor*, April 1, 1977, 1; "Labor Helps Oust 2 Unified Incumbents," *Racine Labor*, April 8, 1977, 1, 15; "New Day Dawns," *Racine Labor*, April 8, 1977, 4.

75. "Jenkins, Happel Walk Out of Closed Meeting," *Racine Labor*, June 17, 1977, 1; "Happel Attacks Ad as Money Misuse," *Racine Labor*, July 22, 1977, 1.

76. Shelton, *Teacher Strike!*; Phillips-Fein, *Fear City*.

77. "State Employes Aim to Bring Up Low End," *Racine Labor*, July 8, 1977, 1, 2; "Mediator Named in State Talks," *Racine Labor*, July 15, 1977, 1, 11; "Strike Issues Explained," *Racine Labor*, July 15, 1977, 4.

Chapter 6. Racine's Labor Community and Deindustrialization

1. Collins and Mayer, *Both Hands Tied*, 2010, 5, 23, 34–39; "Economy Slides, Welfare Rolls Grow," *Racine Labor*, July 18, 1980, 3; "1,000 Here to Lose UC Pay Sept. 25," *Racine Labor*, August 6, 1982, 1, 10.

2. Stein, *Pivotal Decade*, 263–264; McCartin, *Collision Course*, 9, 10; "Joblessness in Racine 2nd Highest in State," *Racine Labor*, August 29, 1980, 9; "4.4% Cuts to Hit Families on Aid," *Racine Labor*, December 19, 1980, 1; "Jobless Workers Angry, Frustrated," *Racine Labor*, February 20, 1981, 1.

3. "Burger King Project Non-Union; Boycott Set," *Racine Labor*, January 11, 1980, 1; "Editorial Cartoon," *Racine Labor*, January 18, 1980, 3.

Notes to Chapter 6

4. Lichtenstein, *State of the Union*, 117–118.

5. "Burger King Project Non-Union; Boycott Set," *Racine Labor*, January 11, 1980, 1; "Editorial Cartoon," *Racine Labor*, January 18, 1980, 3; "Burger King Pickets Banned by Court Order," *Racine Labor*, February 1, 1980, 1; "It's Time to Fry Burger King," *Racine Labor*, February 1, 1980, 4; "Boycott Burger King: An Open Letter to Racine's Working People," *Racine Labor*, February 22, 1980, 1; "Burger King Shifts Policy; Boycott Off," *Racine Labor*, June 6, 1980, 1, 2.

6. "UAW Local 37 Strikes Young Radiator," *Racine Labor*, July 3, 1981, 1, 12.

7. "Talks Renewed in Young Strike," *Racine Labor*, August 28, 1981, 12, 13; "Local 37 Ratifies Pact with Young," *Racine Labor*, October 2, 1981, 1, 8.

8. NAACP, Racine Branch, WHS, General Correspondence, Boxes 3–5; Racine NAACP history, Box 6, Folder 2; Committee Meetings, Box 6, Folder 7; General Correspondence, Box 4, Folder 3.

9. "Minority Teachers Meet to Increase Involvement," *Racine Labor*, February 27, 1981, 3; "REA's Black Caucus Gives Scholarship," *Racine Labor*, June 13, 1980, 4.

10. SEIU District 925 Collection, "Organizing: Midwest Field Offices, 1985," WPR, Box 2, Folder 18.

11. "50 Hear Forum Speakers Decry Discrimination," *Racine Labor*, June 12, 1981, 10, 11. Community Forum on Race Relations in Racine County, Wisconsin, "Race Relations and Equal Opportunity in Racine County, Wisconsin," https://www.usccr.gov/pubs/sac/wi0301/ch3.htm, accessed December 2012.

12. "Class Action Suit Charges City Bias," *Racine Labor*, August 21, 1981, 1, 5; "Bias Suit Moves Forward," *Racine Labor*, March 19, 1982, 5; "UAW Local 553 Calls on A-Center to Hire Black," *Racine Labor*, May 2, 1980, 1, 5, 10; "Follow-up: Update on Previous Stories," *Racine Labor*, August 7, 1981, 10.

13. "Local 244 Gets Three Year Pact with Massey-Ferguson," *Racine Labor*, March 14, 1980, 1; "MF to Lay Off 1500," *Racine Labor*, April 25, 1980, 3; "UAW Officials Say MF Collapse Unlikely," *Racine Labor*, September 12, 1980, 1, 8; "Local 244 agrees to concessions to Massey," *Racine Labor*, November 21, 1980, 3.

14. "Massey Bosses Escape Layoffs Despite Pact," *Racine Labor*, April 10, 1981, 3; "Office Layoffs a Blow to UAW 244," *Racine Labor*, December 24, 1981, 3; "MF Workers Angered by Short Notice on Shutdown," *Racine Labor,* February 26, 1982, 3; "Massey Workers Agree on Contract Concessions," *Racine Labor*, April 23, 1982, 7; "Despite Assurances, MF Workers Ready to Fight," *Racine Labor*, October 29, 1982, 1, 6; "MF Workers Plan Dec. 4 Jobs Rally," *Racine Labor*, November 5, 1982, 1, 11.

15. "Workers Reject Concessions to Massey-Ferguson 2 to 1," *Racine Labor*, August 19, 1983, 1.

16. For case studies of communities fighting to save plants see Thomas Fuechtmann, *Steeples and Stacks: Religion and Steel, Crisis in Youngstown* (Cambridge: Cambridge University Press, 1989); Staughton Lynd, *The Fight against Shutdowns: Youngstown's Steel Mill Closings* (San Pedro: Singlejack

Notes to Chapter 6

Books, 1982); Dale A. Hathaway, *Can Workers Have a Voice? The Politics of Deindustrialization in Pittsburgh* (University Park: Pennsylvania State University Press, 1993); Bruce Nissen, ed., *Fighting for Jobs: Case Studies of Labor, Community Coalitions Confronting Plant Closings* (Albany: State University of New York Press, 1995); Jeremy Brecher, *Banded Together: Economic Democratization in the Brass Valley* (Urbana: University of Illinois Press, 2011); Michael Stewart Foley, *Front Porch Politics: The Forgotten Heyday of American Activism in the 1970s and 1980s* (New York: Hill and Wang, 2013), 179–260.

17. Kathryn Marie Dudley, *The End of the Line: Lost Jobs, New Lives in Postindustrial America* (Chicago: University of Chicago Press, 1994); Sherry Lee Linkon and John Russo, *Steeltown USA: Work & Memory in Youngstown* (Lawrence: University Press of Kansas, 2002); Steven High, *Industrial Sunset: The Making of North America's Rust Belt, 1969–1984* (Toronto: University of Toronto Press, 2003).

18. "Jobless Workers Angry, Frustrated," *Racine Labor*, February 20, 1981, 1.

19. "Despite Assurances, MF Workers Ready to Fight," *Racine Labor*, October 29, 1982, 1, 6.

20. "UAW 244 Angrily Responds to MF," *Racine Labor*, November 11, 1983, 1, 5.

21. "Job Security Spurs Jacobsen Strike," *Racine Labor*, May 6, 1983, 1, 19.

22. "Job Security Spurs Jacobsen Strike," *Racine Labor*, May 6, 1983, 1, 19; "UAW 556 Gains Job Protections," *Racine Labor*, May 13, 1983, 1, 4.

23. I use Dionicio Nodin Valdes's term to describe the anti-Mexican rhetoric in popular discourse during the 1980s and 1990s. *Barrios Nortenos: St. Paul and Midwestern Mexican Communities in the Twentieth Century* (Austin: University of Texas Press, 2000), 245–262, quote on page 255.

24. Mae M. Ngai, *Impossible Subjects: Illegal Aliens and the Making of Modern America* (Princeton: Princeton University Press, 2004), 266.

25. MacLean, *Freedom Is Not Enough*, 185.

26. Valdes, *Barrios Nortenos*, 215–216, 245–255; Ngai, *Impossible Subjects*, 265–269; MacLean, *Freedom*, 225–261; Sean Wilentz, *The Age of Reagan: A History, 1974–2008* (New York: HarperCollins, 2008), 167–198.

27. "UAW 553 Chief Rips Raid on Immigrants," *Racine Labor*, June 29, 1984, 1, 5; "UAW 553 Rips Press, INS on Raids," *Racine Labor*, July 6, 1984, 1, 4; "Hispanics Angered, Saddened by Raids," *Racine Labor*, July 1984, 5; "UAW 553 Rips New Immigrant Raid," *Racine Labor*, July 20, 1984, 2; "Labor, Hispanics Decry Raids by INS Agents," *Racine Labor*, July 27, 1984, 13; "UAW 553 to Fight for 2 'Aliens' Jobs," *Racine Labor*, September 28, 1984, 3; Ngai, *Impossible Subjects*, 267.

28. Freeman, *American Empire*, 48, 347.

29. "Randall's Store Workers Ratify First Contract," *Racine Labor*, June 11, 1982, 7; "Sentry Workers Vote for Union," *Racine Labor*, August 6, 1982, 2.

30. See Chapter Three.

192 Notes to Chapter 6

31. Al Hartog, "Join the Labor Run for United Way," *Racine Labor*, August 8, 1980, 3.

32. "Labor Effort Raises $5,000 for the Hungry," *Racine Labor*, March 25, 1983, 1; "Postal Workers Hold Own Food Drive," *Racine Labor*, March 25, 1983, 3.

33. MacLean, *Freedom*, 225, 226; Wilentz, *The Age of Reagan*, 134–137; Van Gosse, "Postmodern America: A New Democratic Order in the Second Gilded Age," in *The World the Sixties Made: Politics and Culture in Recent America*, eds. Van Gosse and Richard Moser (Philadelphia: Temple University Press, 2003), 12.

34. "250,000–500,000 Rally in Washington," *Racine Labor*, September 25, 1981, 1, 7, 11; McCartin, *Collision Course*, 254, 318.

35. "250,000–500,000 Rally in Washington," *Racine Labor*, September 25, 1981, 1, 7, 11.

36. Russ Whitesel, "Creation of a Citizens Utility Board (CUB)" in Chapter 72, Laws of 1979 Information Memorandum by Wisconsin Legislative Council Staff, Madison, WI (Dec 1979).

37. "Local Citizen/Labor Energy Coalition Forming," *Racine Labor*, June 12, 1981, 6; "Newly-Elected Valeo Seeks to Build Cub," *Racine Labor*, February 6, 1981, 1, 5; "CUB to Battle $141 Million Electric Hike," *Racine Labor*, March 13, 1981, 3.

38. "CUB Wins Significant Victory in WEPCO Rate Increase Decision," CUB Bulletin Alert, Sept. 1981; Racine NAACP, letter from Thomas to Strohl, September 29, 1980, WHS, Box 4, Folder 2.

39. "Interest Grows in Feb. 16 Job Hearing Here," *Racine Labor*, February 5, 1982, 1, 5; "Local Jobless Rate at 16.3%, State's Highest," *Racine Labor*, June 4, 1982, 1.

40. "Interest Grows in Feb. 16 Job Hearing Here," *Racine Labor*, February 5, 1982, 1, 5; "Local Jobless Rate at 16.3%, State's Highest," *Racine Labor*, June 4, 1982, 1; "March Set Sept. 5 to Protest Joblessness," *Racine Labor*, August 27, 1982, 3.

41. "Training Program Being Set Up for Case's Laid-off," *Racine Labor*, August 10, 1984, 5; "Program RESTOREs Hope for Case," *Racine Labor*, January 18, 1985, 3, 12; "UAW 180 to Apply for TAA Benefits," *Racine Labor*, August 1, 1986, 1, 6.

42. Pferdehirt, *Blue Jenkins*, 121–123.

43. Dudley, *End of the Line*, 154–155.

44. "Historic Case IH Pact Sets 100% Job Security," *Racine Labor*, May 15, 1987, 1, 7.

45. "Strike Deadline Nears at Case," *Racine Labor*, May 1, 1987, 1, 2; "Historic Case IH Pact Sets 100% Job Security," *Racine Labor*, May 15, 1987, 1, 7; "Skilled Trades Express Rage at New Case Pact," *Racine Labor*, May 22, 1987, 3, 20; "Layoffs Hit about 23 SkilledTrades Workers at Case," *Racine Labor*, March 18, 1988, 8.

Notes to Chapter 6   193

46. "Labor Welcomes Zayre Workers," *Racine Labor*, January 27, 1984, 1, 13; "United Way Offers Help for Workers," *Racine Labor*, August 13, 1982, 1.

47. Windham, *Knocking on Labor's Door*.

48. Ron Thomas, interview with author, July 11, 2014, Racine, WI.

49. "'Unity Party' to Celebrate SEIU Victory at Westview," *Racine Labor*, October 23, 1987, 2.

50. "Labor Songfest Delights crowd of over 1000," *Racine Labor*, October 3, 1986, 16.

51. Tony Rogers, "Concert in Kenosha to Aid Labor," *Chicago Tribune*, September 17, 1986.

52. Dick Weissman, *Which Side are You on? An Inside History of the Folk Music Revival in America* (New York: Continuum, 2005), 10, 54, 57, 59, 151–156; Peter Dreier and Dick Flacks, "Protest Music and Peoples Movements: The Tradition Continues," *Common Dreams*, accessed May 29, 2014, http://www.common dreams.org/view/2014/05/26?print.

53. "UAW 180 Plans Meal, Food Drive for P-40 Strikers," *Racine Labor*, May 22, 1987, 1.

54. Valdes, *Barrios Nortenos*, 228–231.

55. Valdes, *Barrios Nortenos*, 228–231.

56. Valdes, *Barrios Nortenos*, 228–231; "Cudahy Closing to Cost 850 Jobs," *Racine Labor*, April 27, 1984, 1, 12; "Cudahy Workers Accept Final Offer," *Racine Labor*, August 3, 1984, 1; "Cudahy Workers' Struggle Goes On," *Racine Labor*, August 17, 1984, 4; Freeman, *American Empire*, 359–360.

57. "Racine Conference to Look at Industrial Unions' History," *Racine Labor*, April 11, 1986, 3; "Labor History Meeting Set in Racine May 10," *Racine Labor*, April 25, 1986, 8; Darryl Holter, "Veteran Labor Leaders Tell Story of Unionism," *Racine Labor*, May 23, 1986, 5.

58. "St. Luke's Workers Gain Pay Hikes," *Racine Labor*, July 23, 1982.

59. "SEIU Local 150 Co-Sponsors Ethiopia Fundraiser," *Racine Labor*, December 21, 1984; "SEIU Local 150 Joins in Ethiopia Fund Drive," *Racine Labor*, March 1, 1985.

60. "SEIU 150 joins WAC," *Racine Labor*, February 1, 1985.

61. "Local 150, 1985," SEIU Executive Office: John Sweeney Records, WPR, Box 26, Folder 12.

62. "Labor Roundtable Shares Concerns of Unions," *Racine Labor*, March 22, 1985.

63. "St. Luke's Workers Seek to Catch up on Wages," *Racine Labor*, April 12, 1985.

64. "Study Says St. Luke's Pay Ranks at Bottom," *Racine Labor*, April 26, 1985; "Go to St. Luke's, the Union Hospital: SEIU 150," *Racine Labor*, April 26, 1985.

65. Fink and Greenberg, *Upheaval in the Quiet Zone*, xi, 78–82.

66. "St. Luke's Workers Beat Back Concessions Push," *Racine Labor*, May 17, 1985.

194 Notes to Chapter 6

67. "St. Luke's Workers Beat Back Concessions Push," *Racine Labor*, May 17, 1985.

68. Peter Seybold, "St. Luke's Slams Door on Aides," *Racine Labor*, June 28, 1985.

69. Karen Brodkin Sacks, *Caring by the Hour: Women, Work, and Organizing at Duke Medical Center* (Urbana: University of Illinois Press, 1988), 189–207.

70. "St. Luke's Not Abiding by Rulings, SEIU Charges," *Racine Labor*, January 9, 1987, 5; "SEIU 150 Hopes to Settle Issues at Jan. 21 Meet," *Racine Labor*, January 16, 1987, 2, 16; "Agreement May Emerge for St. Luke's Nursing Aides," *Racine Labor*, February 6, 1987, 3; "Mediator to Assist Talks Between St. Luke's, SEIU 150," *Racine Labor*, May 8, 1987, 16; "SEIU Sets Training Session for Members on March 21," *Racine Labor*, March 13, 1987, 2; "St. Luke's Workers Get Update on Talks," *Racine Labor*, May 15, 1987, 2; "SEIU 150 Seeks Better Relations, Pay at St. Luke's," *Racine Labor*, May 22, 1987, 20; "SEIU 150 to Press Ahead for Pay Hike at St. Luke's," *Racine Labor*, June 5, 1987, 10; "SEIU 150 Pleased with Meeting," *Racine Labor*, June 12, 1987, 1.

71. Collins and Mayer, *Both Hands Tied*, 2–3, 37–39.

72. "SEIU Wins Major Case at St. Luke's Hospital," *Racine Labor*, July 10, 1987, 1, 8; "SEIU Hopes Victory Will Lead to Better Relations," *Racine Labor*, September 25, 1987, 1, 4; "SEIU 150 Gets Pay Hikes in Pact with St. Luke's," *Racine Labor*, May 13, 1988, 3.

73. SEIU Organizing Department Records, "Health Care Locals," WPR, Box 6, Folder 2; "Healthcare Organizing," Box 6, Folder 4.

74. "76% at Westview Sign Up for SEIU," *Racine Labor*, August 7, 1987, 1; "Workers Seek Union to Solve Crisis," *Racine Labor*, August 14, 1987, 1, 5; "Westview Workers Seek Recognition," *Racine Labor*, August 21, 1987, 1, 8.

75. "Workers Happy with Sept. 4 Union Vote at Westview," *Racine Labor*, August 28, 1987, 11.

76. "Workers Happy with Sept. 4 Union Vote at Westview," *Racine Labor*, August 28, 1987, 11; "Sept. 12 Hearing Examines Nursing-home Reform Issue," *Racine Labor*, August 28, 1987, 1; "SEIU Optimistic on Vote at Westview," *Racine Labor*, September 5, 1987, 5; "97% Vote 'SEIU' at Westview," *Racine Labor*, September 11, 1987, 1, 11.

77. "Workers to Fight Harris Metals Move to Tenn.," *Racine Labor*, August 14, 1987, 1, 5; "Workers Set Two-part Strategy for Fighting Harris Move to Tennessee," *Racine Labor*, August 21, 1987, 1, 5.

78. "Our History," Jobs with Justice, accessed April 20, 2014, http://www.jwj.org/about-us/our-history.

79. "Spirit of Resurgence at 1987 Labor Fest," *Racine Labor*, September 11, 1987, 1, 12.

80. "Spirit of Resurgence at 1987 Labor Fest," *Racine Labor*, September 11, 1987, 1, 12; NAACP Supports Labor's Cause," *Racine Labor*, September 4, 1987, 3.

81. "Strohl Asks Harris Owner to Reconsider Move to Tenn.," *Racine Labor*,

September 11, 1987, 3; "Boilermakers Plan Major Public Action to Protest Harris Move to Tenn.," *Racine Labor*, September 18, 1987, 1, 9; "Rally Tonight Rips Harris' 'Take the Money & Run,'" *Racine Labor*, September 25, 1987, 1; "Rally Puts Heat on Harris for Moving Jobs," *Racine Labor*, October 2, 1987, 1, 8.

82. "$200 Severance pay Labeled 'Disgusting'," *Racine Labor*, October 2, 1987, 1, 4; "Boilermakers To Vote on Severance Offer Sunday," *Racine Labor*, October 16, 1987, 7; "Harris Ups Severance Offer," *Racine Labor*, October 9, 1987, 3; "Dignity Before Money: Boilermakers Reject Offer," *Racine Labor*, October 23, 1987, 1, 4.

83. "Dignity Before Money: Boilermakers Reject Offer," *Racine Labor*, October 23, 1987, 1, 4.

84. "Boilermakers Vote Sunday on Improved Severance Pay," *Racine Labor*, November 13, 1987, 3; "Harris Workers Approved Beefed-up Severance Pact," *Racine Labor*, November 20, 1987, 6; "Training Help Available for Harris Metals Workers," *Racine Labor*, November 6, 1987, 3.

85. "Wisconsin Labor Management Conference, Milwaukee, April 12, 1989," SEIU Executive Office: John Sweeney, WPR, Box 119, Folder 31.

86. "'New Directions for Labor' Conference Set for May 7," *Racine Labor*, April 22, 1988, 2; "'New Directions' Offers New Tactics, Strategies," *Racine Labor*, April 29, 1988, 2; "Local Results Cheer Up Democrats in Racine," *Racine Labor*, November 11, 1988, 1, 12; "Jobs Shanghaied, UAW 1007 sets March," *Racine Labor*, November 3, 1989, 1, 4; "AFL-CIO Sets Nov. 14 Forum to Build Unity," *Racine Labor*, November 3, 1989, 1; "Momentum Builds for Dec. 2 Jobs Rally," *Racine Labor*, November 17, 1989, 1, 4; "Western Tries Threats to Undermine UAW Boycott," *Racine Labor*, December 1, 1989, 4; "Rally Gains Support," *Racine Labor*, December 1, 1989, 1, 5; "Labor, Community Rally Against Shift of Jobs," *Racine Labor*, December 15, 1989, 1, 4; Freeman, *American Empire*, 409–410; Wilentz, *The Age of Reagan*, 266–273; "AFSCME Local 67 Wins a Battle on Contracting Out," *Racine Labor*, March 11, 1988, 9; "Thompson Blocking Bill on Retirement," *Racine Labor*, March 18, 1988, 1, 11; "AFSCME 67 Gets 2% Pay Hikes in Both Years of Pact," *Racine Labor*, March 18, 1988, 3; "6000 Public Workers Rip Thompson Stance," *Racine Labor*, March 25, 1988, 1, 11; "Historic Choice Before Workers on April 5th," *Racine Labor*, April 1, 1988, 1, 16; "Dukakis Takes State in Worker Oriented Primary," *Racine Labor*, April 8, 1988, 1; "Local Results Generally Good for Labor Movement," *Racine Labor*, April 8, 1988, 3.

Conclusion

1. Dorothy Sue Cobble, "Introduction," in *The Sex of Class: Women Transforming American Labor*, ed. Dorothy Sue Cobble (Ithaca: ILR Press, 2007), 8; Keeanga-Yamahtta Taylor, *From #BlackLivesMatter to Black Liberation* (Chicago: Haymarket Books, 2016); Robin D.G. Kelley, "The Freedom Struggle Is a Labor Struggle, Then & Now," *Against the Current*, https://againstthecurrent

.org/atc210/the-freedom-struggle-is-a-labor-struggle-then-now/, accessed June 19, 2021.

2. Battista, *The Revival of Labor*, 13; Nelson Lichtenstein, *State of the Union: A Century of American Labor*, 255–256.

3. Cobble, 6; Ruth Milkman, "Two Worlds of Unionism: Women and the New Labor Movement," in *The Sex of Class*, 79–80.

4. Naomi R Williams and Sheri Davis-Faulkner, "Worker Mobilization and Political Engagement: A Historical Perspective," in *Revaluing Work(ers): Toward a Democratic and Sustainable Future*, eds. Tobias Schulze-Cleven and Todd E. Vachon (Champaign, IL: Labor and Employment Relations Association, 2021); Barbara Ransby, *Making All Black Lives Matter: Reimagining Freedom in the Twenty-First Century* (Berkeley: University of California Press, 2018).

5. See Tamara L. Lee and Maite Tapia, "A Critical Industrial Relations Approach to Understanding Contemporary Worker Uprising," *Work and Occupations* 50, no. 3: 393–399; Tamara L. Lee and Maite Tapia, "Intersectional Organizing: Building Solidarity through Radical Confrontation," *Industrial Relations* 62, no. 1: 78–111; Tamara L. Lee and Maite Tapia, "Confronting Race and Other Social Identity Erasures: The Case for Critical Industrial Relations Theory," *ILR Review* 74 no. 3 (May 2021): 637–662; Tamara L. Lee, Sheri Davis-Faulkner, Naomi R Williams and Maite Tapia, eds. *A Racial Reckoning in Industrial Relations: Storytelling as Revolution from Within* (Champaign, IL: Labor and Employment Relations Association, 2022).

6. See for example, Annelise Orleck, *"We Are All Fast-Food Workers Now": The Global Uprising Against Poverty Wages* (Boston: Beacon Press, 2018); Erica Smiley and Sarita Gupta, *The Future We Need: Organizing for a Better Democracy in the Twenty-First Century* (Ithaca: ILR Press, 2022).

7. Richard Bensinger, "Unionization Strategies and Recent Developments in Organizing the South," (paper presented at the annual meeting of the Labor Research Action Network, Washington, DC, June 16, 2014).

8. Thompson, *Whose Detroit?* 8.

Bibliography

Archives

Wayne State University, Detroit, MI:
  UAW Local 180 Collection. Walter P. Reuther (WPR) Library.
Wisconsin State Historical Society (WHS), Madison, WI:
  Documenting the Midwestern Origins of the 20th-Century Women's
    Movement, 1987–1992.
  Harvey Kitzman Papers.
  Jenkins, William. Interview by George H. Roeder.
  Racine NAACP.
  Racine Trades and Labor Council (RTLC) records.
  University of Wisconsin–Parkside. Business Survey Records.
  Whiteside, Paul. Interview by James Cavanaugh.
  Wisconsin Labor Oral History Project, 1981–1982.

Primary Sources

Heritage Research Center, "WWII Industrial Facilities: Authorized Feder-
  ally Funded Facilities." http://www.heritageresearch.com/ourlibrary/
  databases/wwii/industries/wisconsin.htm.
J. I. Case Company. *CASE: A Case History*. Racine: Case Company, n.d.
Racine (WI) Journal-Times (newspaper).
Racine (WI) Labor (newspaper).

Secondary Sources

Bailey, Beth, and David Farber, eds. *America in the Seventies*. Lawrence: University Press of Kansas, 2004.

Bibliography

Balto, Simon E. "'Occupied Territory': Police Repression and Black Resistance in Postwar Milwaukee." *Journal of African American History* 98, no. 2 (Spring 2013): 229–252.

Battista, Andrew. *The Revival of Labor Liberalism*. Urbana: University of Illinois Press, 2008.

Beadling, Tom, Pat Cooper, Grace Palladino, and Peter Pieragostini, eds. *A Need for Valor: The Roots of the Service Employees International Union, 1902–1992*. Washington, DC: SEIU, 1992.

Bluestone, Barry, and Bennett Harrison. *The Deindustrialization of America: Plant Closings, Community Abandonment, and the Dismantling of Basic Industry*. NY: Basic Books, 1982.

Borgwardt, Elizabeth. *A New Deal for the World: America's Vision for Human Rights*. Cambridge: Harvard University Press, 2005.

Boyle, Kevin. *The UAW and the Heyday of American Liberalism 1945–1968*. Ithaca: Cornell University Press, 1995.

Brecher, Jeremy. *Banded Together: Economic Democratization in the Brass Valley*. Urbana: University of Illinois Press, 2011.

Brenner, Aaron, Robert Brenner, and Cal Winslow, eds. *Rebel Rank and File: Labor Militancy and Revolt from Below During the Long 1970s*. New York: Verso, 2010.

Brinkley, Alan. *The End of Reform: New Deal Liberalism in Recession and War*. New York: Vintage Books, 1995.

Buenker, John. *Invention City: The Sesquicentennial History of Racine*. Racine: Racine Heritage Museum, 1998.

Burckel, Nicholas C., ed. *Racine: Growth and Change in a Wisconsin County*. Racine: Racine County Board of Supervisors, 1977.

Bussel, Robert. *Fighting for Total Person Unionism: Harold Gibbons, Ernest Calloway, and Working-Class Citizenship*. Urbana: University of Illinois Press, 2015.

Caldwell, Patrick. "The County that Swings Wisconsin." *The American Prospect*. October 25, 2012.

Chen, Anthony. *The Fifth Freedom: Jobs, Politics, and Civil Rights in the United States, 1941–1972*. Princeton University Press, 2009.

Clark, Daniel J. *Disruption in Detroit: Autoworkers and the Elusive Postwar Boom*. Urbana: University of Illinois Press, 2018.

Cobble, Dorothy Sue. *The Other Women's Movement: Workplace Justice and Social Rights in Modern America*. Princeton University Press, 2004.

Cobble, Dorothy Sue, ed. *The Sex of Class: Women Transforming American Labor*. Ithaca: ILR Press, 2007.

Cohen, Lizabeth. *Making a New Deal: Industrial Workers in Chicago, 1919–1939*. Cambridge: Cambridge University Press, 1990.

Coleman, Vernon. "Labor Power and Social Equality: Union Politics in a Changing Economy." *Political Science Quarterly* 103, no. 4 (Winter, 1988–1989): 687–705.

Bibliography

Collins, Jane L., and Victoria Mayer. *Both Hands Tied: Welfare Reform and the Race to the Bottom in the Low-Wage Labor Market*. University of Chicago Press, 2010.

Colton, Joel, and Stuart Bruchey, eds. *Technology, the Economy, and Society: The American Experience*. New York: Columbia University Press, 1987.

Connell, Tula. *Conservative Counterrevolution: Challenging Liberalism in 1950s Milwaukee*. Urbana: University of Illinois Press, 2016.

Cowie, Jefferson. *Capital Moves: RCA's Seventy-Year Quest for Cheap Labor*. Ithaca: Cornell University Press, 1999.

Cowie, Jefferson. *The Great Exception: The New Deal and the Limits of American Politics*. Princeton University Press, 2016.

Cowie, Jefferson. *Stayin' Alive: The 1970s and the Last Days of the Working Class*. New York: The New Press, 2010.

Cowie, Jefferson, and Joseph Heathcott, eds. *Beyond the Ruins: The Meanings of Deindustrialization*. Ithaca: ILR Press, 2003.

Davis, Angela Y. *Women, Race and Class*. New York: Random House, 1981.

Dudley, Kathryn Marie. *The End of the Line: Lost Jobs, New Lives in Postindustrial America*. Chicago: University of Chicago Press, 1994.

Enke, Finn. *Finding the Movement: Sexuality, Contested Space, and Feminist Activism*. Durham: Duke University Press, 2007.

Fink, Leon, and Brian Greenberg. *Upheaval in the Quiet Zone: 1199SEIU and the Politics of Health Care Unionism*. 2nd ed. Urbana: University of Illinois Press, 2009.

Foley, Michael Stewart. *Front Porch Politics: The Forgotten Heyday of American Activism in the 1970s and 1980s*. New York: Hill and Wang, 2013.

Freeman, Joshua B. *American Empire: The Rise of a Global Power, the Democratic Revolution at Home: 1945–2000*. New York: Penguin Books, 2012.

Friedman, Tami. "'Acute Depression in the Age of Plenty': Capital Migration, Economic Dislocation, and the Missing 'Social Contract' of the 1950s." *Labor: Studies in Working Class History of the Americas* 8, no. 4 (January 2011): 89–113.

Frymer, Paul. *Black and Blue: African Americans, the Labor Movement, and the Decline of the Democratic Party*. Princeton University Press, 2008.

Fuechtmann, Thomas. *Steeples and Stacks: Religion and Steel, Crisis in Youngstown*. Cambridge: Cambridge University Press, 1989.

Fure-Slocum, Eric. *Contesting the Postwar City: Working-Class and Growth Politics in 1940s Milwaukee*. Cambridge University Press, 2013.

Gilpin, Toni. *The Long Deep Grudge: A Story of Big Capital, Radical Labor, and Class War in the American Heartland*. Chicago: Haymarket Books, 2020.

Gordon, Colin Gordon. *New Deals: Business, Labor, and Politics in America, 1920–1935*. Cambridge: Cambridge University Press, 1994.

Gordon, Robert J. *The Rise and Fall of American Growth: The U.S. Standard of Living Since the Civil War*. Princeton University Press, 2016.

Gosse, Van, and Richard Moser, eds. *The World the Sixties Made: Politics and Culture in Recent America*. Philadelphia: Temple University Press, 2003.

Gould, William B. "Black Workers Inside the House of Labor." *Annals of the American Academy of Political and Social Science* 407 (May 1973): 78–90.

Hahamovitch, Cindy. *No Man's Land: Jamaican Guestworkers in America and the Global History of Deportable Labor*. Princeton University Press, 2011.

Hall, Jacquelyn Dowd. "The Long Civil Rights Movement and the Political Uses of the Past." *JAH* 91, no. 4 (Mar 2005): 1233–1263.

Haney, Richard C. "The Rise of Wisconsin's New Democrats: A Political Realignment in the Mid-Twentieth Century." *The Wisconsin Magazine of History* 58, no. 2 (Winter, 1974–1975): 90–106.

Harris, Howell John. *The Right to Manage: Industrial Relations Policies of American Business in the 1940s*. Madison, WI: University of Wisconsin Press, 1982.

Hathaway, Dale A. *Can Workers Have a Voice?: The Politics of Deindustrialization in Pittsburgh*. University Park, PA: Pennsylvania State University Press, 1993.

Harvey, David. *Justice, Nature and the Geography of Difference*. Malden, MA: Blackwell Publishing, 1996.

Hayes, Robert H., and William J. Abernathy. "Managing Our Way to Economic Decline." *Harvard Business Review* 58, no. 4 (1980): 67–77.

High, Steven. *Industrial Sunset: The Making of North America's Rust Belt, 1969–1984*. Toronto: University of Toronto Press, 2003.

Horowitz, Roger. *"Negro and White, Unite and Fight!" A Social History of Industrial Unionism in Meatpacking, 1930–90*. Urbana: University of Illinois Press, 1997.

Jones, William P. *The March on Washington: Jobs, Freedom, and the Forgotten History of Civil Rights*. New York: W.W. Norton & Co., 2013.

Jones, William P. "The Unknown Origins of the March on Washington: Civil Rights Politics and the Black Working Class." *Labor: Studies in Working-Class History of the Americas* 7, no. 3 (2010): 33–52.

Kelley, Blair LM. *Black Folk: The Roots of the Black Working Class*. New York: Liveright Publishing Corporation, 2023.

Kelley, Robin D.G. "The Freedom Struggle Is a Labor Struggle, Then & Now." *International Viewpoint*, January 2021. https://internationalviewpoint.org/spip.php?article6986.

Kersten, Andrew. *Race, Jobs, and the War: The FEPC in the Midwest, 1941–46*. Urbana: University of Illinois Press, 2000.

Korstad, Robert, and Nelson Lichtenstein. "Opportunities Found and Lost: Labor, Radicals, and the Early Civil Rights Movement." *JAH* 75 (Dec 1985): 786–811.

Lee, Tamara L. and Maite Tapia. "A Critical Industrial Relations Approach to Understanding Contemporary Worker Uprising." *Work and Occupations* 50, no. 3: 393–399.

Bibliography

Lee, Tamara L. and Maite Tapia. "Confronting Race and Other Social Identity Erasures: The Case for Critical Industrial Relations Theory." *ILR Review* 74, no. 3 (May 2021): 637–662.

Lee, Tamara L. and Maite Tapia. "Intersectional Organizing: Building Solidarity through Radical Confrontation." *Industrial Relations* 62, no. 1:78–111.

Lee, Tamara L., Sheri Davis-Faulkner, Naomi R Williams, and Maite Tapia, eds. *A Racial Reckoning in Industrial Relations: Storytelling as Revolution from Within.* (Champaign, IL: Labor and Employment Relations Association, 2022.

Levinson, Marc. *An Extraordinary Time: The End of the Postwar Boom and the Return of the Ordinary Economy.* New York: Basic Books, 2016.

Lichtenstein, Nelson. *Labor's War at Home: The CIO in World War II.* Cambridge: Cambridge University Press, 1982.

Lichtenstein, Nelson. *The Most Dangerous Man in Detroit: Walter Reuther and the Fate of American Labor.* New York: Basic Books, 1995.

Lichtenstein, Nelson. *State of the Union: A Century of American Labor.* Princeton University Press, 2002.

Linkon, Sherry Lee, and John Russo. *Steeltown USA: Work & Memory in Youngstown.* Lawrence: University Press of Kansas, 2002.

Lynd, Staughton. *The Fight against Shutdowns: Youngstown's Steel Mill Closings.* San Pedro: Singlejack Books, 1982.

Mackenzie, G. Calvin, and Robert Weisbrot. *The Liberal Hour: Washington and the Politics of Change in the 1960s.* New York: Penguin Press, 2008.

MacLean, Nancy. *Freedom Is Not Enough: The Opening of the American Workplace.* Cambridge: Harvard University Press, 2006.

McCartin, Joseph. *Collision Course: Ronald Reagan, the Air Traffic Controllers, and the Strike that Changed America.* Oxford: Oxford University Press, 2011.

McCartin, Joseph. "'A Wagner Act for Public Employees': Labor's Deferred Dream and the Rise of Conservatism, 1970–1976." *Journal of American History* 95, no. 1 (June 2008): 123–148.

McGirr, Lisa. *Suburban Warriors: The Origins of the New American Right.* Princeton University Press, 2001.

Mckee, Guian A. *The Problem of Jobs: Liberalism, Race, and Deindustrialization in Philadelphia.* Chicago: University of Chicago Press, 2008.

Meier, August, and Elliott Rudwick. *Black Detroit and the Rise of the UAW.* New York: Oxford University Press, 1979.

Milkman, Ruth. *L.A. Story: Immigrant Workers and the Future of the U.S. Labor Movement.* New York: Russell Sage Foundation, 2006.

Moten, Crystal Marie. *Continually Working: Black Women, Community Intellectualism, and Economic Justice in Postwar Milwaukee.* Nashville: Vanderbilt University Press, 2023.

Ngai, Mae M. *Impossible Subjects: Illegal Aliens and the Making of Modern America.* Princeton University Press, 2004.

Nissen, Bruce, ed. *Fighting for Jobs: Case Studies of Labor, Community*

Coalitions Confronting Plant Closings. Albany: State University of New York Press, 1995.

Orleck, Annelise. *Storming Caesar's Palace: How Black Mothers Fought Their Own War on Poverty*. Boston: Beacon Press, 2005.

Orleck, Annelise. *"We Are All Fast-Food Workers Now": The Global Uprising Against Poverty Wages*. Boston: Beacon Press, 2018.

Orleck, Annelise, and Lisa Gayle Hazirjian, eds. *The War on Poverty: A New Grassroots History, 1964–1980*. Athens, GA: University of Georgia Press, 2011.

Ozanne, Robert W. *The Labor Movement in Wisconsin: A History*. Madison: State Historical Society of Wisconsin, 1984.

Pferdehirt, Julia. *Blue Jenkins: Working for Workers*. Madison: Wisconsin Historical Society Press, 2011.

Phillips, Lisa. *A Renegade Union: Interracial Organizing and Labor Radicalism*. Urbana: University of Illinois Press, 2013.

Phillips-Fein, Kim. *Invisible Hands: The Making of the Conservative Movement from the New Deal to Reagan*. New York: W.W. Norton, 2009.

Phillips-Fein, Kim. *Fear City: New York's Fiscal Crisis and the Rise of Austerity Politics*. New York: Metropolitan Books, 2017.

Pizzigati, Sam, and Fred J. Solowey, eds. *The New Labor Press: Journalism for a Changing Union Movement*. New York: ILR Press, 1992.

Ransby, Barbara. *Making All Black Lives Matter: Reimagining Freedom in the Twenty-First Century*. Berkeley: University of California Press, 2018.

Reichard, Hugh. "Racine Again." *Ammunition* 4, no. 3 (March 1946): 18–19.

Reverby, Susan, and David Rosner. *Health Care in America: Essays in Social History*. Philadelphia, PA: Temple University Press, 1979.

Rustin, Bayard. "The Blacks and the Unions." *Harper's Magazine*. May 1971.

Sacks, Karen Brodkin. *Caring by the Hour: Women, Work, and Organizing at Duke Medical Center*. Urbana: University of Illinois Press, 1988.

Schulze-Cleven, Tobias, and Todd E. Vachon, ed. *Revaluing Work(ers): Toward a Democratic and Sustainable Future*. Champaign, IL: Labor and Employment Relations Association, 2021.

Self, Robert O. *American Babylon: Race and the Struggle for Postwar Oakland*. Princeton University Press, 2003.

Shannon, Lyle W., and Judith L. McKim. "Attitudes Toward Education and the Absorption of Immigrant Mexican-Americans and Negroes in Racine." *Education and Urban Society* 6, no. 3 (May 1974): 333–354.

Shelton, Jon. *Teacher Strike! Public Education and the Making of a New American Political Order*. Urbana: University of Illinois Press, 2017.

Shermer, Elizabeth Tandy. "Origins of the Conservative Ascendancy: Barry Goldwater's Early Senate Career and the Delegitimization of Organized Labor." *JAH* 95 (Dec 2008): 678–709.

Sherry, Michael. *In the Shadow of War: The United States Since the 1930s*. New Haven: Yale University Press, 1997.

Bibliography

Slater, Joseph E. *Public Workers: Government Employee Unions, the Law, and the State, 1900–1962*. Ithaca: ILR Press, 2004.

Smiley, Erica, and Sarita Gupta, *The Future We Need: Organizing for a Better Democracy in the Twenty-First Century*. Ithaca: ILR Press, 2022.

Stein, Judith. *Pivotal Decade: How the United States Traded Factories for Finance in the Seventies*. New Haven: Yale University Press, 2010.

Stein, Judith. *Running Steel Running America: Race, Economic Policy, and the Decline of Liberalism*. Chapel Hill: University of North Carolina Press, 1998.

Sugrue, Thomas J. *The Origins of the Urban Crisis: Race and Inequality in Postwar Detroit*. 2nd ed. Princeton University Press, 2005.

Taylor, Keeanga-Yamahtta. *From #BlackLivesMatter to Black Liberation*. Chicago: Haymarket Books, 2016.

Thompson, Heather Ann. *Whose Detroit? Politics, Labor, and Race in a Modern American City*. Ithaca: Cornell University Press, 2001.

Thompson, Heather Ann. "Why Mass Incarceration Matters: Rethinking Crisis, Decline, and Transformation in Postwar American History." *JAH* 97, no. 3 (Dec 2010): 703–734.

Trotter, Joe William, Jr. *Black Milwaukee: The Making of An Industrial Proletariat, 1915–45*. 2nd ed. Urbana: University of Illinois Press, 2007.

Turner, Lowell, et al., ed. *Rekindling the Movement: Labor's Quest for Relevance in the 21st Century*. Ithaca: ILR Press, 2001.

Uphoff, Walter. *Kohler on Strike: Thirty Years of Conflict*. Boston: Beacon Press, 1966.

Valdes, Dionicio Nodin. *Barrios Nortenos: St. Paul and Midwestern Mexican Communities in the Twentieth Century*. Austin: University of Texas Press, 2000.

Weissman, Dick. *Which Side are You on? An Inside History of the Folk Music Revival in America*. New York: Continuum, 2005.

Wilentz, Sean. *The Age of Reagan: A History, 1974–2008*. New York: HarperCollins, 2008.

Williams, Naomi R. "Sustaining Labor Politics in Hard Times: Race, Labor, and Coalition Building in Racine, Wisconsin." *Labor: Studies in Working-Class History*, 18, no. 2: 41–63.

Windham, Lane. *Knocking on Labor's Door. Union Organizing in the 1970s and the Roots of a New Economic Divide*. Chapel Hill: University of North Carolina Press, 2017.

Index

Act 10 (Wisconsin), 3, 9
AFSCME Local 63, 49
agriculture, 6–7, 129, 144. *See also* J. I.
  Case Company
Akron, OH, 6
Allegheny Ludlum Industries, 83
Alliance for Labor, 110
Allis Chalmers Manufacturing
  Company, 24, 68
Amazon company, 161
American Civil Liberties Union, 133
American Federation of Labor (AFL),
  2, 5, 7, 20–27, 37, 53, 56, 77–79,
  91–102, 141–44, 161; and merger
  with CIO, 60–61. *See also* Congress
  of Industrial Organizations (CIO);
  Racine County AFL-CIO
American Federation of State,
  County and Municipal Employees
  (AFSCME), 49, 53, 77, 104, 127–28
American Federation of Teachers
  (AFT), 49. *See also* education
American Motors Company, 54, 91,
  96, 144
Aspin, Les, 142–43, 153–55
Austin, MN, 147
automation, 55, 61, 64, 80–81

Baldwin, Tammy, 2
banking, 90–91
Barbish, Jack, 81

B. D. Eisendrath Tannery, 55, 83
Beatty, Don, 78–80, 119–23
Belle City Malleable, 24, 32–35, 45,
  68–70, 95, 111–14, 133–39, 147–48
Bettendorf, IA, 111
Beyer, William H., 83, 98, 105
Black Lives Matter movement, 161
Black workers, 1–20, 31–38, 41, 61, 68,
  79, 87–117, 132–39; and migration, 4,
  19, 31–35, 79, 117, 130, 138, 161; and
  women, 39, 78
Blada, Mitch, 136
Bluestone, Barry, 13–14
Boilermakers Local 1703, 153–56
Brown, Manny, 75
Buhler, Ed, 137
Building Service Employees Interna-
  tional Union (BSEIU), 7, 49, 77–81,
  86
Burdick, Art, 117, 121–24
Burger King, 130–31
Burman, Bruce, 141
Bush, George H. W., 157
Bush, George W., 1
Bussel, Robert, 20, 74

Caldwell, Patrick, 1–2, 12
Calloway, Ernest, 20
Canada, 134
capitalism, 13–14, 160. *See also* corporate power

206 Index

Carey, James B., 81
Caribbean workers, 34–35
Case, Jerome I., 26
Case Company. *See* J. I. Case
  Company
Caterpillar Company, 68
Catlin, Mark, 52
Change to Win (CTW), 161
Cherkasky, Bill, 70
Chicago, IL, 1, 6–7, 19, 28, 36, 78,
  94–96, 138–39
Christensen, Loretta, 5, 39, 76–77, 95
church/religion, 48, 92, 100, 125, 133,
  135, 143. *See also* Young Women's
  Christian Association (YWCA)
Citizen-Labor Energy Coalition,
  142–43
citizenship (economic), 8–9, 13, 20–27,
  41, 61, 104–6, 143, 160
Citizens Utility Board (CUB), 142
Civil Rights Act (1964), 78
civil rights movements, 2–9, 26, 33, 41,
  71, 78, 89–102, 125, 133, 146, 161–62.
  See also women's rights movements
Clausen, Leon R., 26–30
Cold War, 13, 26, 50, 138, 160
collective bargaining, 3, 8, 14–17,
  25–27, 43, 49, 64–79
Collins, Jane, 2–3
Commission on Human Rights
  (Racine), 87, 91
Communist Party/Communism, 25,
  44, 50–52. *See also* Socialist Party/
  socialism
Concerned Minority Citizens Group,
  100
Congress of Industrial Organizations
  (CIO), 2, 7, 21, 25, 33–38, 50–56,
  77–79, 161; and merger with AFL,
  60–61
conservatism, 2, 4, 9–27, 43–53, 59,
  104–8, 141–56
Consumer Price Index, 49
contingent workers, 161
Cooks, Victor, 147
corporate power, 2–10, 24–25, 45, 54,
  106, 129, 145–47, 159. *See also* corporate restructuring

corporate restructuring, 10–17, 44–46,
  54–56, 61, 64, 80–86, 111, 146, 153.
  See also corporate power
Cowie, Jefferson, 10
Cudahy, Patrick, 146, 154
Cupery, Steve, 149–50
CWA Local 4611, 154

Day, Clara, 40
DeBruin, Cookie, 141
declension narrative, 2, 12–14, 160. *See
  also* historiography
deindustrialization (general), 1–6,
  11–17, 54, 105, 129–30, 159–62. *See
  also* Racine: deindustrialization
DeLaat, Tony, 69
Delgado, Gilbert, 146
democracy, 4, 8–13, 20–30, 43–44, 48,
  64–73, 86, 104, 118
Democratic Party (national), 2, 8, 10,
  13, 22, 26, 70, 156–59
Democratic Party (Wisconsin), 2–5,
  17–23, 43, 52–53, 61–70, 94, 142–43.
  See also Nelson, Gaylord
Department of Health and Social Ser-
  vices, 129
Department of Public Works, 49
DeRosier, Barbara, 122–23
Des Moines, Iowa, 134–35
Detroit, MI, 32–36, 45, 66, 84, 106,
  134–35, 173n42
Diaz, Moises, 68
Dorman, Henry, 125
Dorn, Anthony, 125
Dowd Hall, Jacquelyn, 9
Doyle, James, 23
Dremel, Ted, 152–53
Dreyfus, Lee, 129
Dr. John Bryant Neighborhood
  Center, 87
Dukakis, Michael, 156–57
Duke Medical Center, 151
Dunmore Company, 112–14

Eagle Hall (Racine), 59
Economic Bill of Rights, 13
education, 4, 74–82, 87, 91, 98, 105–10,
  124–33

Index

Eisenhower, Dwight D., 46
Emergency Labor Importation Program, 34
Enke, Finn, 174n51
Executive Order 8802, 33

Fair Employment Practices Committee (FEPC), 33
Fair Labor Standards Act (FLSA), 78–79
Faucett, Tom, 77
federal government, 7–9, 13, 24, 30–35, 106, 129, 139, 145–46. *See also* New Deal
Feick, Brenda, 148–49
feminism, 38, 40, 67, 78, 141, 174n51. *See also* gender; women workers
Fields, Morris, 65
Fight for $15 movement, 161
Fink, Leon, 117, 120
firefighters, 7, 51, 77–78, 106–7, 112, 121
Floyd, George, 161
Flynn, Gerald, 53
Ford Motor Company, 32–33
foreign workers, 34–35. *See also* immigration; migration
Fought, Dick, 137–39
Franklin Community Center (Racine), 98
freedom, 13, 29. *See also* democracy
Fure-Slocum, Eric, 169n86

Garvey, Ed, 155
Gary, IN, 6, 139
Gateway Technical Institute, 143, 156
gender, 3 17, 20, 38 41, 61, 67, 78, 86–103, 117–18. *See also* feminism; women workers
General Motors, 10, 45
Gephardt, Richard, 142
Gibbons, Harold, 20
Goldwater, Barry, 59
Great Depression, 5, 7, 21, 26, 63, 160
Great Society programs, 115–16
Grede, William, 66, 70–71
Greenberg, Brian, 120
Greene Manufacturing, 77

Greenhouse, Pat, 71
grocery stores, 139–40
Groppi, James, 100
Gupta, Sarita, 161–62

Habermas, George, 56
Haener, Dorothy, 39
Hamilton-Beach Company, 83–85, 112, 117
Hamilton, Louis, 112
Happel, Marv, 126–27
Harris Metals, 148, 153–56
Harrison, Bennett, 13–14
Hartmann Luggage Company, 83
Hartog, Al, 140
Harvey, David, 76
Harvey, Richard, 106–7
Heitzer, Arthur, 81, 123
Heitzer, Michael, 81
Herron, Albert, 148, 153–56
Hess, Robert, 113
Heymanns, Charles, 60, 79, 147
Hill, Augusta, 96
historiography, 3–14, 24–25, 32–34, 43, 74, 78, 89–90, 161–62; and declension narrative, 2, 12–14, 160
Holston, Ruth, 151
Hoover, Herbert, 28
Horlick High School (Racine), 132
Horlicks Corporation, 40, 83
Hormel, 147
Hospital Workers' Union Local 1199, 120–21, 149
housing, 4, 10, 14, 37–38, 97–101, 129
Houston, TX, 14
Howard Industries, 40, 112
Howell Elementary School (Racine), 108–10
Huck, Gary, 130
Huck, Kenneth L., 99, 105–6
Hudson Company, 54
Humble, Jack H., 87, 92

IAFF Local 321, 106–8
immigration, 5, 117, 130, 137–39, 161. *See also* migration
Immigration and Naturalization Service (INS), 130, 137–39

Index

industrial unionism, 21, 48–49, 61, 81. *See also* Congress of Industrial Organizations (CIO)
Industrial Workers of the World (IWW), 50
International Association of Machinists (IAM), 100
International Harvester, 68
Ironworkers Local 8, 130
Iverson, Dan, 148–53
Iverson, George, 83–84

Jackson, Jesse, 156
Jacobsen Manufacturing, 83, 137, 141
Jenkins, Frank, 31–32, 34–37
Jenkins, William, 19, 45, 64, 113; background, 4, 6, 31; and job training programs, 143–44; leadership of, 19, 31–36, 72–74, 87–101, 143–48; and school board, 126–27
J. I. Case Company, 5, 7, 24, 76, 82, 113, 116, 129, 144; history of, 26–27; and management, 9, 20, 29–30, 40, 44, 65–71, 111, 144; and plants/plant closings, 29, 55, 67, 83, 111; strikes against, 9, 20, 28–31, 63–73, 86, 113; and workers' rights, 26–30, 40, 58–59, 66, 71–73. *See also* UAW Local 180
Jobs with Justice, 154
job training, 115–17, 143–44, 155–56
John Deere Company, 68
John Oster Manufacturing Company, 82
Johnson, Erling, 55
Johnson, Lyndon B., 78, 94, 116
Johnson, Richard, 131–32
Johnson, Roma, 77
Johnson, Russ, 77
Jones, Sam, 133
Jones, William P., 78
journalism, 1, 6, 16, 19, 22, 41

Kamla, Geraldine, 39
Kansas City, MO, 36
Kennedy, John F., 58, 95
Kennedy, Robert, 58
Kenosha, WI, 6, 21, 54, 68, 91–96, 131–33, 140–46

Kern County Land Company, 83
Kerner Commission, 99
King, Martin Luther Jr., 125
Kirkland, Lane, 141
Kitzman, Arthur, 47
Kitzman, Edrie, 76
Kitzman, Harvey, 5, 27–30, 36–52, 64–66, 74–76, 94–97
Kiwanis Club, 89
Knights of Labor, 7, 20
Kohler, Herbert V., 59
Kohler Company, 44, 53, 57–60, 147; strikes against, 57–60, 64–65, 86
Kongstvedt, Gerald, 125
Korstad, Robert, 34
Kovac, Ellen, 103, 117–18, 122–24
Kozlik, Paul, 113

Labaj, S. V., 48
Labor and Public Welfare Committee, 58, 70
Labor Day events, 15, 21, 39, 57, 113, 143–45, 154, 156
labor feminists. *See* feminism, women workers
labor history. *See* historiography
labor-liberal coalition, 2, 8–13, 23, 64–85, 93–106, 127, 156–57, 160. *See also* Democratic Party; liberalism/liberals; New Deal
Labor Songfest, 145–47
La Follette, Philip, 49
La Follette, Robert M., 52
La Guardia, Fiorello, 30
Lakeside Malleable, 37
Latine students, 109
Latine workers, 9, 15–16, 79, 89–99, 114–17, 132–39
law and order rhetoric, 28–29, 70
law/lawyers, 3, 51–59, 78–82, 106, 123–27, 160
lawsuits, 3, 53–59, 74, 106, 123, 135
layoffs, 1, 3, 10–13, 54–55, 82–83, 111, 129–36, 143–51
League of Women Voters, 88, 91–92
Lee, Tamara, 161
LGBTQIA+, 16
liberalism/liberals, 9–13, 17, 20, 25–26, 87–101, 127, 159. *See also* Democratic

Index

Party; labor-liberal coalition; New Deal
Lichtenstein, Nelson, 8, 24–25, 34, 167n28
Lindberg Corporation, 155
Love, Thomas, 133

Mack, Keith, 108, 132
Madison, WI, 77, 141, 156
March on Washington Movement, 33–34, 88, 94–95
Margosian, Michael, 108
Martin, Trayvon, 161
Marxism, 50. *See also* Communist Party/Communism; Socialist Party/socialism
Massey-Harris-Ferguson Company, 24, 54–55, 134–37, 145, 151
Mathieus, Bob, 76
May, Steve, 14
McCarthy, Eugene, 70
McCarthy, Joseph, 51–52, 146
McCartin, Joseph, 11
McClellan Committee hearings, 59
McClennan, Howard, 126
McDonald, David J., 81
McFetridge, William, 78
McNeil, Lowell, 126
Meany, George, 60–61
meatpacking workers, 28, 36, 94, 146–47
Meier, August, 32
Memphis, TN, 136
Mexican/Mexican American workers, 11, 16, 34, 68, 115, 137–38, 147. *See also* Latine workers
Miami, FL, 154
middleclass, 11, 36, 105
migration, 4, 19, 31–35, 79, 117, 130, 138, 161. *See also* immigration
Milwaukee, WI, 6–8, 33–34, 36, 54, 68, 78, 147
Minority Involvement Committee (MIC), 132
Modine Manufacturing Company, 29, 44–48, 103, 111
Modine, A. B., 46
Morrison, Laura, 14
Moss, Obry, 90–91

Moten, Crystal, 8
Motor Castings Company (West Allis), 111
Municipal Employees Relations Act (MERA), 43, 53, 61, 77, 108
Murray, Pauli, 78

Nader, Ralph, 142
Nash Motors, 54
National Association for the Advancement of Colored People (NAACP), 4–5, 16, 32–37, 56, 74, 87–109, 132, 141
National Association of Letter Carriers, 140
National Association of Manufacturers (NAM), 24–25, 59
National Association of Social Workers, 101
National Education Association (NEA), 108
National Labor Relations Act, 24–27, 43–45, 79, 117
National Labor Relations Board (NLRB), 25, 57–59, 69, 71, 84, 120–24, 145, 152–53
National Organization for Women (NOW), 39
Naugatuck Valley Project, 135
Negro American Labor Council, 94, 96
Neleon Brothers and Strom Company, 24
Nelson, Gaylord, 23, 43, 53–56, 61, 66–72, 82–84, 142
neoliberalism, 159
Newby, David, 153
New Deal, 6, 8–9, 12–30, 43, 47, 59–61, 70, 96, 105, 159
New Left, 92
New Voice, 161
New York, NY, 30, 120, 127
Norman, Loren, 22, 90

Oakland, CA, 27, 106
Obama, Barack, 1–2, 87
older workers, 73–74, 80–84, 141
Olson, Dick, 121
Olson, Steve, 47

210 Index

oral histories, 14, 16–17
Oster Manufacturing, 39
Owens, Corinne. *See* Reid-Owens,
  Corinne

Partach, Pauline, 85
Pettit, Dean, 118
Phillips-Fein, Kim, 59
Pittsburgh, PA, 127
plant closings, 5, 10–14, 44, 54–64,
  82–83, 104, 112, 132–36, 154–60
police/policing, 11, 51, 78, 87–90,
  99–107, 118, 121
Professional Air Traffic Controllers
  Organization (PATCO), 141
progressive politics (WI), 22–23,
  52–53, 60, 70. *See also* Democratic
  Party (Wisconsin)
Project Breakthru, 115
Proxmire, William, 52–53, 61, 70, 142

race, 3–20, 31–41, 61, 68, 86–116,
  130–41, 160–61
Racine, WI: deindustrialization of, 1–17,
  44, 54, 104, 112, 129–62; description of, 1–2, 5–6, 11; history of, 6–17,
  20–21; and population statistics, 24,
  31, 36, 41; and tourism, 2, 159
Racine Common Council, 37, 49–53,
  76–77, 91, 104–8, 112
Racine County AFL-CIO, 35, 116, 126,
  142. *See also* American Federation
  of Labor (AFL)
Racine County Welfare Board, 114
Racine County Workers Committee, 7
Racine Education Association (REA),
  74, 91, 108–10, 118, 124–26, 132. *See
  also* education; Racine Unified
  School Board
Racine Job Service, 143
Racine Labor Center, 44, 67, 74–75, 92,
  110, 133, 137, 145–53; creation of, 56;
  description of, 1–3
Racine Steel Castings. *See* Belle City
  Malleable
Racine Trades and Labor Council
  (RTLC), 21–22, 51, 61, 76–77, 95
Racine Unified School Board, 78,
  104–10, 125–28, 132. *See also*

education; Racine Education
  Association
Racine Vocational and Adult School,
  80
radio, 22, 63, 66, 99
Rae Motor Company, 73
railroads, 11
Rainfair, 39
Randolph, A. Philip, 33, 93, 96
Raschke, Louis, 46
Reagan, Ronald, 138, 141–45
REA Local 325 (Racine), 108, 110
recall election. *See* Wisconsin guber-
  natorial recall
Reichard, Hugh, 21
Reid-Owens, Corinne, 5, 37, 41, 87–101,
  108, 132, 154
Reiter, Matthew M., 52
religion. *See* church/religion
Republican Party (national), 1, 19, 46,
  59. *See also* Reagan, Ronald
Republican Party (Wisconsin), 3, 19,
  22–23, 43–52
retirement, 49, 73–74, 80–82, 156
Reuther, Walter, 28, 44, 51, 59, 82,
  94–95
Reynolds, John, 23
right-to-work laws, 9, 25, 43, 52, 59
Rizzo, Jim, 70
Rizzo, Sam, 23, 66, 83, 94, 113, 116
Rockford, IL, 111
Roosevelt, Franklin D., 13, 19, 24, 29,
  33, 61. *See also* New Deal
Rudwick, Elliott, 32
Rust Belt, 5, 14, 129. *See also*
  deindustrialization
Rustin, Bayard, 93
Ryan, Paul, 1

Sacks, Karen Brodkin, 151
Scheible, Herbert C., 84, 117, 123
Schultz, Charles, 60
Schwartz, Ben, 51
Schwartz, Jay, 100, 117–23
Seeger, Pete, 146
SEIU Local 150, 103–4, 117–25, 145–61
SEIU Local 152, 109–13, 125
Service Employees International
  Union (SEIU), 3, 16, 103–28

Service Employment Redevelopment (SER), 115–16
service workers, 3, 6–15, 78–80, 101–28, 139, 145–61. *See also* SEIU Local 150; St. Luke's Hospital
Sheboygan, WI, 57–59. *See also* Kohler Company
Shelton, Jon, 127
Shermer, Elizabeth Tandy, 59
Smedegaard, Paul, 143
Smiley, Erica, 161–62
Smith, Beverly, 122
Socialist Party/socialism, 26, 58. *See also* Communist Party/Communism
South Lafayette Neighborhood Group, 87
Southside Community Center (Racine), 98
Spanish Center (Racine), 115–16
Sparks, Kelly, 145–48
Sperry Gyroscope Company, 24
Standard Foundry, 111–12
Stanton, Howard, 126
Starbucks coffee, 161
St. Louis, MO, 20, 74
St. Luke's Hospital, 3, 21, 79–82, 103–6, 117–28, 148–59
St. Mary's Hospital, 159
Stop Outlandish Spending (SOS), 105–8
strikebreakers, 15, 31–33, 68–71
Strohl, Joseph, 154–55
Sullivan, George, 81
Sunbeam Corporation, 82
Support Excellence in Education (SEE), 107–8
Sweeney, John, 156, 161, 167n28
Sykes, Coronett, 153

Taft-Hartley Act (1947), 23–25, 43, 46, 50–52, 130–31, 160
Tapia, Maite, 161
taxes, 2, 4, 10, 14, 54, 60, 75, 84, 105–9
teachers. *See* education; Racine Unified School Board
Teamsters Hall (Racine), 75
Teamsters union, 21–22, 40, 51, 59, 130, 161
Tenneco Company, 83, 144

Thomas, Julian, 89–91, 99, 108, 132
Thomas, P. B., 20
Thomas, Ron, 134, 145, 148, 151, 155
Thompson, Carl, 23
Thompson, Harold J., 23, 46, 76, 82
Thompson, Tommy, 153, 156
Thomson, Vernon, 70
Tighe, Robert, 107, 116
total person unionism, 64, 74, 77
Trotter, Joe William, Jr., 89
Truman, Harry, 23
Twin Disc Clutch Company, 24

UAW Local 37, 131
UAW Local 60, 111
UAW Local 72 (Kenosha), 144
UAW Local 82, 29, 46–49, 103–4, 111
UAW Local 85, 45, 73
UAW Local 180, 7, 19–40, 47–72, 111–13, 140–48, 159
UAW Local 234, 37
UAW Local 244, 134–36
UAW Local 391, 45
UAW Local 553, 19, 32, 35–37, 70, 92, 112–14, 133
UAW Local 556, 137, 141
UAW Local 557, 83
UAW Local 642, 112–13
UAW Local 833 (Sheboygan), 57–60
UAW Local 841, 112
UAW Local 1007, 73, 116
UAW Local 1296, 73
UAW Political Action Committee, 126
UAW Region 10, 5, 28, 46, 63, 96
UFCW Local 1444, 140, 144–46
UFCW Local P-40, 145–47
unemployment, 8, 10, 54–55, 80–82, 115–16, 123–33, 140–44
union dues, 3, 52, 72
Union Hall, 21, 75–76
unionization trends (general), 2–3, 7–13, 25–33, 43, 50, 107–8, 145
United Auto Workers (UAW), 3, 7, 16–38, 56–59, 94, 142, 156, 162; and conventions, 40, 55; and fair employment practices, 33–34, 38–39, 68, 88, 91–93; and international, 44, 46, 55, 64, 66, 95, 113, 162. *See also UAW Locals*

Index

United Electrical Workers (UEW), 38, 50, 142
United Food and Commercial Workers, 161
United Fund, 101
United Nations, 30
United Public Workers Local 249, 49–51
United Steel Workers of America, 81
United Way, 63, 140
UNITE HERE, 161
University of Wisconsin School for Workers, 39, 81
University of Wisconsin–Madison, 2–3, 75
University of Wisconsin–Parkside, 126–28, 141, 146
Urban League, 32, 36, 88, 91, 97, 143
U.S. Department of Mediation and Conciliation, 48
U.S. Supreme Court, 59. *See also* law/lawyers; lawsuits

Valeo, Tony, 4–6, 47, 58, 63–72, 94, 142
Vietnam War, 116, 146

wages, 8, 43, 51, 79–80, 104–8, 117
Wagner Act. *See* National Labor Relations Act
Walker, Scott, 1–4, 9
Walker Manufacturing, 45, 73–74, 83
Walsh, Brenda,155
Ware, Robert, 132
War on Poverty, 115–16
Washington, D.C., 141
Webster, Mike, 148, 154–55
Webster Electric, 39, 45
welfare, 8, 129, 141
Wendt, Francis, 23, 29–30, 52–53, 77
Western Printing Company, 39, 73, 77, 116, 157
Westview Nursing Home, 145, 148, 151–54
Whiteside, Paul Jr., 9, 21–22, 140, 148
Wilkie, Horace, 23
Williams, Sloan, 91
Wimpress, James, 136
Windham, Lane, 10, 145

Wirtz, Willard, 79
Wisconsin Action Coalition (WAC), 148
Wisconsin AFL-CIO, 77, 82, 87–98, 107, 110; and fair employment practices, 95–99
Wisconsin Democrats. *See* Democratic Party (Wisconsin)
Wisconsin Education Association, 132
Wisconsin Employment Relations Commission, 39–40, 53–54, 73, 79–85, 124–25, 140
Wisconsin gubernatorial recall, 1–2, 9
Wisconsin Industrial Commission, 40, 55, 73–74, 95
Wisconsin Labor History Society, 147
Wisconsin Labor Management Conference, 156
Wisconsin Legislature, 1, 75
Wisconsin Public Service Commission, 142
Wisconsin Republicans. *See* Republican Party (Wisconsin)
Wisconsin State Employment Services (WSES), 115
Wisconsin Supreme Court, 74
Witt, Jane, 2
Wolf, John B., 48
Women's Civic Council of Racine, 91–92
women's rights movements, 2–3, 9, 17, 40–41. *See also* civil rights movements
Women's Trade Union League (Racine), 39
women workers, 8–19, 78, 84–87, 152, 161; early union activity, 38–41, 61; leadership, 78, 87, 117; and limited job opportunities, 79, 84–87; and St. Luke's Hospital strike, 3, 104, 117–18. *See also* gender; Reid-Owens, Corinne; women's rights movements
Wooley, LeRoy, 90, 92
Workers Industrial Union, 7
Working America organization, 2, 6
Works Progress Administration (WPA), 7, 21

Index

World War I, 33
World War II, 4, 7–8, 13, 17–40, 49, 61, 160
Worley, Leroy, 108

Yale University, 133
Young Radiator, 131

Youngstown, OH, 135
Young Women's Christian Association (YWCA), 5, 37, 87

Zayre Department Stores, 144–46
Zierten, Scott, 141

NAOMI R WILLIAMS is an assistant professor of labor studies and employment relations at Rutgers University.

The University of Illinois Press
is a founding member of the
Association of University Presses.

Composed in 10.5/13 Mercury Text
with Avenir display
by Jim Proefrock
at the University of Illinois Press

University of Illinois Press
1325 South Oak Street
Champaign, IL 61820-6903
www.press.uillinois.edu